Further Pure 1

Hugh Neill and Douglas Quadling

Series editor Hugh Neill

CAMBRIDGE UNIVERSITY PRESS
Cambridge, New York, Melbourne, Madrid, Cape Town, Singapore, São Paulo

Cambridge University Press
The Edinburgh Building, Cambridge CB2 2RU, UK

www.cambridge.org
Information on this title: www.cambridge.org/9780521548984

First published 2004
Reprinted 2005 (twice)

Printed in the United Kingdom at the University Press, Cambridge

A catalogue record for this publication is available from the British Library

ISBN-13 978-0-521-54898-4 paperback
ISBN-10 0-521-54898-5 paperback

Contents

Introduction

Cambridge Advanced Mathematics has been written especially for the OCR modular examinations. It consists of one book or half-book corresponding to each module. This book is the first Further Pure Mathematics module, FP1.

The book opens with an unusual chapter entitled 'Preliminaries'. The purpose of this chapter is to introduce some notation and ideas concerned with sets of numbers, and proof. The chapter is meant for reference when it is needed: there are no exercises.

The remainder of the book is divided into chapters roughly corresponding to specification headings. Occasionally a section includes an important result that is difficult to prove or is outside the specification. These sections are marked with an asterisk (∗) in the section heading, and there is usually a sentence early on explaining precisely what it is that the student needs to know.

Chapter 1, on simultaneous equations, contains examples and exercises where the solutions are unique and also examples and exercises where there is either no solution or the solution is not unique. It may be advisable, in the first instance, to leave Sections 1.3 onwards which deal with non-unique solutions and come back to them later. However, Chapter 2 requires the (unique) solution of a set of three equations with three unknowns.

Occasionally within the text paragraphs appear in a grey box. These paragraphs are usually outside the main stream of the mathematical argument, but may help to give insight, or suggest extra work or different approaches.

The authors have assumed that the students have access to graphic calculators and that students will use them throughout the course to assist their learning of mathematics.

Numerical work is presented in a form intended to discourage premature approximation. In ongoing calculations inexact numbers appear in decimal form like 3.456... , signifying that the number is held in a calculator to more places than are given. Numbers are not rounded at this stage; the full display could be, for example, 3.456 123 or 3.456 789. Final answers are then stated with some indication that they are approximate, for example '1.23 correct to 3 significant figures'.

There are plenty of exercises, and each chapter contains a miscellaneous exercise which includes some questions of examination standard. The authors thank Charles Parker, Lawrence Jarrett, Jean Matthews and Tim Cross, the OCR examiners who contributed to these exercises. There are also two revision exercises, with many questions taken from OCR examination papers, and two practice examination papers.

The authors also thank Robert Leslie and Eveline Johnstone, who read the book very carefully and made many extremely useful comments, and OCR and Cambridge University Press for their help in producing this book. However, the responsibility for the text, and for any errors, remains with the authors.

0 Some preliminaries

The reason for this unusual chapter number and title is that this is not a chapter in the usual sense of this book. It contains a number of things which you might well have seen before, in which case you can skip it and go straight to Chapter 1, and just use this for occasional reference.

If you haven't seen the material before, skim it quickly, go on to Chapter 1 and come back to it when you need to.

This chapter consists of

* some new notation
* some details about methods of proof and disproof.

0.1 Notation for numbers

When you have been working with functions, an expression which occurs frequently is 'where x is a real number'.

There is a special notation for this, which is '$x \in \mathbb{R}$'.

The symbol '$\in$' stands for 'belongs to' or 'is a member of', and the symbol '$\mathbb{R}$' stands for 'the set of real numbers'.

In a similar way, when you are dealing with sequences, such as an arithmetic or a geometric sequence, the sequence is often called u_1, u_2, u_3 etc. In this case the subscripts 1, 2, 3... are natural numbers which are denoted by the symbol $\mathbb{N}$.

Thus, to say that $n \in \mathbb{N}$ means that n can be a whole number greater than 0. (Some authors allow $\mathbb{N}$ to include the number 0, but this will never be the case in this book.)

0.2 Modulus notation

Suppose that you want to find the difference between the heights of two people. With numerical information, the answer is quite straightforward: if their heights are 160 cm and 170 cm, you would answer 10 cm; and if their heights were 170 cm and 160 cm, you would still answer 10 cm.

But how would you answer the question if their heights were H cm and h cm? The answer is, it depends which is bigger: if $H > h$, you would answer $(H - h)$ cm; if $h > H$ you would answer $(h - H)$ cm; and if $h = H$ you would answer 0 cm, which is either $(H - h)$ cm or $(h - H)$ cm.

Questions like this, in which you want an answer which is always positive or zero, lead to the idea of the modulus.

> The **modulus** of x, written $|x|$ and pronounced 'mod x', is defined by
>
> $|x| = x \quad$ if $x \geq 0$,
> $|x| = -x \quad$ if $x < 0$.

Using the modulus notation, you can now write the difference in heights as $|H - h|$ whether $H > h$, $h > H$ or $h = H$.

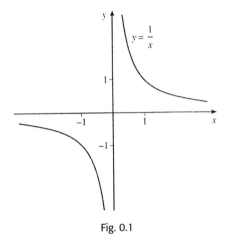

Another situation when the modulus is useful is when you talk about numbers which are large numerically, but which are negative, such as -1000 or $-1\,000\,000$. These are 'negative numbers with large modulus'.

For example, for large positive values of x, the value of $\frac{1}{x}$ approaches 0. The same is true for negative values of x with large modulus. So you can say that, when $|x|$ is large, $\left|\frac{1}{x}\right|$ is close to zero; or in a numerical example, when $|x| > 1000$, $\left|\frac{1}{x}\right| < 0.001$. (See Fig. 0.1.)

Fig. 0.1

0.3 Implication

It is extremely useful to have a way of shortening the argument 'If A, then B', where A and B are mathematical statements. Examples of such arguments with statements A and B might be

'If $x = 5$, then $x^2 = 25$',

and

'If XYZ is a triangle and angle $X = 90°$, then $XY^2 + XZ^2 = YZ^2$'.

These statements can be rewritten using the symbol $\Rightarrow$ as

$x = 5 \quad \Rightarrow \quad x^2 = 25,$

and

XYZ is a triangle and $X = 90° \quad \Rightarrow \quad XY^2 + XZ^2 = YZ^2.$

The $\Rightarrow$ sign is read as 'implies'. If the statement on the left is true, then the statement on the right is true.

Notice that if the statement on the left is not true, nothing is said about the statement on the right. The use of $\Rightarrow$ in the statement $0 = 1 \Rightarrow 1 = 2$ is perfectly correct. If the statement on the left is true, the statement on the right follows logically. This is not a particularly helpful piece of deduction, because $0 = 1$ is false!

If you link several statements together by a chain of implications, as

$$A \Rightarrow B \Rightarrow C \Rightarrow \cdots \Rightarrow K,$$

then you can deduce that $A \Rightarrow K$. In this way you can sometimes prove a whole theorem through a number of small steps.

Sometimes the sign is reversed, as $\Leftarrow$, which is read as 'is implied by'. So $A \Rightarrow B$ can also be written as $B \Leftarrow A$.

It sometimes happens that $A \Rightarrow B$ and $A \Leftarrow B$. You can then combine $\Rightarrow$ and $\Leftarrow$, to write

$$A \Leftrightarrow B$$

where the symbol $\Leftrightarrow$ means 'implies and is implied by'. This means that the two statements are completely equivalent; if either one is known to be true, so is the other. So $\Leftrightarrow$ is often read as 'is logically equivalent to' or as 'if and only if'.

For example, when doing algebra, you can add the same number to both sides of an equation, so that

$$x = y \Rightarrow x + z = y + z.$$

It is also true that

$$x = y \Leftarrow x + z = y + z, \quad \text{or} \quad x + z = y + z \Rightarrow x = y.$$

So you can write

$$x = y \Leftrightarrow x + z = y + z.$$

But there are some important algebraic steps which cannot be reversed in this way. For example, the step

$$x = y \Rightarrow xz = yz$$

is valid, but it is not true that

$$x = y \Leftarrow xz = yz, \quad \text{or} \quad xz = yz \Rightarrow x = y,$$

since z could be zero, and then x and y need not be equal.

Another non-reversible step is squaring both sides of an equation. You can write

$$x = y \Rightarrow x^2 = y^2, \quad \text{but not} \quad x = y \Leftarrow x^2 = y^2.$$

The correct reverse implication is

$$\begin{aligned} x^2 = y^2 \Rightarrow\ & x^2 - y^2 = 0 \\ \Rightarrow\ & (x - y)(x + y) = 0 \\ \Rightarrow\ & \text{either } x - y = 0 \text{ or } x + y = 0 \\ \Rightarrow\ & \text{either } x = y \text{ or } x = -y. \end{aligned}$$

These points are important when you solve equations. It is very tempting to join up the steps in a solution with $\Leftrightarrow$ signs without thinking. But you can easily reach a wrong conclusion if one of the implications is not reversible.

Example 0.3.1
Solve the equation $\sqrt{2x + 1} = \sqrt{x} - 5$.

$$\begin{aligned} \sqrt{2x + 1} = \sqrt{x} - 5 \Rightarrow\ & 2x + 1 = (\sqrt{x} - 5)^2 \\ \Leftrightarrow\ & 2x + 1 = x - 10\sqrt{x} + 25 \\ \Leftrightarrow\ & 10\sqrt{x} = 24 - x \\ \Rightarrow\ & 100x = (24 - x)^2 \\ \Leftrightarrow\ & 100x = 576 - 48x + x^2 \\ \Leftrightarrow\ & x^2 - 148x + 576 = 0 \\ \Leftrightarrow\ & (x - 4)(x - 144) = 0 \\ \Leftrightarrow\ & \text{either } x = 4 \text{ or } x = 144. \end{aligned}$$

But in fact, neither $x = 4$ nor $x = 144$ satisfies the equation $\sqrt{2x + 1} = \sqrt{x} - 5$. With $x = 4$ the left side is $\sqrt{9} = 3$ and the right side is $\sqrt{4} - 5 = -3$. With $x = 144$ the left side is $\sqrt{289} = 17$, and the right side is $\sqrt{144} - 5 = 7$. It follows that the equation has no solution.

The point is that solving equations is a two-way process. You need to show both that

if x satisfies the equation, then x would have certain values

and that

if x has one of these values, then it satisfies the equation.

With a simple equation such as

$$2x + 3 = 7 - 3x \quad \Leftrightarrow \quad 3x + 2x = 7 - 3 \quad \Leftrightarrow \quad x = 0.8,$$

all the steps are equivalence steps, so that both parts of the solution are included in the single chain of reasoning. (But it is still a good idea to check that $x = 0.8$ does satisfy the original equation, to make sure you haven't made a mistake.)

But in Example 0.3.1 above there are two non-reversible steps,

(a) $\sqrt{2x + 1} = \sqrt{x} - 5 \quad \Rightarrow \quad 2x + 1 = (\sqrt{x} - 5)^2$

and   (b) $10\sqrt{x} = 24 - x \quad \Rightarrow \quad 100x = (24 - x)^2.$

You can easily check that when $x = 4$ the equation on the right of (a) is satisfied, but the equation on the left is not; and when $x = 144$ the equation on the right of (b) is satisfied, but the equation on the left is not.

There are actually four different equations,

(i) $\sqrt{2x+1} = \sqrt{x} - 5$ (ii) $-\sqrt{2x+1} = \sqrt{x} - 5$

(iii) $\sqrt{2x+1} = -\sqrt{x} - 5$ (iv) $-\sqrt{2x+1} = -\sqrt{x} - 5$

all of which after two squarings lead to $100x = (24 - x)^2$, and thence to $x = 4$ or $x = 144$. Equation (ii) has $x = 4$ as a root; (iv) has $x = 144$; and (i) and (iii) have no solution.

Example 0.3.2

Solve the simultaneous equations $2x - 5y = 3$, $10y - 4x = -5$.

$$2x - 5y = 3 \text{ and } 10y - 4x = -5 \quad \Rightarrow \quad 2(2x - 5y) + (10y - 4x) = 2 \times 3 + (-5)$$
$$\Rightarrow \quad 4x - 10y + 10y - 4x = 6 - 5$$
$$\Rightarrow \quad 0 = 1.$$

This is *not* a 'proof' that $0 = 1$. It would have been wrong to write down a sequence of equations ending with the statement 'Therefore $0 = 1$'. The advantage of the $\Rightarrow$ notation is that nowhere in the chain of reasoning is it asserted that any of the statements are true; only that *if* the first statement is true, then so is the last.

The correct interpretation of this example is that if there were numbers x and y such that $2x - 5y = 3$ and $10y - 4x = -5$, then 0 would equal 1. Since you know that 0 does not equal 1, the conclusion is that there are no numbers x and y satisfying these simultaneous equations. That is, the equations have no solution. This is an example of proof by contradiction which you will see more about in the next section.

Solving equations is an act of faith. You begin by assuming that there is a solution, and use the rules of algebra to find out what it must be. If you end up with an answer (or answers), you must check that it does (or they do) satisfy the equation. You do this either by making sure that all the steps can be joined by $\Leftrightarrow$ and not just $\Rightarrow$, or by direct substitution. If you end up with a false statement, then the equation has no solution.

0.4 Proof by contradiction

Sometimes it is not possible to find a way of proving a theorem by deduction, and a more roundabout method of proof has to be used.

A typical form for such an argument is:

$A, B, C, \ldots$ are already known to be true.

If K were not true, one of $A, B, C, \ldots$ would not be true.

Therefore K is true.

That is, you look at the proposition you want to prove, and investigate the effect of assuming the opposite is true. If this leads you to a contradiction, then it follows that the original proposition is true. This technique is known as **proof by contradiction**.

Example 0.4.1
(a) Prove that the square of an odd number is odd.
(b) Prove that, if the square of a natural number is odd, the number itself is odd.

(a) This can be proved deductively. Any odd number can be written as $2m + 1$, where $m \in \mathbb{N}$. Then

$$(2m + 1)^2 = (2m)^2 + 2(2m) + 1$$
$$= 4m^2 + 4m + 1$$
$$= 2(2m^2 + 2m) + 1.$$

Since $m \in \mathbb{N}$, $2m^2 + 2m \in \mathbb{N}$, so that $(2m + 1)^2$ can be written as $2k + 1$, where $k \in \mathbb{N}$. Therefore $(2m + 1)^2$ is an odd number.

(b) The argument in part (a) cannot be reversed, so an indirect approach (proof by contradiction) is used.

Let n be a natural number whose square is odd. Then, if n were not odd, it would be even, so you could write n as $2m$, where $m \in \mathbb{N}$. But

$$n = 2m \quad \Rightarrow \quad n^2 = 4m^2 = 2(2m^2),$$
$$\Rightarrow \quad n^2 = 2k, \text{ where } k = 2m^2.$$

So if n were even, n^2 would be even, which contradicts the definition of n^2. It follows that n is not even, so n is odd.

0.5   Counterexamples

The previous two sections were about methods of proving that a statement is true, but occasionally you might want to show that a statement is false. A particularly good way to do this is by using a **counterexample**.

Here is an example (of a counterexample!).

Example 0.5.1
Suppose you were asked to disprove the statement:

'All prime numbers are odd'.

Then all you need to do is to say

'2 is a prime number and 2 is even'.

The counterexample is 2, and this one counterexample (in this case the only one) shows that the statement is false.

Example 0.5.2

Is the statement. 'The lowest common multiple (LCM) of two positive integers m and n is mn' true or false?

The statement is false.

Let $m = 2$ and $n = 4$. Then the LCM of m and n is 4, but $mn = 8$.

Example 0.5.3

For all positive integers n, $n^2 + n + 41$ is prime. Prove that this statement is untrue.

When $n = 41$, $n^2 + n + 41 = 41^2 + 41 + 41 = 41(41 + 1 + 1) = 41 \times 43$.

Hence when $n = 41$, $n^2 + n + 41$ is not prime, and the statement is untrue.

1 Sets of linear equations

This chapter is about technique for solving sets of linear equations systematically. When you have completed it you should know

- how to find the unique solution of a set of linear equations if there is one
- the meaning of the terms 'consistent' and 'inconsistent' as applied to linear equations
- how to find all the solutions of a set of linear equations when the solution is not unique.

This chapter looks in more detail at simultaneous equations and takes them further than you have taken them before. At first you may wish to read only as far as Sections 1.1 and 1.2 and to work Exercise 1A. The ideas in the remaining sections are developed further in Chapters 4 and 10 and you will probably need to return to this chapter before starting them.

1.1 Simultaneous linear equations

You already know how to solve a pair of simultaneous equations with two unknowns, such as

$$\left. \begin{array}{l} 2x + y = 9 \\ 3x - y = 11 \end{array} \right\}.$$

An equation like $2x + y = 9$ is called a linear equation. This is to distinguish it from equations like $x + y + y^2 = 4$, or $x^4 - xy + 2y^3 = 1$, which contain powers or products of the unknowns.

> A **linear equation** with two unknowns x, y is an equation of the form
>
> $$ax + by = c,$$
>
> where a, b and c are numbers.

An equation of this form is called linear because it is usually the equation of a straight line. But you can see from the definition that equations such as $0x + 0y = 1$ and $0x + 0y = 0$ are also linear equations, even though they are not equations of straight lines.

A single linear equation such as $2x + y = 9$ is satisfied by many pairs of values of x and y: for example,

$$x = 3, y = 3; \qquad x = 0, y = 9; \qquad x = 4, y = 1; \qquad x = \tfrac{1}{2}, y = 8,$$

and many more. Similarly the linear equation $3x - y = 11$ is satisfied by many pairs of values, such as

$$x = 3\tfrac{2}{3}, y = 0; \qquad x = 4, y = 1; \qquad x = 2, y = -5; \qquad x = 3, y = -2.$$

But there is only one pair of numbers which satisfy both of the equations

$$\left. \begin{array}{l} 2x + y = 9 \\ 3x - y = 11 \end{array} \right\}$$

simultaneously. This is the pair

$$x = 4, y = 1.$$

It is called the **solution** of the pair of **simultaneous linear equations**.

This chapter investigates the solution of sets of linear equations. The set may consist of just one equation, or a pair of equations, or three or more equations. If there is more than one equation, then the solution has to satisfy all the equations simultaneously.

Before looking at detailed methods of finding the solution, you need to decide what kind of numbers x and y can be. Some problems only make sense if x and y are positive integers; in that case the complete solution of the equation $2x + y = 9$ would be the four pairs

$$x = 1, y = 7; \quad x = 2, y = 5; \quad x = 3, y = 3; \quad x = 4, y = 1.$$

In other applications x and y might be restricted to all integers, or to rational numbers. But in this chapter it will be assumed that x and y can be real numbers of any kind. This will include pairs such as

$$x = 5\tfrac{1}{7}, y = -1\tfrac{2}{7} \quad \text{and} \quad x = 3 + \sqrt{2}, \; y = 3 - 2\sqrt{2}.$$

1.2 Sets of equations with unique solutions

Two equations and two unknowns

When you have a pair of simultaneous linear equations to solve, you probably start by asking the question 'will it be easier to eliminate x or y?'. For example, in solving the equations

$$\left. \begin{array}{r} 2x + y = 9 \\ 3x - y = 11 \end{array} \right\}.$$

at the beginning of Section 1.1, you would spot that by adding the two equations the unknown y will disappear. So you would add the first equation to the second, and replace the pair of equations by the equivalent pair

$$\left. \begin{array}{r} 2x + y = 9 \\ 5x = 20 \end{array} \right\}.$$

The second equation gives $x = 4$. Then substituting this in the first equation, $y = 9 - 2 \times 4 = 1$.

But if you wanted to program a computer to solve the equations, you might do it differently. It isn't worth training a computer to distinguish between 'easy' and 'hard' arithmetic. It is more efficient to choose a set procedure which will work whatever the numbers are. So you might program it always to begin by eliminating x. To do this, subtract $\tfrac{3}{2}$ times the first equation (that is, $3x + \tfrac{3}{2}y = \tfrac{27}{2}$) from the second to get

$$\left. \begin{array}{r} 2x + y = 9 \\ \left(-1 - \tfrac{3}{2}\right) y = \left(11 - \tfrac{27}{2}\right) \end{array} \right\}.$$

The second equation is

$$-\tfrac{5}{2}y = -\tfrac{5}{2},$$

which gives $y = 1$. Then substituting this in the first equation, $2x = 9 - 1 = 8$, so $x = 4$. What has happened here is that a pair of equations

$$\left.\begin{array}{l} ax + by = p \\ cx + dy = q \end{array}\right\}$$

has been replaced by an equivalent set, of the form

$$\left.\begin{array}{l} kx + ly = r \\ my = s \end{array}\right\}.$$

At this stage, provided that neither m nor k is zero, you can solve the final equation and then substitute the value into the first equation to obtain a unique solution. However, if either m nor k is zero, there is no solution, or there are infinitely many solutions. These are discussed in Sections 1.3 and 1.4; in this section, the solution is always unique.

When the equations are in the form

$$\left.\begin{array}{l} kx + ly = r \\ my = s \end{array}\right\},$$

they are said to be in **triangular form**. Triangular form is a useful first stage in the solution of linear equations.

This technique will generalise to sets of equations with more than two unknowns.

Example 1.2.1

Solve the equations $\left.\begin{array}{l} 2x + 3y = 1 \\ 4x - y = 9 \end{array}\right\}.$

There are three allowable operations that you can perform on these equations and obtain a set of equations which is equivalent. You may:

- multiply an equation by a non-zero number
- subtract a multiple of one equation from another
- exchange two equations.

The resulting set of equations will have exactly the same solutions as the original set. The symbol $\Leftrightarrow$ is used to denote that two sets of equations are equivalent, that is, they have the same solutions.

Here is one way to solve the given equations.

Subtracting twice the first equation from the second, leaving the first equation as it is, gives

$$\left.\begin{array}{l} 2x + 3y = 1 \\ 4x - y = 9 \end{array}\right\} \quad \Leftrightarrow \quad \left.\begin{array}{l} 2x + 3y = 1 \\ 0x - 7y = 7 \end{array}\right\}.$$

The equations are now in triangular form.

Dividing the second equation by –7 gives

$$\left.\begin{array}{l} 2x + 3y = 1 \\ 4x - y = 9 \end{array}\right\} \quad \Leftrightarrow \quad \left.\begin{array}{l} 2x + 3y = 1 \\ 0x - 7y = 7 \end{array}\right\} \quad \Leftrightarrow \quad \left.\begin{array}{l} 2x + 3y = \;\;1 \\ y = -1 \end{array}\right\}.$$

When you get to the last stage, you can tell that the equations have a unique solution with $y = -1$ and then, by substituting in the other equation, that $x = 2$.

The equations have the solution $x = 2, y = -1$.

It is useful to have some notation for showing what operations have been carried out as you move from step to step. The notation $r_2' = r_2 - 2r_1$ will be used to indicate that the new row 2 has been obtained by taking the old row $2 - 2 \times$ old row 1. The next and following examples will use this notation, which is self-explanatory.

Example 1.2.2

Solve the equations $\left.\begin{array}{l} 3x + 4y = 95 \\ 4x - 3y = 60 \end{array}\right\}.$

$$\left.\begin{array}{l} 3x + 4y = 95 \\ 4x - 3y = 60 \end{array}\right\} \quad \Leftrightarrow \quad \left.\begin{array}{l} 12x + 16y = 380 \\ 12x - 9y = 180 \end{array}\right\} \quad \begin{array}{l} r_1' = 4r_1 \\ r_2' = 3r_2 \end{array}$$

$$\Leftrightarrow \quad \left.\begin{array}{l} 12x + 16y = \;\;\;380 \\ -25y = -200 \end{array}\right\} \quad r_2' = r_1 - r_2$$

$$\Leftrightarrow \quad \left.\begin{array}{l} 12x + 16y = 380 \\ y = \;\;\;8 \end{array}\right\} \quad r_2' = -\tfrac{1}{25}r_2$$

At this stage, you can substitute $y = 8$ in the original first equation, to find that $3x + 4 \times 8 = 75$, giving $3x + 32 = 95$ and $x = 21$.

The equations have the solution $x = 21, y = 8$.

You can use the same notation and approach for three equations and three unknowns.

Three equations and three unknowns

When solving three equations in three unknowns, it is even more important to be systematic than in previous cases. Here is an example.

Example 1.2.3

Solve the equations $\left.\begin{array}{l} 2x + y - z = 2 \\ x - 2y + 3z = 7 \\ 3x + 5y - z = 0 \end{array}\right\}.$

In this example it is a good idea to exchange the first two equations, since it is easier to make the x-coefficients in the second and third equations 0 if the coefficient of x in the first equation is 1. After this step the x-coefficients are made 0 in turn. Then the last equation ($11y - 10z = -21$) is multiplied by 5 to avoid fractions when making the y-coefficient equal to 0. Thus:

$$\left.\begin{array}{l} 2x + y - z = 2 \\ x - 2y + 3z = 7 \\ 3x + 5y - z = 0 \end{array}\right\} \Leftrightarrow \left.\begin{array}{l} x - 2y + 3z = 7 \\ 2x + y - z = 2 \\ 3x + 5y - z = 0 \end{array}\right\} \quad \begin{array}{l} r_1' = r_2 \\ r_2' = r_1 \end{array}$$

$$\Leftrightarrow \left.\begin{array}{rl} x - 2y + 3z = & 7 \\ 0x + 5y - 7z = & -12 \\ 0x + 11y - 10z = & -21 \end{array}\right\} \quad \begin{array}{l} r_2' = r_2 - 2r_1 \\ r_3' = r_3 - 3r_1 \end{array}$$

$$\Leftrightarrow \left.\begin{array}{rl} x - 2y + 3z = & 7 \\ 5y - 7z = & -12 \\ 55y - 50z = & -105 \end{array}\right\} \quad r_3' = 5r_3$$

$$\Leftrightarrow \left.\begin{array}{rl} x - 2y + 3z = & 7 \\ 5y - 7z = & -12 \\ 0y + 27z = & 27 \end{array}\right\} \quad r_3' = r_3 - 11r_2$$

$$\Leftrightarrow \left.\begin{array}{rl} x - 2y + 3z = & 7 \\ 5y - 7z = & -12 \\ z = & 1 \end{array}\right\} \quad r_3' = \tfrac{1}{27}r_3$$

From the third equation $z = 1$; substitute this value in the second equation to find $y = -1$, and then substitute both these values in the first equation to find $x = 2$.

These equations are satisfied uniquely by $x = 2$, $y = -1$, $z = 1$.

Notice how the method proceeds systematically. The x-coefficient in the first equation is used to eliminate the x terms in the second and third equations; then the y-coefficient in the second equation is used to eliminate the y term in the third equation. You should aim to do this each time, but you may have to interchange a pair of equations first. For example, the first equation may not contain a term in x.

Exercise 1A

1 Use the notation and method of Example 1.2.2 to solve the following equations.

(a) $\left.\begin{array}{l} x + 4y = 5 \\ 3x + 15y = 9 \end{array}\right\}$ (b) $\left.\begin{array}{l} 2x - 3y = 11 \\ -11x + 2y = 12 \end{array}\right\}$ (c) $\left.\begin{array}{l} 16x - y = 4 \\ -11x + y = 1 \end{array}\right\}$

2 Use the notation and method of Example 1.2.3 to solve the following equations.

(a) $\left.\begin{array}{l} x + 3y - 4z = 10 \\ x + 4y - 2z = 9 \\ 3x + 5y + 2z = 12 \end{array}\right\}$ (b) $\left.\begin{array}{l} x - 2y + 4z = 12 \\ -3x + 4y - z = -1 \\ 2x + 5y + 2z = -3 \end{array}\right\}$ (c) $\left.\begin{array}{l} 3x - 2y + 4z = 4 \\ 2x + 3y - 5z = 7 \\ 4x - 2y - 3z = 6 \end{array}\right\}$

(d) $\left.\begin{array}{l} y + z = 4 \\ x + 3y + z = 5 \\ 2x - 2y - z = 3 \end{array}\right\}$ (e) $\left.\begin{array}{l} y + z = 4 \\ x + y = 5 \\ x + z = 3 \end{array}\right\}$ (f) $\left.\begin{array}{l} 5x + 2y - 3z = 9 \\ 4x - 5y + 5z = 8 \\ 3x - 8y + 7z = 5 \end{array}\right\}$

1.3   Sets of equations with two unknowns where the solution is not unique

In the previous section you saw how to solve two linear equations with two unknowns and three linear equations with three unknowns when the set of equations have a single solution. But you might find that you have a situation with one equation with two unknowns. How do you find the solution of an equation such as $2x + 3y = 6$?

One equation and two unknowns

Geometrically, if the values of x and y are plotted on a graph, the equation represents a line. There are infinitely many points on the line, and there are infinitely many pairs of values of x and y which satisfy the equation.

If you put $y = t$ in the equation $2x + 3y = 6$, you get

$$2x = 6 - 3t$$

that is

$$x = 3 - \tfrac{3}{2}t.$$

So the solution can be written as

$$x = 3 - \tfrac{3}{2}t,$$
$$y = \quad\ t.$$

It is helpful to write the expressions on the right side in columns, with the terms involving t in the same vertical line.

Each time you substitute any real number for t, you get a different pair of values of x and y which satisfy the equation. To emphasise this, the solution can be written more precisely as

$$\left. \begin{array}{l} x = 3 - \tfrac{3}{2}t \\ y = \quad\ t \end{array} \right\}, \quad t \in \mathbb{R}.$$

The symbol $\in$ means 'belongs to', and $\mathbb{R}$ denotes the set of real numbers. So this states that the solution of the equation is given by the formulae $x = 3 - \tfrac{3}{2}t$, $y = t$ where t is any real number. The variable t is called a **parameter**.

Although this is the complete solution, there are many different ways of writing it.

- You may prefer a form of the solution which doesn't involve fractions. By writing t as $2s$, the term $\tfrac{3}{2}t$ can be replaced by $3s$. Since, if t is a real number then s is a real number, and vice versa, the solution could be written

$$\left. \begin{array}{l} x = 3 - 3s \\ y = \quad\ 2s \end{array} \right\}, \quad s \in \mathbb{R}.$$

- Instead of beginning by putting $y = t$, you could put $x = u$. Then

$$3y = 6 - 2x = 6 - 2u, \quad \text{giving} \quad y = 2 - \tfrac{2}{3}u.$$

You would then write the solution as

$$\left.\begin{array}{l} x = \quad u \\ y = 2 - \frac{2}{3}u \end{array}\right\}, \quad u \in \mathbb{R}.$$

And again, you could avoid fractions by replacing u by $3v$, which gives

$$\left.\begin{array}{l} x = \quad 3v \\ y = 2 - 2v \end{array}\right\}, \quad v \in \mathbb{R}.$$

- Try substituting

$$\left.\begin{array}{l} x = -3 + 3w \\ y = \quad 4 - 2w \end{array}\right\}, \quad w \in \mathbb{R}$$

in the equation $2x + 3y = 6$. You will find that it satisfies the equation for any value of w. This is just one more of the many possible ways of writing the solution.

Although all these solutions look different, they give exactly the same pairs of values for x and y. For example, $t = -2$ and $s = -1$, $u = 6$ and $v = 2$, and $w = 3$ all give the pair $x = 6, y = -2$.

Example 1.3.1
Solve the equation $4x - 3y = 12$ for x and y.

Put $y = t$. Then $4x = 12 + 3t$, giving $x = 3 + \frac{3}{4}t$.

The solution can be written as
$$\left.\begin{array}{l} x = 3 + \frac{3}{4}t \\ y = \quad\quad t \end{array}\right\}, \quad t \in \mathbb{R}.$$

However, this solution is not very tidy. As the solution for x involves a division by 4 you can see that if instead of putting $y = t$ you put $y = 4u$, then the solution can be written as

$$\left.\begin{array}{l} x = 3 + 3u \\ y = \quad\; 4u \end{array}\right\}, \quad u \in \mathbb{R}.$$

It does not matter whether you give the first solution, the second solution, or some other solution which looks completely different; two apparently different looking answers may both be correct.

It doesn't matter what letter you give for the parameter.

Two equations and two unknowns

Sometimes a set of two equations with two unknowns may not have a unique solution. For example the value of m in the triangular set of equations

$$\left.\begin{array}{l} kx + ly = r \\ \quad\quad my = s \end{array}\right\}$$

referred to just before Example 1.2.1 may be 0. Here are two examples.

Example 1.3.2

Solve the equations $\left.\begin{array}{r} -x + 2y = 0 \\ 2x - 4y = -4 \end{array}\right\}$.

When you add twice the top equation to the bottom equation you find that

$$\left.\begin{array}{r} -x + 2y = 0 \\ 2x - 4y = -4 \end{array}\right\} \quad \Leftrightarrow \quad \left.\begin{array}{r} -x + 2y = 0 \\ 0x + 0y = -4 \end{array}\right\} \quad r_2' = r_2 + 2r_1.$$

The second equation, which is simply $0 = 4$, is a contradiction (see Example 0.3.2). This shows that the original equations have no solution because there are no values of x and y which can make $0 = 4$. The equations are said to be **inconsistent**.

Example 1.3.3

Solve the equations $\left.\begin{array}{r} -2x + 4y = 1 \\ 4x - 8y = -2 \end{array}\right\}$.

When you add twice the top equation to the bottom equation you find that

$$\left.\begin{array}{r} -2x + 4y = 1 \\ 4x - 8y = -2 \end{array}\right\} \quad \Leftrightarrow \quad \left.\begin{array}{r} -2x + 4y = 1 \\ 0x + 0y = 0 \end{array}\right\} \quad r_2' = r_2 + 2r_1$$

The equation $0x + 0y = 0$ is true for all values of x and y, so the equations just reduce to $-2x + 4y = 1$, which is the type of equation in Example 1.3.1. If you put $y = t$, where t is a parameter, then

$$x = 2t - \tfrac{1}{2}.$$

So the solution can be written as $\left.\begin{array}{l} x = -\tfrac{1}{2} + 2t \\ y = \phantom{-\tfrac{1}{2} + {}} t \end{array}\right\}, \quad t \in \mathbb{R}.$

You can interpret the various cases of the type of solution to a set of two linear equation with two unknowns geometrically. In Example 1.2.1 with a unique solution the two equations represent two straight lines which are not parallel and so meet in a point. In Example 1.3.2, the two straight lines are parallel and do not meet, so there is no solution. In Example 1.3.3, the two equations represent the same line, so there are infinitely many points in common.

These situations are illustrated in the three parts of Fig. 1.1.

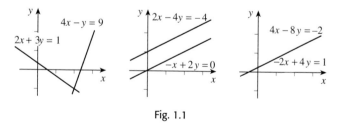

Fig. 1.1

There are other ways of writing the solution to the equations in Example 1.3.3. You could easily have put $x = t$, and then found that $y = \tfrac{1}{4}(2t + 1)$.

Here is a summary of the three types of solution. The word 'point' is used to mean a pair of values of the unknowns.

When solving linear equations there are three possible outcomes:

- the solution may be a single point;
- the solution may consist of infinitely many points;
- there may be no points satisfying the equations.

In the first two cases the equations are said to be **consistent**; when there is no solution (the third case) the equations are said to be **inconsistent**.

If the solution consists of a single point it is said to be **unique**.

1.4 Sets of equations with three unknowns where the solution is not unique

One or two equations and three unknowns

If there are three unknowns, x, y and z, an equation of the form

$$ax + by + cz = d$$

is called a linear equation in three unknowns. But there is a trap here. If (x, y, z) are the coordinates of a point in three-dimensional geometry, this equation doesn't represent a line, but a plane. 'Linear' is now just a description of the equation, not the geometry.

The method for solving the equation $x + 2y + 3z = 6$ is similar to that for solving an equation with two unknowns described in Section 1.3.

Example 1.4.1
Solve the equation $x + 2y + 3z = 6$.

You can let y and z have any values and then find x. Putting $y = s$ and $z = t$ you get $x = 6 - 2s - 3t$. The solution can therefore be written as

$$\left. \begin{array}{l} x = 6 - 2s - 3t \\ y = \quad\quad s \\ z = \quad\quad\quad t \end{array} \right\} , \quad s, t \in \mathbb{R}.$$

Example 1.4.2
Solve the equations $\left. \begin{array}{l} x + 2y + 3z = 6 \\ 2x + 3y + \ z = 7 \end{array} \right\}$.

$$\left. \begin{array}{l} x + 2y + 3z = 6 \\ 2x + 3y + \ z = 7 \end{array} \right\} \quad \Leftrightarrow \quad \left. \begin{array}{l} x + 2y + 3z = \ 6 \\ 0x - \ y - 5z = -5 \end{array} \right\} \quad r_2' = r_2 - 2r_1$$

$$\Leftrightarrow \quad \left. \begin{array}{l} x + \ 2y + 3z = 6 \\ \quad\quad y + 5z = 5 \end{array} \right\} \quad r_2' = r_2 \div (-1)$$

You can let z have any value and find x and y. Putting $z = t$ you get $y = 5 - 5t$ and $x = 6 - 2(5 - 5t) - 3t = -4 + 7t$. The solution is therefore

$$\left.\begin{array}{l} x = -4 + 7t \\ y = 5 - 5t \\ z = t \end{array}\right\}, \quad t \in \mathbb{R}.$$

Three equations and three unknowns

These examples show situations with three equations and three unknowns where either there is no solution or the solution is not unique.

Example 1.4.3

Solve the equations $\left.\begin{array}{r} x - y + z = 2 \\ 2x + 3y - z = 4 \\ 3x + 7y - 3z = 5 \end{array}\right\}$.

$$\left.\begin{array}{r} x - y + z = 2 \\ 2x + 3y - z = 4 \\ 3x + 7y - 3z = 5 \end{array}\right\} \Leftrightarrow \left.\begin{array}{r} x - y + z = 2 \\ 0x + 5y - 3z = 0 \\ 0x + 10y - 6z = -1 \end{array}\right\} \quad \begin{array}{l} r'_2 = r_2 - 2r_1 \\ r'_3 = r_3 - 3r_1 \end{array}$$

$$\Leftrightarrow \left.\begin{array}{r} x - y + z = 2 \\ 5y - 3z = 0 \\ 0y + 0z = -1 \end{array}\right\} \quad r'_3 = r_3 - 2r_2$$

$$\Leftrightarrow \left.\begin{array}{r} x - y + z = 2 \\ 5y - 3z = 0 \\ 0 = -1 \end{array}\right\}.$$

The last equation shows that these equations are inconsistent and therefore have no solution.

Example 1.4.4

Solve the equations $\left.\begin{array}{r} x - y + z = 2 \\ 2x + 3y - z = 4 \\ 3x + 7y - 3z = 6 \end{array}\right\}$.

$$\left.\begin{array}{r} x - y + z = 2 \\ 2x + 3y - z = 4 \\ 3x + 7y - 3z = 6 \end{array}\right\} \Leftrightarrow \left.\begin{array}{r} x - y + z = 2 \\ 0x + 5y - 3z = 0 \\ 0x + 10y - 6z = 0 \end{array}\right\} \quad \begin{array}{l} r'_2 = r_2 - 2r_1 \\ r'_3 = r_3 - 3r_1 \end{array}$$

$$\Leftrightarrow \left.\begin{array}{r} x - y + z = 2 \\ 5y - 3z = 0 \\ 0y + 0z = 0 \end{array}\right\} \quad r'_3 = r_3 - 2r_2$$

$$\Leftrightarrow \left.\begin{array}{r} x - y + z = 2 \\ 5y - 3z = 0 \\ 0 = 0 \end{array}\right\}.$$

These equations are consistent. To solve them put $z = 5t$ where t is a parameter. In the second equation, $y = 3t$, and then, substituting in the first equation, $x = -2t + 2$. The solution can be written as

$$\left. \begin{array}{rl} x = & 2 - 2t \\ y = & 3t \\ z = & 5t \end{array} \right\}, \quad t \in \mathbb{R}.$$

Example 1.4.5

Solve the equations $\left. \begin{array}{r} x - y + z = 2 \\ 2x - 2y + 2z = 4 \\ 3x - 3y + 3z = 6 \end{array} \right\}$.

Using the same methods as previously, you quickly see that

$$\left. \begin{array}{r} x - y + z = 2 \\ 2x - 2y + 2z = 4 \\ 3x - 3y + 3z = 6 \end{array} \right\} \Leftrightarrow \left. \begin{array}{r} x - y + z = 2 \\ 0x - 0y + 0z = 0 \\ 0x - 0y + 0z = 0 \end{array} \right\} \quad \begin{array}{l} r_2' = r_2 - 2r_1 \\ r_3' = r_3 - 3r_1 \end{array}$$

$$\Leftrightarrow \left. \begin{array}{r} x - y + z = 2 \\ 0 = 0 \\ 0 = 0 \end{array} \right\} .$$

These equations can be solved by the method used in Example 1.4.1. Put $y = s$ and $z = t$, giving $x = 2 + s - t$. So the solution can be written as

$$\left. \begin{array}{rl} x = & 2 + s - t \\ y = & s \\ z = & t \end{array} \right\}, \quad s, t \in \mathbb{R}.$$

Example 1.4.6

Solve the equations $\left. \begin{array}{r} 2x - y + 3z = -1 \\ x - 2y - 4z = 1 \\ 2x - 7y - 19z = k \end{array} \right\}$, giving your answers in terms of k.

$$\left. \begin{array}{r} 2x - y + 3z = -1 \\ x - 2y - 4z = 1 \\ 2x - 7y - 19z = k \end{array} \right\} \Leftrightarrow \left. \begin{array}{r} x - 2y - 4z = 1 \\ 2x - y + 3z = -1 \\ 2x - 7y - 19z = k \end{array} \right\} \quad \begin{array}{l} r_1' = r_2 \\ r_2' = r_1 \end{array}$$

$$\Leftrightarrow \left. \begin{array}{r} x - 2y - 4z = 1 \\ 3y + 11z = -3 \\ -3y - 11z = k - 2 \end{array} \right\} \quad \begin{array}{l} r_2' = r_2 - 2r_1 \\ r_3' = r_3 - 2r_1 \end{array}$$

$$\Leftrightarrow \left. \begin{array}{r} x - 2y - 4z = 1 \\ 3y + 11z = -3 \\ 0y + 0z = k - 5 \end{array} \right\} \quad r_3' = r_3 + r_2$$

At this stage you can see that if $k \neq 5$, the equations are inconsistent, and there are no points satisfying the equations.

If $k = 5$, put $z = 3t$, giving $3y = -3 - 33t$, so $y = -1 - 11t$. And then $2x = -1 + (-1 - 11t) - 9t = -2 - 20t$, giving $x = -1 - 10t$.

So, if $k = -3$, then

$$\left.\begin{array}{r} x = -1 - 10t \\ y = -1 - 11t \\ z = \qquad 3t \end{array}\right\}, \quad t \in \mathbb{R},$$

and if $k \neq 5$, there is no solution.

Sometimes it may be convenient to give a solution in terms of one of the existing variables.

Example 1.4.7

Solve the equations $\left.\begin{array}{r} x + 2y + 3z = 8 \\ x - 3y + 5z = 0 \\ x - 8y + 7z = -8 \end{array}\right\}$, giving x and y in terms of z.

Working in the usual way,

$$\left.\begin{array}{r} x + 2y + 3z = 8 \\ x - 3y + 5z = 0 \\ x - 8y + 7z = -8 \end{array}\right\} \Leftrightarrow \left.\begin{array}{r} x + 2y + 3z = 8 \\ -5y + 2z = -8 \\ -10y - 4z = -16 \end{array}\right\} \begin{array}{l} r_2' = r_2 - r_1 \\ r_3' = r_3 - r_1 \end{array}$$

$$\Leftrightarrow \left.\begin{array}{r} x + 2y + 3z = 8 \\ -5y + 2z = -8 \\ 0 = 0 \end{array}\right\} \quad r_3' = r_3 - 2r_2$$

At this stage, you can rewrite the equations as

$$\left.\begin{array}{r} x + 2y = 8 - 3z \\ -5y = -8 - 2z \end{array}\right\}.$$

Then $y = \frac{1}{5}(8 + 2z)$ and, substituting for x in the first equation gives

$$x = 8 - 3z - 2y$$
$$= 8 - 3z - \frac{2}{5}(8 + 2z)$$
$$= \frac{24}{5} - \frac{19}{5}z = \frac{1}{5}(24 - 19z).$$

So the solution is $x = \frac{1}{5}(24 - 19z)$, $y = \frac{1}{5}(8 + 2z)$.

1.5* Geometric interpretation

You will see in FP3 that an equation such as $x - 3y + 4z = 2$ represents a plane, and that the equation $x - 3y + 4z = a$, where a is any real number, represents a plane parallel to the plane $x - 3y + 4z = 2$.

You can then interpret the solutions of Example 1.2.3 and Examples 1.4.3 to 1.4.5 geometrically.

In Example 1.2.3, the equations represent three planes which meet in a single point.

In Example 1.4.3, the equations represent three planes which meet in a prism-shape. This is illustrated in Fig. 1.2, where you can see that the three planes have no common point.

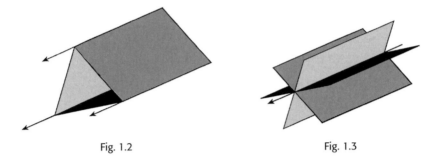

Fig. 1.2   Fig. 1.3

In Example 1.4.4, the three planes meet in a line, as in Fig. 1.3. The equations are then satisfied by infinitely many points, all lying along the common line of intersection.

In Example 1.4.5, the three equations are identical and all represent the same plane. This explains why two parameters are needed: they describe the two-dimensional nature of the solution.

Exercise 1B

1 Use the triangular form method to find the solution, if it exists, of each of the following sets of equations.

(a) $\begin{aligned} x - y &= 2 \\ -x + y &= -2 \end{aligned}$

(b) $\begin{aligned} 2x - y &= 1 \\ 4x - 2y &= 3 \end{aligned}$

(c) $\begin{aligned} 3x - y &= 0 \\ -6x + 2y &= 0 \end{aligned}$

(d) $\begin{aligned} 2x - 4y &= 6 \\ -4x + 8y &= -12 \end{aligned}$

(e) $\begin{aligned} x + 3y &= 6 \\ 6x + 18y &= 12 \end{aligned}$

(f) $\begin{aligned} 5x - 3y &= 10 \\ -10x + 6y &= -20 \end{aligned}$

2 Solve, where possible, each of the following sets of equations.

(a) $\begin{aligned} x - y + z &= 3 \\ 2x + y - 2z &= 5 \end{aligned}$

(b) $\begin{aligned} 2x - y - z &= 5 \\ x + y - z &= -1 \end{aligned}$

(c) $\begin{aligned} 2x + y - 3z &= 2 \\ -4x - 2y + 6z &= -1 \end{aligned}$

(d) $\begin{aligned} 2x + y - 3z &= 2 \\ -4x - 2y + 6z &= -4 \end{aligned}$

(e) $x + y - z = 3$

(f) $\begin{aligned} x - 2y + z &= 0 \\ x + y - 2z &= 3 \end{aligned}$

(g) $3x - 4y + 5z = 0$

(h) $\begin{aligned} 3x + y - 2z &= 4 \\ -9x - 3y + 6z &= 12 \end{aligned}$

(i) $\begin{aligned} 3x + y - 2z &= 4 \\ -9x - 3y + 6z &= -12 \end{aligned}$

3 Solve, where possible, each of the following sets of equations.

(a) $\begin{aligned} x + y - z &= 4 \\ 2x - y - 6z &= 6 \\ x - 2y + 3z &= -6 \end{aligned}$

(b) $\begin{aligned} 2x - y + 3z &= 5 \\ x + 3y - 2z &= 4 \\ y - z &= 2 \end{aligned}$

(c) $\begin{aligned} x + y + 2z &= 5 \\ 2x - y + z &= 1 \\ x - 2y - z &= -4 \end{aligned}$

(d) $\begin{aligned} y - z &= 2 \\ x + 2y &= 3 \\ x \quad + 2z &= -1 \end{aligned}$

(e) $\begin{aligned} y + z &= 2 \\ x + y &= 3 \\ x + 2y + z &= 5 \end{aligned}$

(f) $\begin{aligned} 2x - y - z &= 3 \\ x + 2y - 3z &= 4 \\ 2x + y + z &= -11 \end{aligned}$

4 Solve each of the following sets of equations in terms of k.

(a) $\left.\begin{array}{r} x - y + z = 2 \\ x + y - z = 4 \\ x + y + z = k \end{array}\right\}$

(b) $\left.\begin{array}{r} 2x + y - z = 8 \\ x + y - 2z = -5 \\ 3x + 2y - 3z = k \end{array}\right\}$

(c) $\left.\begin{array}{r} y - z = 2 \\ x + 2y - z = 9 \\ 2x + 3y - z = k \end{array}\right\}$

5 Solve the following sets of equations expressing x and y in terms of z.

(a) $\left.\begin{array}{r} 2x + y + 5z = 8 \\ x + y - 3z = 0 \\ x \quad + 8z = 8 \end{array}\right\}$

(b) $\left.\begin{array}{r} x + 2y + 3z = 4 \\ 4x + 5y + 6z = 1 \\ 7x + 8y + 9z = -2 \end{array}\right\}$

(c) $\left.\begin{array}{r} y + z = 3 \\ x - y \quad = 4 \\ x \quad + z = 7 \end{array}\right\}$

Miscellaneous exercise 1

1 Find the solution of the pair of equations $\left.\begin{array}{r} 2x + 3y = 4 \\ -4x - 6y = -8 \end{array}\right\}$.

2 Solve the equation $3x + 2y - 5z = 0$.

3 Solve the equations $\left.\begin{array}{r} x + 3y + 5z = 0 \\ -x + 2y + 4z = 0 \end{array}\right\}$.

4 Solve the equations

(a) $\left.\begin{array}{r} 3x - y - 2z = 14 \\ 2x + y - z = 7 \\ 4x - y + 3z = 7 \end{array}\right\}$

(b) $\left.\begin{array}{r} 2x + 3y - z = 8 \\ 3x + y - z = 8 \\ 4x - y - z = 8 \end{array}\right\}$

(c) $\left.\begin{array}{r} x - y - z = 1 \\ 2x - y - z = 2 \\ 3x - y - z = 3 \end{array}\right\}$

(d) $\left.\begin{array}{r} y - 2z = 0 \\ 2x + 3y = 18 \\ x + 2y - z = 9 \end{array}\right\}$

(e) $\left.\begin{array}{r} x - 2y + 2z = 5 \\ 2x - y - 2z = 1 \\ 2x + 2y + z = 1 \end{array}\right\}$

(f) $\left.\begin{array}{r} y - z = 1 \\ x + z = 2 \\ x + y = 3 \end{array}\right\}$

5 Solve each of the following sets of equations in terms of k.

(a) $\left.\begin{array}{r} x - 3y = 4 \\ -4x + 12y = k \end{array}\right\}$

(b) $\left.\begin{array}{r} x - y = 3 \\ 3x + y = k \end{array}\right\}$

(c) $\left.\begin{array}{r} y = 3 \\ x + y = k \end{array}\right\}$

6 Solve each of the following sets of equations in terms of k.

(a) $\left.\begin{array}{r} x + y + z = 1 \\ 2x + 2y + z = 2 \\ 3x + 3y + z = k \end{array}\right\}$

(b) $\left.\begin{array}{r} z = 1 \\ x - y + z = 2 \\ y + z = k \end{array}\right\}$

(c) $\left.\begin{array}{r} x + y + z = 1 \\ x + y + z = 2k \\ x + y + z = k^2 \end{array}\right\}$

7 Solve the equations $\left.\begin{array}{r} kx + y + z = 1 \\ x + ky + z = 1 \\ x + y + kz = p \end{array}\right\}$

(a) when $k = -2$ and $p = -2$,   (b) when $k = 1$ and $p = 1$.

8 Solve the equations $\left.\begin{array}{r} -x + 8y = kx \\ 5x - 4y = ky \end{array}\right\}$ for the cases

(a) $k = -9$,   (b) $k = 4$.

2 Summing series

This chapter is about finding formulae for the sums of series. When you have completed it, you should

- be able to sum series where the rth term is a polynomial in r of degree 3 or less
- be able to use a method based on differences to sum certain kinds of series
- be able to tell in simple cases when a series converges and, if it does, to find the sum to infinity.

Before you start this chapter you should read C2 Chapter 2.

2.1 Sum of squares of the first n natural numbers

In C2 Section 2.2 it was shown that $1 + 2 + \cdots + n = \frac{1}{2}n(n+1)$. In sigma notation this can be written $\sum_{r=1}^{n} r = \frac{1}{2}n(n+1)$.

Also $\sum_{r=1}^{n} 1$ means $\overbrace{1 + 1 + 1 + \cdots + 1}^{n\text{ of these}}$, which is clearly equal to n.

As $1 = r^0$ and $r = r^1$, you could write these two results as

$$\sum_{r=1}^{n} r^0 = n,$$

and
$$\sum_{r=1}^{n} r^1 = \frac{1}{2}n(n+1).$$

Can you find similar formulae for

$$\sum_{r=1}^{n} r^2 = 1^2 + 2^2 + \cdots + n^2$$

and
$$\sum_{r=1}^{n} r^3 = 1^3 + 2^3 + \cdots + n^3?$$

From the formula $\sum_{r=1}^{n} r^0 = n$, you can see that

$$\sum_{r=1}^{n} r^0 = n \times \text{a polynomial of degree 0 in } n,$$

and from the formula $\sum_{r=1}^{n} r^1 = \frac{1}{2}n(n+1)$ that

$$\sum_{r=1}^{n} r^1 = n \times \text{a polynomial of degree 1 in } n.$$

This suggests that $\sum_{r=1}^{n} r^2 = n \times$ a polynomial of degree 2 in n.

So try making the assumption that $\sum_{r=1}^{n} r^2$ can be written in the form

$$\sum_{r=1}^{n} r^2 = n(A + Bn + Cn^2)$$

where A, B and C are constants, and see if you can find A, B and C.

The polynomial $A + Bn + Cn^2$ has been written in ascending order of powers of n because it makes the calculation which follows simpler. At the end of the calculation it has been put back in descending order.

This is the same as assuming that $\sum_{r=1}^{n} r^2 = An + Bn^2 + Cn^3$.

Putting $n = 1, \ 2, \ $ and 3 in turn, this means that

$$\left. \begin{array}{l} 1^2 = A \times 1 + B \times 1^2 + C \times 1^3 \\ 1^2 + 2^2 = A \times 2 + B \times 2^2 + C \times 2^3 \\ 1^2 + 2^2 + 3^2 = A \times 3 + B \times 3^2 + C \times 3^3 \end{array} \right\},$$

that is,

$$\left. \begin{array}{rcl} A + B + C &=& 1 \\ 2A + 4B + 8C &=& 5 \\ 3A + 9B + 27C &=& 14 \end{array} \right\}.$$

Solving these by the method of Section 1.6,

$$\left. \begin{array}{rcl} A + B + C &=& 1 \\ 2A + 4B + 8C &=& 5 \\ 3A + 9B + 27C &=& 14 \end{array} \right\} \Leftrightarrow \left. \begin{array}{rcl} A + B + C &=& 1 \\ 2B + 6C &=& 3 \\ 6B + 24C &=& 11 \end{array} \right\} \begin{array}{l} r'_2 = r_2 - 2r_1 \\ r'_3 = r_3 - 3r_1 \end{array}$$

$$\Leftrightarrow \left. \begin{array}{rcl} A + B + C &=& 1 \\ 2B + 6C &=& 3 \\ 6C &=& 2 \end{array} \right\} \ r'_3 = r_3 - 3r_2$$

You can now see that $C = \frac{1}{3}$; substituting this into the second and first equations gives $B = \frac{1}{2}$ and $A = \frac{1}{6}$.

This suggests that $\sum_{r=1}^{n} r^2 = \frac{1}{6}n + \frac{1}{2}n^2 + \frac{1}{3}n^3$.

Reverting to descending order of powers for the polynomial, and factorising, gives

$$\sum_{r=1}^{n} r^2 = \frac{1}{3}n^3 + \frac{1}{2}n^2 + \frac{1}{6}n$$

$$= \frac{1}{6}n(2n^2 + 3n + 1)$$

$$= \frac{1}{6}n(n+1)(2n+1).$$

Note that this derivation is not a proof. All it shows is that, if $\sum\limits_{r=1}^{n} r^2$ is a cubic polynomial, then $\sum\limits_{r=1}^{n} r^2 = \frac{1}{6}n(n+1)(2n+1)$. However, it is encouraging that $1^2 + 2^2 + 3^2 + 4^2 + 5^2 = 55$ and $\frac{1}{6} \times 5(5+1)(2 \times 5 + 1) = \frac{1}{6} \times 5 \times 6 \times 11 = 55$. You will find a proof of the result in Section 2.3.

Example 2.1.1

Find the sum $1^2 + 2^2 + \cdots + 144^2$.

Putting $n = 144$ in $\sum\limits_{r=1}^{n} r^2 = \frac{1}{6}n(n+1)(2n+1)$,

$$\sum_{r=1}^{144} r^2 = \frac{1}{6} \times 144 \times 145 \times 289 = 1\,005\,720.$$

Example 2.1.2

Find the sum of the series $1 \times 2 + 2 \times 3 + 3 \times 4 + \cdots + n(n+1)$.

The rth term of this series is $r(r+1)$. So the sum is

$$\sum_{r=1}^{n} r(r+1) = \sum_{r=1}^{n} (r^2 + r)$$

$$= \sum_{r=1}^{n} r^2 + \sum_{r=1}^{n} r \qquad \text{(using the addition rule; see C2 Section 2.7).}$$

Now you can use the formulae for $\sum\limits_{r=1}^{n} r^2$ and $\sum\limits_{r=1}^{n} r$, so

$$\sum_{r=1}^{n} r^2 + \sum_{r=1}^{n} r = \frac{1}{6}n(n+1)(2n+1) + \frac{1}{2}n(n+1)$$

$$= n(n+1)\left(\frac{1}{6}(2n+1) + \frac{1}{2}\right)$$

$$= n(n+1) \times \frac{1}{6}(2n+1+3)$$

$$= \frac{1}{6}n(n+1)(2n+4)$$

$$= \frac{1}{6}n(n+1) \times 2(n+2)$$

$$= \frac{1}{3}n(n+1)(n+2).$$

Therefore $1 \times 2 + 2 \times 3 + 3 \times 4 + \cdots + n(n+1) = \frac{1}{3}n(n+1)(n+2)$.

It is worth checking this for a small value of n. Putting $n = 2$, the left side is $1 \times 2 + 2 \times 3 = 8$. The right side is $\frac{1}{3} \times 2 \times (2+1) \times (3+1) = 8$.

You can use this method in a variety of ways. Here are two more examples.

Example 2.1.3
Find the sum $(n+1)^2 + (n+2)^2 + \cdots + (2n)^2$.

Method 1   Notice that this is the sum $1^2 + 2^2 + 3^2 + \cdots + n^2 + \cdots + (2n)^2$ with the first n terms subtracted, which can be written as
$$(1^2 + 2^2 + \cdots + (2n)^2) - (1^2 + 2^2 + \cdots + n^2).$$

Using the formula for $\sum_{r=1}^{n} r^2$,

$$(1^2 + 2^2 + \cdots + (2n)^2) - (1^2 + 2^2 + \cdots + n^2)$$
$$= \sum_{r=1}^{2n} r^2 - \sum_{r=1}^{n} r^2$$
$$= \tfrac{1}{6}(2n)((2n)+1)(2(2n)+1) - \tfrac{1}{6}n(n+1)(2n+1)$$
$$= \tfrac{1}{6}(2n)(2n+1)(4n+1) - \tfrac{1}{6}n(n+1)(2n+1)$$
$$= \tfrac{1}{6}n(2n+1)(2(4n+1)-(n+1))$$
$$= \tfrac{1}{6}n(2n+1)(7n+1).$$

Method 2   This method, which is not so efficient, expresses the rth term in the form $(n+r)^2$.

Then the series $(n+1)^2 + (n+2)^2 + \cdots + (2n)^2$ can be written in the form

$$(n+1)^2 + (n+2)^2 + \cdots + (2n)^2 = \sum_{r=1}^{n}(n+r)^2$$
$$= \sum_{r=1}^{n}(n^2 + 2nr + r^2)$$
$$= \sum_{r=1}^{n} n^2 + \sum_{r=1}^{n} 2nr + \sum_{r=1}^{n} r^2 \quad \text{(addition rule)}$$
$$= n^2 \sum_{r=1}^{n} 1 + 2n \sum_{r=1}^{n} r + \sum_{r=1}^{n} r^2 \quad \text{(multiple rule)}$$
$$= n^2 \times n + 2n \times \tfrac{1}{2}n(n+1) + \tfrac{1}{6}n(n+1)(2n+1)$$
$$= n(n^2 + n(n+1) + \tfrac{1}{6}(n+1)(2n+1))$$
$$= \tfrac{1}{6}n(6n^2 + 6n(n+1) + (n+1)(2n+1))$$
$$= \tfrac{1}{6}n(14n^2 + 9n + 1) = \tfrac{1}{6}n(2n+1)(7n+1).$$

Where the multiple rule is used, it is important to notice that you can take n out of the summation because it is a constant, but you cannot do the same for the summation variable r.

Example 2.1.4

Find the sum of the series $1^2 - 2^2 + 3^2 - 4^2 + \cdots + (2n-1)^2 - (2n)^2$.

Method 1   Using a method which involves adding $2(2^2 + 4^2 + \cdots + (2n)^2)$ and then subtracting it gives

$$1^2 - 2^2 + 3^2 - 4^2 + \cdots + (2n-1)^2 - (2n)^2$$
$$= 1^2 + 2^2 + 3^2 + 4^2 + \cdots + (2n-1)^2 + (2n)^2$$
$$\qquad - 2(2^2 + 4^2 + \cdots + (2n)^2)$$
$$= 1^2 + 2^2 + \cdots + (2n)^2 - 2 \times 2^2(1^2 + 2^2 + \cdots + n^2)$$
$$= \sum_{r=1}^{2n} r^2 - 8 \sum_{r=1}^{n} r^2$$
$$= \tfrac{1}{6}(2n)((2n)+1)(2(2n)+1) - 8 \times \tfrac{1}{6}n(n+1)(2n+1)$$
$$= \tfrac{1}{3}n(2n+1)(4n+1) - \tfrac{4}{3}n(n+1)(2n+1)$$
$$= \tfrac{1}{3}n(2n+1)((4n+1) - 4(n+1))$$
$$= \tfrac{1}{3}n(2n+1) \times (-3) = -n(2n+1).$$

Method 2   If you pair off the terms as

$$(1^2 - 2^2) + (3^2 - 4^2) + \cdots + ((2n-1)^2 - (2n)^2),$$

the rth bracket is

$$(2r-1)^2 - (2r)^2.$$

which is $4r^2 - 4r + 1 - 4r^2 = -4r + 1$.

Thus the series is

$$\sum_{r=1}^{n}(-4r+1) = -4\sum_{r=1}^{n} r + \sum_{r=1}^{n} 1$$
$$= -4 \times \tfrac{1}{2}n(n+1) + n$$
$$= -2n(n+1) + n$$
$$= n(-2n - 2 + 1)$$
$$= -n(2n+1).$$

You can check this result by putting $n = 1$ or $n = 2$.

Exercise 2A

1 Use the formulae for $\sum_{r=1}^{n} 1$, $\sum_{r=1}^{n} r$ and $\sum_{r=1}^{n} r^2$ to find the following sums.

(a) $1^2 + 2^2 + \cdots + 100^2$

(b) $2 \times 3 + 3 \times 4 + \cdots + 99 \times 100$

(c) $(1 + 1^2) + (2 + 2^2) + \cdots + (20 + 20^2)$

2 Use the formulae for $\sum\limits_{r=1}^{n} 1$, $\sum\limits_{r=1}^{n} r$ and $\sum\limits_{r=1}^{n} r^2$ to find the following sums.

(a) $\sum\limits_{r=0}^{n} (r+1)$ (b) $\sum\limits_{r=1}^{n} (2r+1)$ (c) $\sum\limits_{r=1}^{n} (3r^2+1)$

3 Write down the formulae for $\sum\limits_{r=1}^{n} 1$ and $\sum\limits_{r=1}^{n} r$. Use these formulae to write down the sum of the arithmetic series a, $a+d$, $a+2d$, $\ldots$, $a+(n-1)d$.

Verify that your answer agrees with the formula $\frac{1}{2}n(2a+(n-1)d)$ given in C2 Section 2.5.

4 (a) Find $\sum\limits_{r=1}^{142} (7r)$.

(b) Find the sum of the multiples of 7 which are less than 10 000.

5 Find the sum of

(a) the squares of the integers less than 100 which are divisible by 3,

(b) the squares of the integers less than 100 which are not divisible by 3.

6 Find the sum of n terms of the series

$$(p-1)(p+1) + (p-2)(p+2) + (p-3)(p+3) + \ldots.$$

7 Find the sum of the series $1 \times n + 2 \times (n-1) + \cdots + n \times 1$.

2.2 Sum of cubes of the first n natural numbers

You could try a method similar to the one for finding $\sum\limits_{r=1}^{n} r^2$ to find a formula for $\sum\limits_{r=1}^{n} r^3$. You could say that you expect it to be a polynomial of degree 4 in n, and then attempt to find the coefficients. But this would involve solving 4 equations with 4 unknowns. Happily you are spared this approach by a stroke of luck. If you examine the corresponding values of $\sum\limits_{r=1}^{n} r^3$ and $\sum\limits_{r=1}^{n} r$ you find a surprising relationship.

$$\sum_{r=1}^{1} r^3 = 1^3 = 1 \qquad\qquad \sum_{r=1}^{1} r = 1$$

$$\sum_{r=1}^{2} r^3 = 1^3 + 2^3 = 9 \qquad\qquad \sum_{r=1}^{2} r = 1 + 2 = 3$$

$$\sum_{r=1}^{3} r^3 = 1^3 + 2^3 + 3^3 = 36 \qquad\qquad \sum_{r=1}^{3} r = 1 + 2 + 3 = 6$$

$$\sum_{r=1}^{4} r^3 = 1^3 + 2^3 + 3^3 + 4^3 = 100 \qquad\qquad \sum_{r=1}^{4} r = 1 + 2 + 3 + 4 = 10$$

This suggests that $\sum\limits_{r=1}^{n} r^3 = \left(\sum\limits_{r=1}^{n} r\right)^2$.

If you check this for $n=5$, you find that $\sum\limits_{r=1}^{5} r = 15$ and $\sum\limits_{r=1}^{5} r^3 = 225$, so the relation $\sum\limits_{r=1}^{n} r^3 = \left(\sum\limits_{r=1}^{n} r\right)^2$ holds for $n = 1, \ldots, 5$. It actually holds for all n, so $\sum\limits_{r=1}^{n} r^3 = \frac{1}{4}n^2(n+1)^2$.

The sums of the early powers of the natural numbers are

$$\sum_{r=1}^{n} 1 = \overbrace{1 + 1 + \cdots + 1}^{n \text{ of these}} = n,$$

$$\sum_{r=1}^{n} r = 1 + 2 + \cdots + n = \tfrac{1}{2}n(n+1),$$

$$\sum_{r=1}^{n} r^2 = 1^2 + 2^2 + \cdots + n^2 = \tfrac{1}{6}n(n+1)(2n+1),$$

$$\sum_{r=1}^{n} r^3 = 1^3 + 2^3 + \cdots + n^3 = \tfrac{1}{4}n^2(n+1)^2.$$

Note that the result $\sum_{r=1}^{n} r^3 = \tfrac{1}{4}n^2(n+1)^2$ has not been proved. A proof is asked for in Miscellaneous exercise 2 Question 10.

Example 2.2.1

Find a formula for $1 \times 2 \times 4 + 2 \times 3 \times 5 + \cdots + n(n+1)(n+3)$.

The rth term is $r(r+1)(r+3)$, so the sum of the series is $\sum_{r=1}^{n} r(r+1)(r+3)$.

As $r(r+1)(r+3) = r^3 + 4r^2 + 3r$, the required sum is

$$\sum_{r=1}^{n} r(r+1)(r+3) = \sum_{r=1}^{n}(r^3 + 4r^2 + 3r) = \sum_{r=1}^{n}r^3 + 4\sum_{r=1}^{n}r^2 + 3\sum_{r=1}^{n}r$$

$$= \tfrac{1}{4}n^2(n+1)^2 + 4 \times \tfrac{1}{6}n(n+1)(2n+1) + 3 \times \tfrac{1}{2}n(n+1)$$

$$= \tfrac{1}{12}n(n+1)(3n(n+1) + 8(2n+1) + 18)$$

$$= \tfrac{1}{12}n(n+1)(3n^2 + 19n + 26).$$

As a check, put $n = 1$. The left side is $1 \times 2 \times 4 = 8$, and the right side is $\tfrac{1}{12} \times 1 \times 2 \times (3 + 19 + 26) = 8$.

Example 2.2.2

Calculate   (a) $2^3 + 4^3 + 6^3 + \cdots + 30^3$,   (b) $1^3 + 3^3 + 5^3 + \cdots + 29^3$.

(a) Start by taking out the factor 2^3 which is common to all the terms. Then

$$2^3 + 4^3 + 6^3 + \cdots + 30^3 = 2^3(1^3 + 2^3 + 3^3 + \cdots + 15^3)$$

$$= 8\sum_{r=1}^{15} r^3$$

$$= 8 \times \tfrac{1}{4} \times 15^2 \times 16^2$$

$$= 115\,200.$$

(b) Insert the even terms which are missing, and then subtract them.

$$1^3 + 3^3 + 5^3 + \cdots + 29^3 = 1^3 + 2^3 + 3^3 + 4^3 + 5^3 + \cdots + 30^3$$
$$- (2^3 + 4^3 + 6^3 + \cdots + 30^3)$$
$$= \sum_{r=1}^{30} r^3 - 115\,200 \qquad \text{(from part (a))}$$
$$= \tfrac{1}{4} \times 30^2 \times 31^2 - 115\,200$$
$$= 101\,025.$$

Exercise 2B

1 Use the formulae for $\sum_{r=1}^{n} 1$, $\sum_{r=1}^{n} r$, $\sum_{r=1}^{n} r^2$ and $\sum_{r=1}^{n} r^3$ to find the following sums.

   (a) $1 \times 2 \times 3 + 2 \times 3 \times 4 + \cdots + 98 \times 99 \times 100$

   (b) $2 \times 3 \times 4 + 3 \times 4 \times 5 \ldots + 99 \times 100 \times 101$

2 Use the formulae for $\sum_{r=1}^{n} 1$, $\sum_{r=1}^{n} r$, $\sum_{r=1}^{n} r^2$ and $\sum_{r=1}^{n} r^3$ to find the following sums.

   (a) $\displaystyle\sum_{r=1}^{n} r^2 (r - 1)$ (b) $\displaystyle\sum_{r=1}^{n} r^2 (2r - 1)$ (c) $\displaystyle\sum_{r=1}^{2n} r^2 (r - 1)$ (d) $\displaystyle\sum_{r=1}^{n+1} r^2 (2r - 1)$

3 (a) Find $\displaystyle\sum_{r=1}^{50} (2r)^3$.

   (b) Find the sum of the cubes of the even numbers less than 100.

4 Find the sum of the cubes of the integers less than 100 which are not divisible by 5.

5 Find the sum of the series $1 \times 2^2 + 2 \times 3^2 + \cdots + n(n + 1)^2$.

6 Find the sum of n terms of the series $1^2 \times 3 + 2^2 \times 4 + 3^2 \times 5 + \ldots$.

7 Find the sum of the series $1 \times n^2 + 2 \times (n - 1)^2 + \cdots + n \times 1^2$.

8 Calculate the following sums.

   (a) $\displaystyle\sum_{r=1}^{100} r(r + 2)(r + 3)$ (b) $\displaystyle\sum_{r=1}^{100} r(r^2 - 1)$ (c) $\displaystyle\sum_{r=1}^{100} r(r + 3)(r + 6)$

2.3 A method based on differences

In this section you will see a method which can be useful for summing series. Suppose for the moment that you know the formulae for $\sum_{r=1}^{n} 1$ and $\sum_{r=1}^{n} r$, and that you want one for $\sum_{r=1}^{n} r^2$.

Consider the equation $(r + 1)^3 - r^3 = 3r^2 + 3r + 1$. If you swap the sides and write it for values of r starting from 1 and going up to n, you get

$$
\begin{array}{rclcl}
3 \times 1^2 & + & 3 \times 1 & + 1 = & 2^3 & - & 1^3 \\
3 \times 2^2 & + & 3 \times 2 & + 1 = & 3^3 & - & 2^3 \\
3 \times 3^2 & + & 3 \times 3 & + 1 = & 4^3 & - & 3^3 \\
& \vdots & & \vdots & \vdots & & \vdots \\
3(n-1)^2 & + & 3(n-1) & + 1 = & n^3 & - & (n-1)^3 \\
3n^2 & + & 3n & + 1 = & (n+1)^3 & - & n^3
\end{array}
$$

Now add downwards.

$$
\begin{array}{rclcl}
3 \times 1^2 & + & 3 \times 1 & + 1 = & \cancel{2^3} & - & 1^3 \\
3 \times 2^2 & + & 3 \times 2 & + 1 = & \cancel{3^3} & - & \cancel{2^3} \\
3 \times 3^2 & + & 3 \times 3 & + 1 = & \cancel{4^3} & - & \cancel{3^3} \\
& \vdots & & \vdots & \vdots & & \vdots \\
3(n-1)^2 & + & 3(n-1) & + 1 = & \cancel{n^3} & - & \cancel{(n-1)^3} \\
3n^2 & + & 3n & + 1 = & (n+1)^3 & - & \cancel{n^3}
\end{array}
$$

$$
3\sum_{1}^{n} r^2 + 3\sum_{1}^{n} r + n = (n+1)^3 - 1^3
$$

The left side is $3\sum\limits_{r=1}^{n} r^2 + 3\sum\limits_{r=1}^{n} r + \sum\limits_{r=1}^{n} 1$. On the right side, most of the terms cancel, leaving $(n+1)^3 - 1^3 = (n+1)^3 - 1$. Therefore

$$
3\sum_{r=1}^{n} r^2 + 3\sum_{r=1}^{n} r + \sum_{r=1}^{n} 1 = (n+1)^3 - 1.
$$

If you transfer $\sum\limits_{r=1}^{n} 1$ and $3\sum\limits_{r=1}^{n} r$ to the right side of the equation, and substitute for the known formulae,

$$
\begin{aligned}
3\sum_{r=1}^{n} r^2 &= (n+1)^3 - 1 - 3\sum_{r=1}^{n} r - \sum_{r=1}^{n} 1 \\
&= (n+1)^3 - 1 - \tfrac{3}{2}n(n+1) - n \\
&= (n+1)^3 - \tfrac{3}{2}n(n+1) - (1+n) \\
&= (n+1)\left((n+1)^2 - \tfrac{3}{2}n - 1\right) \\
&= (n+1)\left(n^2 + 2n + 1 - \tfrac{3}{2}n - 1\right) \\
&= (n+1)\left(n^2 + \tfrac{1}{2}n\right) = \tfrac{1}{2}n(n+1)(2n+1).
\end{aligned}
$$

Therefore, on dividing by 3, $\sum\limits_{r=1}^{n} r^2 = \tfrac{1}{6}n(n+1)(2n+1)$.

It is helpful to look more carefully at this process, which relies on the original equation that enables the right side to cancel when you add the terms.

Suppose a function $g(r)$, defined for $r \in \mathbb{N}$, can be written in the form $f(r + 1) - f(r)$ where $f(r)$ is a function also defined for $r \in \mathbb{N}$. Then you can write

$$
\begin{aligned}
g(1) &= f(2) - f(1) \\
g(2) &= f(3) - f(2) \\
g(3) &= f(4) - f(3) \\
&\ \vdots \\
g(n-1) &= f(n) - f(n-1) \\
g(n) &= f(n+1) - f(n)
\end{aligned}
$$

and adding downwards gives

$$
\sum_{r=1}^{n} g(r) = f(n+1) - f(1).
$$

Thus, this gives you a method for summing the series $\sum_{r=1}^{n} g(r)$.

> **Difference method**
> If $g(r) = f(r + 1) - f(r)$ for $r \in \mathbb{N}$, then
> $$
> \sum_{r=1}^{n} g(r) = f(n+1) - f(1).
> $$

Example 2.3.1

Verify that $\dfrac{1}{r} - \dfrac{1}{r+1} = \dfrac{1}{r(r+1)}$. Hence show that $\displaystyle\sum_{r=1}^{n} \dfrac{1}{r(r+1)} = \dfrac{n}{n+1}$.

$$
\frac{1}{r} - \frac{1}{r+1} = \frac{1 \times (r+1) - 1 \times r}{r(r+1)} = \frac{r+1-r}{r(r+1)} = \frac{1}{r(r+1)}.
$$

The expression $\dfrac{1}{r(r+1)} = \dfrac{1}{r} - \dfrac{1}{r+1}$ is of the form $g(r) = f(r+1) - f(r)$ with $g(r) = \dfrac{1}{r(r+1)}$ and $f(r) = -\dfrac{1}{r}$. Therefore, summing, $\displaystyle\sum_{r=1}^{n} g(r) = f(n+1) - f(1)$; that is,

$$
\sum_{r=1}^{n} \frac{1}{r(r+1)} = -\frac{1}{n+1} - \left(-\frac{1}{1}\right) = 1 - \frac{1}{n+1} = \frac{(n+1)-1}{n+1} = \frac{n}{n+1}.
$$

Example 2.3.2

Show that $b^r - b^{r-1} = (b-1)b^{r-1}$, and use this to find the formula for the sum of a geometric progression.

Expanding the right side gives $b \times b^{r-1} - b^{r-1} = b^r - b^{r-1}$ which is the left side.

Let the geometric progression have first term a and common ratio b.

From the formula above

$$ab^{r-1} = \frac{ab^r - ab^{r-1}}{b-1} = \frac{ab^r}{b-1} - \frac{ab^{r-1}}{b-1}.$$

The expression $ab^{r-1} = \dfrac{ab^r}{b-1} - \dfrac{ab^{r-1}}{b-1}$ is of the form $g(r) = f(r+1) - f(r)$ with

$g(r) = ab^{r-1}$ and $f(r) = \dfrac{ab^{r-1}}{b-1}$. Therefore, summing, $\sum\limits_{r=1}^{n} g(r) = f(n+1) - f(1)$; that is,

$$\sum_{r=1}^{n} ab^{r-1} = \frac{ab^n}{b-1} - \frac{ab^0}{b-1} = \frac{ab^n}{b-1} - \frac{a}{b-1} = \frac{a(b^n - 1)}{b-1}.$$

So $$\sum_{r=1}^{n} ab^{r-1} = \frac{a(b^n - 1)}{b-1}.$$

Example 2.3.3 uses the general idea of differences, but goes back to first principles of cancelling terms which produces the result in the box.

Example 2.3.3

Verify that $\dfrac{1}{r} - \dfrac{2}{r+1} + \dfrac{1}{r+3} = \dfrac{3-r}{r(r+1)(r+3)}$. Hence find an expression for $\sum\limits_{r=1}^{n} \dfrac{3-r}{r(r+1)(r+3)}$

for $n \geqslant 1$.

$$\frac{1}{r} - \frac{2}{r+1} + \frac{1}{r+3} = \frac{1(r+1)(r+3) - 2r(r+3) + 1r(r+1)}{r(r+1)(r+3)}$$

$$= \frac{r^2 + 4r + 3 - 2r^2 - 6r + r^2 + r}{r(r+1)(r+3)}$$

$$= \frac{-r+3}{r(r+1)(r+3)} = \frac{3-r}{r(r+1)(r+3)}.$$

Writing out the terms of the series using this formula, you find the following.

$$\frac{2}{1 \times 2 \times 4} = \frac{1}{1} - \frac{2}{2} + \cancel{\frac{1}{4}}$$

$$\frac{1}{2 \times 3 \times 5} = \frac{1}{2} - \frac{2}{3} + \cancel{\frac{1}{5}}$$

$$\frac{0}{3 \times 4 \times 6} = \frac{1}{3} - \cancel{\frac{2}{4}} + \cancel{\frac{1}{6}}$$

$$\frac{-1}{4 \times 5 \times 7} = \cancel{\frac{1}{4}} - \cancel{\frac{2}{5}} + \cancel{\frac{1}{7}}$$

$$\vdots \qquad \vdots \qquad \vdots \qquad \vdots$$

$$\frac{3-(n-3)}{(n-3)(n-2)n} = \cancel{\frac{1}{n-3}} - \cancel{\frac{2}{n-2}} + \cancel{\frac{1}{n}}$$

$$\frac{3-(n-2)}{(n-2)(n-1)(n+1)} = \cancel{\frac{1}{n-2}} - \cancel{\frac{2}{n-1}} + \frac{1}{n+1}$$

$$\frac{3-(n-1)}{(n-1)n(n+2)} = \cancel{\frac{1}{n-1}} - \cancel{\frac{2}{n}} + \frac{1}{n+2}$$

$$\frac{3-n}{n(n+1)(n+3)} = \cancel{\frac{1}{n}} - \frac{2}{n+1} + \frac{1}{n+3}$$

When you add the terms downwards notice that almost every pair of positive terms with the same denominator on the right side is balanced by a corresponding negative term with the same denominator, and that only terms at the beginning and end remain. You need a little care in keeping track of it all.

$$\sum_{r=1}^{n} \frac{3-r}{r(r+1)(r+3)} = \frac{1}{1} - \frac{2}{2} + \frac{1}{2} - \frac{2}{3} + \frac{1}{3} + \frac{1}{n+3} - \frac{2}{n+1} + \frac{1}{n+2} + \frac{1}{n+1}$$

$$= \frac{1}{6} + \frac{1}{n+3} + \frac{1}{n+2} - \frac{1}{n+1} = \frac{1}{6} + \frac{n^2+2n-1}{(n+1)(n+2)(n+3)}.$$

You can see from the pattern of terms crossed out in the diagram that the sum is valid for $n \geqslant 3$.

But when $n = 1$, $\dfrac{2}{1 \times 2 \times 4} = \dfrac{1}{4}$ and $\dfrac{1}{6} + \dfrac{1^2 + 2 \times 1 - 1}{(1+1)(2+1)(3+1)} = \dfrac{1}{6} + \dfrac{2}{24} = \dfrac{1}{4}$;

and when $n = 2$, $\dfrac{2}{1 \times 2 \times 4} + \dfrac{1}{2 \times 3 \times 5} = \dfrac{1}{4} + \dfrac{1}{30} = \dfrac{17}{60}$ and

$\dfrac{1}{6} + \dfrac{2^2 + 2 \times 2 - 1}{(2+1)(3+1)(4+1)} = \dfrac{1}{6} + \dfrac{7}{60} = \dfrac{17}{60}.$

So the sum is valid for $n \geqslant 1$.

2.4 Convergence of series

Now that you have some series for which you can find the sum, it is natural to ask, does the series converge as n increases? You have seen this situation before.

In C2 Section 6.3, the sum of the geometric series

$$1 + 0.2 + 0.2^2 + \cdots + 0.2^n$$

was shown to tend to a limit because the common ratio. 0.2, lies between –1 and 1. The geometric series is said to be 'convergent'.

The key to the convergence of the geometric series is the behaviour of its sum sequence

$$S_n = \frac{a(1 - 0.2^n)}{1 - 0.2}.$$

This idea can be generalised.

Let $S_n = \sum_{r=1}^{n} u_r$. Then if, as $n \to \infty$, S_n approaches a limit, the series $\sum_{r=1}^{n} u_r$ **converges**. The limit is written as $\sum_{r=1}^{\infty} u_r$.

If this limit is S, then S is said to be the **sum** of the series $\sum_{r=1}^{\infty} u_r$.

Example 2.4.1
Show that the series of triangle numbers $1 + 3 + 6 + 10 + \ldots$ does not converge.

Since the general term t_r of the triangle numbers is given by $t_r = \frac{1}{2}r(r+1)$, the sum function for the triangle numbers is $S_n = \sum\limits_{r=1}^{n} \frac{1}{2}r(r+1)$. Then, using the result of Example 2.1.2,

$$S_n = \tfrac{1}{6}n(n+1)(n+2).$$

Since $S_n = \frac{1}{6}n(n+1)(n+2) > \frac{1}{6}n^3$ and $\frac{1}{6}n^3$ can be made as large as you please by taking n to be large enough, the series of triangle numbers does not converge.

Example 2.4.2
Show that the series $\dfrac{1}{1 \times 2} + \dfrac{1}{2 \times 3} + \cdots + \dfrac{1}{n(n+1)}$ converges to 1 as n tends to infinity.

From Example 2.3.1, the sum function is $S_n = 1 - \dfrac{1}{n+1}$ (which came before $S_n = \dfrac{n}{n+1}$).

You can see that, if n becomes large, $\dfrac{1}{n+1}$ becomes small, so that S_n is only a little less than 1. As $n \to \infty$, $\dfrac{1}{n+1} \to 0$, so $S_n \to 1 - 0 = 1$. Therefore the series converges to 1.

Another way to see that $S_n \to 1$ is to write $S_n = \dfrac{n}{n+1} = \dfrac{1}{1 + \dfrac{1}{n}}$. As n gets large, $\dfrac{1}{n} \to 0$, so $S_n \to 1$.

The method of dividing the numerator and denominator by n is an example of a useful technique for showing that functions of this type approach a limit. For example, if you wish to show that $\dfrac{(n+1)(n+2)(n+3)}{n^3}$ has the limit 1 as $n \to \infty$, then write

$$\dfrac{(n+1)(n+2)(n+3)}{n^3} = \left(1 + \dfrac{1}{n}\right)\left(1 + \dfrac{2}{n}\right)\left(1 + \dfrac{3}{n}\right),$$ and the limit becomes much clearer.

The process of writing down the limit in this way relies on some important results about limits, which are stated here without proof. You may assume these results.

If $\lim\limits_{n\to\infty} u_n = u$ and $\lim\limits_{n\to\infty} v_n = v$, then

$$\lim_{n\to\infty} (u_n \pm v_n) = u \pm v,$$

$$\lim_{n\to\infty} (u_n v_n) = uv,$$

and, provided $v \neq 0$, $\lim\limits_{n\to\infty} \left(\dfrac{u_n}{v_n}\right) = \dfrac{u}{v}.$

In many cases it is not easy to tell whether or not a series converges, because you can only find the sum sequence for a very limited number of series. Other, more advanced methods are then required.

Exercise 2C

1 (a) Show that $\dfrac{1}{2r-1} - \dfrac{1}{2r+1} = \dfrac{2}{(2r-1)(2r+1)}$.

   (b) Find the sum of n terms of the series $\dfrac{2}{1\times3} + \dfrac{2}{3\times5} + \dfrac{2}{5\times7} + \cdots$.

2 (a) Prove that if $f(r) = r!$, then $f(r+1) - f(r) = r \times r!$.

   (b) Sum the series $1\times1! + 2\times2! + 3\times3! + \cdots + n\times n!$.

3 Show that $\dfrac{r-1}{r!} = \dfrac{1}{(r-1)!} - \dfrac{1}{r!}$. Hence show that $\displaystyle\sum_{r=1}^{n} \dfrac{r-1}{r!} = 1 - \dfrac{1}{n!}$.

4 Simplify $\frac{1}{4}r(r+1)(r+2)(r+3) - \frac{1}{4}(r-1)r(r+1)(r+2)$, and use your result to find $\displaystyle\sum_{r=1}^{n} r(r+1)(r+2)$.

5 Simplify $(2r+1)^5 - (2r-1)^5$, and use your result to derive a formula for $\displaystyle\sum_{r=1}^{n} r^4$.

6 Show that $\dfrac{2}{r(r+1)(r+2)} = \dfrac{1}{r(r+1)} - \dfrac{1}{(r+1)(r+2)}$, and hence find $\displaystyle\sum_{r=1}^{n} \dfrac{2}{r(r+1)(r+2)}$.
   Find the sum to infinity of this series.

7 Show that $ra^r - (r-1)a^{r-1} = (a-1)ra^{r-1} + a^{r-1}$. Use this result to find $\displaystyle\sum_{r=1}^{n} ra^{r-1}$.

8 Show that $\dfrac{1}{r-2} - \dfrac{1}{r} = \dfrac{2}{(r-2)r}$ and use this result to show that

$$\sum_{r=3}^{n} \frac{1}{(r-2)r} = \frac{1}{2}\left(\frac{3}{2} - \frac{1}{n-1} - \frac{1}{n}\right).$$

   Find the limit as $n \to \infty$ of $\displaystyle\sum_{r=3}^{n} \dfrac{1}{(r-2)r}$.

9* Show that $\dfrac{\frac{1}{2}}{r-1} + \dfrac{\frac{1}{2}}{r+1} = \dfrac{r}{(r-1)(r+1)}$, and use this result to sum the series

$$S_n = \frac{2}{1\times3} - \frac{4}{3\times5} + \cdots + \frac{(-1)^{n-1}2n}{(2n-1)(2n+1)}. \text{ Calculate } \lim_{n\to\infty} S_n.$$

Miscellaneous exercise 2

1 (a) Find the sum of the multiples of 3 which lie between 1 and 100.

   (b) Find the sum of the numbers between 1 and 100 inclusive which are not multiples of 3.

2 Calculate the values of

   (a) $\displaystyle\sum_{r=1}^{40} (3r-1)$ (b) $\displaystyle\sum_{r=1}^{40} (4r^2 + 2r + 1)$.

3 Calculate $2^2 + 5^2 + 8^2 + \cdots + 98^2$.

4 Calculate the sum of the series $1^2 \times 2 + 2^2 \times 3 + \cdots + 25^2 \times 26$.

5 Prove that the sum of the series $(1 \times 3) + (2 \times 4) + (3 \times 5) + \cdots + n(n+2)$ is $\frac{1}{6}n(n+1)(2n+7)$. (OCR)

6 (a) Use the formulae for $\sum_{k=1}^{n} k$ and $\sum_{k=1}^{n} k^2$ to show that $\sum_{k=1}^{n} (2k-1)^2 = \lambda n(4n^2 - 1)$ where λ is a constant to be determined.

(b) Find the sum of the squares of all the odd numbers between 100 and 200. (OCR)

7 Find the sum of the series $\sum_{n=1}^{100} n(n^2 + 2)$. (OCR)

8 The rth term of a finite series is u_r, and the sum of n terms is denoted by S_n, so $S_n = \sum_{r=1}^{n} u_r$. It is given that $S_n = 2n^2 + 3n$. By considering $S_n - S_{n-1}$, express u_r as a function of r. Also find $\sum_{r=n}^{2n} u_r$. (OCR, adapted)

9 Show that $\dfrac{\frac{1}{2}}{r-1} - \dfrac{\frac{1}{2}}{r+1} = \dfrac{1}{r^2 - 1}$.

Show also that $\sum_{r=2}^{n} \dfrac{1}{r^2 - 1} = \dfrac{3}{4} - \dfrac{2n+1}{2n(n+1)}$. (OCR)

10 If $S_n = 1 \times n + 2(n-1) + 3(n-2) + \cdots + (n-1) \times 2 + n \times 1$, where n is a positive integer, prove that $S_{n+1} - S_n = \frac{1}{2}(n+1)(n+2)$.

Prove that $S_n = \frac{1}{6}n(n+1)(n+2)$. (OCR, adapted)

11 Simplify $r^2(r+1)^2 - (r-1)^2 r^2$.

By considering $\sum_{r=1}^{n} (r^2(r+1)^2 - (r-1)^2 r^2)$, prove that $\sum_{r=1}^{n} r^3 = \frac{1}{4}n^2(n+1)^2$.

12* Show that $\dfrac{1}{r} - \dfrac{2}{r+1} + \dfrac{1}{r+2} = \dfrac{2}{r(r+1)(r+2)}$.

Prove that $\dfrac{1}{1 \times 2 \times 3} + \dfrac{1}{2 \times 3 \times 4} + \cdots + \dfrac{1}{n(n+1)(n+2)} = \dfrac{1}{4} - \dfrac{1}{2(n+1)(n+2)}$. (OCR)

13* Show that $n(n+1)(n+2) - (n-1)n(n+1) = 3n(n+1)$. Hence, or otherwise, find a formula for $S_n = \sum_{r=1}^{n} r(r+1)$. Use this result to prove that $\sum_{r=1}^{n} r^2 = \frac{1}{6}n(n+1)(2n+1)$. Hence, or otherwise, find a formula for the sum to n terms of $4^2 + 7^2 + 10^2 + 13^2 + \dots$. (OCR)

14* (a) Verify that $\dfrac{\frac{1}{2}}{n-1} - \dfrac{1}{n} + \dfrac{\frac{1}{2}}{n+1} = \dfrac{1}{n^3 - n}$.

(b) Find the sum of the series $\sum_{n=2}^{N} \dfrac{1}{n^3 - n}$.

(c) Deduce that the series $\dfrac{1}{6} + \dfrac{1}{24} + \dfrac{1}{60} + \cdots + \dfrac{1}{n^3 - n} + \cdots$ is convergent, and find its sum to infinity. (OCR, adapted)

3 Matrices

This chapter explains why and how matrices are defined, and how to add, subtract and multiply them. When you have completed it, you should

- be able to carry out operations of matrix addition, subtraction and multiplication
- know the terms zero (or null) matrix, and identity (or unit) matrix
- know the meaning of the terms 'singular' and 'non-singular'
- know that under certain circumstances matrices have inverses.

3.1 What is a matrix?

Suppose that you wanted to program a computer to solve a pair of simultaneous linear equations such as

$$\left. \begin{array}{r} x + 2y = 3 \\ 2x + 3y = 4 \end{array} \right\}.$$

What are the essential ingredients of this pair of equations? What information do you need to give to the computer?

Notice that the equations $\left. \begin{array}{r} x + 2y = 3 \\ 2x + 3y = 4 \end{array} \right\}$ are essentially the same as $\left. \begin{array}{r} p + 2q = 3 \\ 2p + 3q = 4 \end{array} \right\}.$

You would not change the way that you solve the equations just because the unknowns are labelled p and q instead of x and y. This suggests that all the necessary information is held by the array of coefficients and symbols

$$\begin{array}{rrrr} 1 & 2 & = & 3 \\ 2 & 3 & = & 4 \end{array}$$

You don't even need the equals signs, provided that you remember what the array means and what the symbols in it stand for. Thus all the information is held by the array

$$\begin{array}{rrr} 1 & 2 & 3 \\ 2 & 3 & 4 \end{array}$$

It turns out to be useful to think of a rectangular array of numbers like this as a single object, called a **matrix**. It is usual to write a matrix in brackets, and to denote it by a single letter written in bold-faced type. Thus $\mathbf{A} = \begin{pmatrix} 1 & 2 & 3 \\ 2 & 3 & 4 \end{pmatrix}$.

A matrix has **rows** and **columns**. In this example, $\mathbf{A}$ has 2 rows and 3 columns and is called a '2 by 3' matrix. The matrix $\mathbf{A}$ is said to have **size** 2×3. If the number of rows is equal to the number of columns, the matrix is **square**. The individual numbers in the matrix are called

elements. A matrix with just one column, such as $\begin{pmatrix} 3 \\ 4 \end{pmatrix}$, is sometimes called a **column matrix**. Similarly a matrix with just one row, such as $(1 \quad 2 \quad 3)$, is called a **row matrix**.

> A **matrix A** is a rectangular array of numbers, called **elements**.
>
> A matrix **A** with m rows and n columns is called an $m \times n$ matrix. If $m = n$, **A** is said to be a **square** matrix.
>
> A matrix with n rows and 1 column is called a **column matrix**.
>
> A matrix with 1 row and n columns is called a **row matrix**.

Matrices can arise from many sources other than simultaneous equations. For example, suppose that Amy and Bob go to a baker's shop to buy cakes, doughnuts and eclairs. The numbers of each that they buy is given by the array of numbers in Table 3.1.

	Cakes	Doughnuts	Eclairs
Amy	2	1	1
Bob	4	0	2

Table 3.1

The array of numbers in Table 3.1 is another example of a matrix. If you wanted to work out the cost, you would strip it of its headings and simply use the numbers in a 'purchase matrix'

$$\mathbf{P} = \begin{pmatrix} 2 & 1 & 1 \\ 4 & 0 & 2 \end{pmatrix}.$$

Suppose that on the next day they make purchases represented by the matrix

$$\mathbf{Q} = \begin{pmatrix} 3 & 0 & 1 \\ 1 & 3 & 1 \end{pmatrix}.$$

Then on the two days together they will have bought $\begin{pmatrix} 5 & 1 & 2 \\ 5 & 3 & 3 \end{pmatrix}$, and it is natural to denote this by $\mathbf{P} + \mathbf{Q}$. Thus

$$\mathbf{P} + \mathbf{Q} = \begin{pmatrix} 2 & 1 & 1 \\ 4 & 0 & 2 \end{pmatrix} + \begin{pmatrix} 3 & 0 & 1 \\ 1 & 3 & 1 \end{pmatrix} = \begin{pmatrix} 5 & 1 & 2 \\ 5 & 3 & 3 \end{pmatrix}.$$

If they make the same purchase **P** on five days the total bought will be

$$5\mathbf{P} = \begin{pmatrix} 10 & 5 & 5 \\ 20 & 0 & 10 \end{pmatrix}.$$

These examples suggest the general definitions of sums and multiples of matrices given in the next section.

3.2 Addition and multiplication by a scalar

Two $m \times n$ matrices **A** and **B** are defined to be **equal** if all the elements in corresponding positions are equal. Two matrices of different sizes cannot be equal.

Thus if you are given that $\begin{pmatrix} a & b \\ c & d \end{pmatrix} = \begin{pmatrix} 0 & 1 \\ 2 & -1 \end{pmatrix}$ you can deduce that $a = 0, b = 1, c = 2$ and $d = -1$. But $\begin{pmatrix} 1 & 2 \\ 3 & 4 \end{pmatrix} \neq \begin{pmatrix} 1 & 3 \\ 2 & 4 \end{pmatrix}$ and $\begin{pmatrix} 1 & 2 \\ 3 & 4 \end{pmatrix} \neq \begin{pmatrix} 1 & 2 & 0 \\ 3 & 4 & 0 \end{pmatrix}$.

Addition

Addition of two $m \times n$ matrices **A** and **B** is performed by adding the corresponding elements.

Thus, if $\mathbf{A} = \begin{pmatrix} 1 & 2 \\ 3 & 4 \end{pmatrix}$ and $\mathbf{B} = \begin{pmatrix} 1 & 3 \\ 2 & 4 \end{pmatrix}$, then their sum

$$\mathbf{A} + \mathbf{B} = \begin{pmatrix} 1 & 2 \\ 3 & 4 \end{pmatrix} + \begin{pmatrix} 1 & 3 \\ 2 & 4 \end{pmatrix} = \begin{pmatrix} 1+1 & 2+3 \\ 3+2 & 4+4 \end{pmatrix} = \begin{pmatrix} 2 & 5 \\ 5 & 8 \end{pmatrix}.$$

You cannot add matrices if they have different sizes.

You can easily check by using numerical examples that:

> For any matrices **A**, **B** and **C** of equal sizes,
>
> $\mathbf{A} + \mathbf{B} = \mathbf{B} + \mathbf{A}$ and $(\mathbf{A} + \mathbf{B}) + \mathbf{C} = \mathbf{A} + (\mathbf{B} + \mathbf{C})$.

To prove that $\mathbf{A} + \mathbf{B} = \mathbf{B} + \mathbf{A}$ and similar properties is straightforward, and left to you.

The zero matrix

The matrix **O**, of any size, in which all the elements are 0, is called the **zero matrix**, or null matrix.

Notice that the 2×2 matrix **O**, that is $\begin{pmatrix} 0 & 0 \\ 0 & 0 \end{pmatrix}$, is different from the 2×3 matrix **O**, that is $\begin{pmatrix} 0 & 0 & 0 \\ 0 & 0 & 0 \end{pmatrix}$. In practice, there is no confusion about the fact that they are both called **O**.

An important property of the zero matrix is that for any matrix **A**, and the zero matrix **O** which is the same size as **A**,

> $\mathbf{A} + \mathbf{O} = \mathbf{O} + \mathbf{A} = \mathbf{A}.$

> In some books the matrix **O** is denoted by **Z** (for zero) or by **0**.

Scalar multiples

You can also multiply a matrix by a number. For example, it seems natural to write $\mathbf{A} + \mathbf{A}$ as $2\mathbf{A}$. If $\mathbf{A} = \begin{pmatrix} 1 & 2 \\ 3 & 4 \end{pmatrix}$, then

$$2\mathbf{A} = \mathbf{A} + \mathbf{A} = \begin{pmatrix} 1 & 2 \\ 3 & 4 \end{pmatrix} + \begin{pmatrix} 1 & 2 \\ 3 & 4 \end{pmatrix} = \begin{pmatrix} 2 & 4 \\ 6 & 8 \end{pmatrix}.$$

If s is any number and $\mathbf{A}$ any $m \times n$ matrix, the product $s\mathbf{A}$ is the $m \times n$ matrix formed by multiplying every element of $\mathbf{A}$ by s. The process is called **multiplying by a scalar**.

It is easy to check the following rules, which you can prove for yourself.

$$1\mathbf{A} = \mathbf{A}, \qquad s(t\mathbf{A}) = (st)\mathbf{A}, \qquad 0\mathbf{A} = \mathbf{O},$$
$$(s + t)\mathbf{A} = s\mathbf{A} + t\mathbf{A}, \qquad s(\mathbf{A} + \mathbf{B}) = s\mathbf{A} + s\mathbf{B}, \qquad s\mathbf{O} = \mathbf{O}.$$

Subtraction

Subtraction of two matrices $\mathbf{A}$ and $\mathbf{B}$ is defined by

$$\mathbf{X} = \mathbf{A} - \mathbf{B} \quad \Leftrightarrow \quad \mathbf{B} + \mathbf{X} = \mathbf{A}.$$

You can easily show that $\mathbf{A} - \mathbf{B} = \mathbf{A} + (-1)\mathbf{B}$.

For these additive and multiple properties, matrices behave just like numbers. Properties that you expect to hold, do hold.

Example 3.2.1

Let $\mathbf{A} = \begin{pmatrix} -1 & -2 \\ 3 & 1 \end{pmatrix}$ and $\mathbf{B} = \begin{pmatrix} 2 & 6 \\ -3 & 4 \end{pmatrix}$. Calculate (a) $\mathbf{A} + \mathbf{B}$, (b) $2\mathbf{A} + 3\mathbf{B}$, (c) $\mathbf{A} - \mathbf{B}$.

$$\begin{aligned}
\text{(a)} \quad \mathbf{A} + \mathbf{B} &= \begin{pmatrix} -1 & -2 \\ 3 & 1 \end{pmatrix} + \begin{pmatrix} 2 & 6 \\ -3 & 4 \end{pmatrix} \\
&= \begin{pmatrix} -1 + 2 & -2 + 6 \\ 3 + (-3) & 1 + 4 \end{pmatrix} \\
&= \begin{pmatrix} 1 & 4 \\ 0 & 5 \end{pmatrix}.
\end{aligned}$$

$$\begin{aligned}
\text{(b)} \quad 2\mathbf{A} + 3\mathbf{B} &= 2\begin{pmatrix} -1 & -2 \\ 3 & 1 \end{pmatrix} + 3\begin{pmatrix} 2 & 6 \\ -3 & 4 \end{pmatrix} \\
&= \begin{pmatrix} -2 & -4 \\ 6 & 2 \end{pmatrix} + \begin{pmatrix} 6 & 18 \\ -9 & 12 \end{pmatrix} \\
&= \begin{pmatrix} -2 + 6 & -4 + 18 \\ 6 + (-9) & 2 + 12 \end{pmatrix} \\
&= \begin{pmatrix} 4 & 14 \\ -3 & 14 \end{pmatrix}.
\end{aligned}$$

(c) $\mathbf{A} - \mathbf{B} = \begin{pmatrix} -1 & -2 \\ 3 & 1 \end{pmatrix} + (-1)\begin{pmatrix} 2 & 6 \\ -3 & 4 \end{pmatrix}$

$\qquad = \begin{pmatrix} -1 & -2 \\ 3 & 1 \end{pmatrix} + \begin{pmatrix} -2 & -6 \\ 3 & -4 \end{pmatrix}$

$\qquad = \begin{pmatrix} -1 + (-2) & -2 + (-6) \\ 3 + 3 & 1 + (-4) \end{pmatrix}$

$\qquad = \begin{pmatrix} -3 & -8 \\ 6 & -3 \end{pmatrix}.$

In practice you will usually shorten such calculations by omitting some of the steps.

Example 3.2.2
Solve for $\mathbf{X}$ the matrix equation $\mathbf{A} + 3\mathbf{X} = 4\mathbf{B}$.

In this example, you must assume that all the matrices are the same size, say $m \times n$, otherwise addition would not be defined.

$$\mathbf{A} + 3\mathbf{X} = 4\mathbf{B} \quad \Leftrightarrow \quad 3\mathbf{X} = 4\mathbf{B} - \mathbf{A}$$
$$\Leftrightarrow \quad \mathbf{X} = \tfrac{1}{3}(4\mathbf{B} - \mathbf{A}).$$

3.3 Multiplying two matrices

The rules for adding two matrices and multiplying a matrix by a scalar were rather obvious. The rule for multiplying two matrices is not at all obvious.

Return to Amy and Bob at the baker's shop. Recall that what they bought was given by the matrix $\mathbf{P} = \begin{pmatrix} 2 & 1 & 1 \\ 4 & 0 & 2 \end{pmatrix}$. Suppose now that there are actually two shops, X and Y, that they could buy at, and that these shops charge prices in pence given by Table 3.2.

	Shop X	Shop Y
Cakes	40	45
Doughnuts	30	25
Eclairs	50	40

Table 3.2

Stripping out the headings gives a cost matrix $\mathbf{C} = \begin{pmatrix} 40 & 45 \\ 30 & 25 \\ 50 & 40 \end{pmatrix}$.

Now suppose that Amy and Bob want to compare how much they would spend in each shop.

Amy would spend $2 \times 40 + 1 \times 30 + 1 \times 50 = 160$ pence in shop X.

Amy would spend $2 \times 45 + 1 \times 25 + 1 \times 40 = 155$ pence in shop Y.

Bob would spend $4 \times 40 + 0 \times 30 + 2 \times 50 = 260$ pence in shop X.

Bob would spend $4 \times 45 + 0 \times 25 + 2 \times 40 = 260$ pence in shop Y.

You could now put these results in a table, as in Table 3.3.

	Shop X	Shop Y
Amy	160	155
Bob	260	260

Table 3.3

The corresponding matrix, $\begin{pmatrix} 160 & 155 \\ 260 & 260 \end{pmatrix}$, obtained by multiplying purchases by costs, is called the product matrix **PC**. Thus

$$\mathbf{PC} = \begin{pmatrix} 2 & 1 & 1 \\ 4 & 0 & 2 \end{pmatrix} \begin{pmatrix} 40 & 45 \\ 30 & 25 \\ 50 & 40 \end{pmatrix}$$

$$= \begin{pmatrix} 2 \times 40 + 1 \times 30 + 1 \times 50 & 2 \times 45 + 1 \times 25 + 1 \times 40 \\ 4 \times 40 + 0 \times 30 + 2 \times 50 & 4 \times 45 + 0 \times 25 + 2 \times 40 \end{pmatrix}$$

$$= \begin{pmatrix} 160 & 155 \\ 260 & 260 \end{pmatrix}.$$

Notice how the individual elements of **PC** are calculated, for example

$$\begin{pmatrix} 2 & 1 & 1 \\ \cdot & \cdot & \cdot \end{pmatrix} \begin{pmatrix} 40 & \cdot \\ 30 & \cdot \\ 50 & \cdot \end{pmatrix} = \begin{pmatrix} 2 \times 40 + 1 \times 30 + 1 \times 50 & \cdot \\ \cdot & \cdot \end{pmatrix}.$$

The element in the first row and first column of **PC** will be called the 'product' of the first row of **P** and the first column of **C**.

More generally, the element in the ith row and jth column of **PC** is the product of the ith row of **P** and the jth column of **C**. Check this for yourself.

This idea of taking the product of rows from the left matrix with columns from the right matrix is central to the multiplication of two matrices. Here are some examples.

Example 3.3.1

Find **AB** and **BA** when $\mathbf{A} = \begin{pmatrix} 1 & 2 \\ 3 & 4 \end{pmatrix}$ and $\mathbf{B} = \begin{pmatrix} 5 & 6 \\ 7 & 8 \end{pmatrix}$.

$$\mathbf{AB} = \begin{pmatrix} 1 & 2 \\ 3 & 4 \end{pmatrix} \begin{pmatrix} 5 & 6 \\ 7 & 8 \end{pmatrix} = \begin{pmatrix} 1 \times 5 + 2 \times 7 & 1 \times 6 + 2 \times 8 \\ 3 \times 5 + 4 \times 7 & 3 \times 6 + 4 \times 8 \end{pmatrix} = \begin{pmatrix} 19 & 22 \\ 43 & 50 \end{pmatrix};$$

$$\mathbf{BA} = \begin{pmatrix} 5 & 6 \\ 7 & 8 \end{pmatrix} \begin{pmatrix} 1 & 2 \\ 3 & 4 \end{pmatrix} = \begin{pmatrix} 5 \times 1 + 6 \times 3 & 5 \times 2 + 6 \times 4 \\ 7 \times 1 + 8 \times 3 & 7 \times 2 + 8 \times 4 \end{pmatrix} = \begin{pmatrix} 23 & 34 \\ 31 & 46 \end{pmatrix}.$$

An important fact emerges from this example. You cannot assume that **AB** and **BA** are equal. In fact, for matrices in general, $\mathbf{AB} \neq \mathbf{BA}$.

In general, the product of the matrices $\begin{pmatrix} a & b \\ c & d \end{pmatrix}$ and $\begin{pmatrix} e & f \\ g & h \end{pmatrix}$ is

$$\begin{pmatrix} a & b \\ c & d \end{pmatrix}\begin{pmatrix} e & f \\ g & h \end{pmatrix} = \begin{pmatrix} ae+bg & af+bh \\ ce+dg & cf+dh \end{pmatrix}.$$

Example 3.3.2

Find the products **AB** and **BA** when $\mathbf{A} = \begin{pmatrix} 2 & -3 & 1 \\ -5 & 2 & -2 \end{pmatrix}$ and $\mathbf{B} = \begin{pmatrix} 1 & 3 \\ 2 & 4 \\ 3 & 6 \end{pmatrix}$.

Although **A** and **B** are not square matrices, you can still use the principle that the element in the ith row and jth column of the product matrix is the product of the ith row of the left matrix with the jth column of the right matrix.

$$\mathbf{AB} = \begin{pmatrix} 2 & -3 & 1 \\ -5 & 2 & -2 \end{pmatrix}\begin{pmatrix} 1 & 3 \\ 2 & 4 \\ 3 & 6 \end{pmatrix}$$

$$= \begin{pmatrix} 2 \times 1 + (-3) \times 2 + 1 \times 3 & 2 \times 3 + (-3) \times 4 + 1 \times 6 \\ (-5) \times 1 + 2 \times 2 + (-2) \times 3 & (-5) \times 3 + 2 \times 4 + (-2) \times 6 \end{pmatrix}$$

$$= \begin{pmatrix} -1 & 0 \\ -7 & -19 \end{pmatrix},$$

and

$$\mathbf{BA} = \begin{pmatrix} 1 & 3 \\ 2 & 4 \\ 3 & 6 \end{pmatrix}\begin{pmatrix} 2 & -3 & 1 \\ -5 & 2 & -2 \end{pmatrix}$$

$$= \begin{pmatrix} 1 \times 2 + 3 \times (-5) & 1 \times (-3) + 3 \times 2 & 1 \times 1 + 3 \times (-2) \\ 2 \times 2 + 4 \times (-5) & 2 \times (-3) + 4 \times 2 & 2 \times 1 + 4 \times (-2) \\ 3 \times 2 + 6 \times (-5) & 3 \times (-3) + 6 \times 2 & 3 \times 1 + 6 \times (-2) \end{pmatrix}$$

$$= \begin{pmatrix} -13 & 3 & -5 \\ -16 & 2 & -6 \\ -24 & 3 & -9 \end{pmatrix}.$$

You can see from this example that **AB** and **BA** are not always the same size. The next example shows that sometimes it is not even possible to multiply two matrices.

Example 3.3.3

Let $\mathbf{A} = \begin{pmatrix} -1 & 2 \\ -3 & -7 \end{pmatrix}$, $\mathbf{B} = \begin{pmatrix} 3 \\ -1 \end{pmatrix}$ and $\mathbf{C} = (2 \quad 5)$. Determine which of the products $\mathbf{A}^2$, **AB**, **AC**, **BA**, $\mathbf{B}^2$, **BC**, **CA**, **CB** and $\mathbf{C}^2$ exist and calculate those which do.

> Why might a matrix product not exist? The product rule for rows and columns relies on the length of the rows of the left matrix matching the length of the columns of the right matrix, otherwise you cannot carry out the product.

$$\mathbf{A}^2 = \begin{pmatrix} -1 & 2 \\ -3 & -7 \end{pmatrix}\begin{pmatrix} -1 & 2 \\ -3 & -7 \end{pmatrix} = \begin{pmatrix} -5 & -16 \\ 24 & 43 \end{pmatrix}; \quad \mathbf{AB} = \begin{pmatrix} -1 & 2 \\ -3 & -7 \end{pmatrix}\begin{pmatrix} 3 \\ -1 \end{pmatrix} = \begin{pmatrix} -5 \\ -2 \end{pmatrix};$$

$$\mathbf{AC} = \begin{pmatrix} -1 & 2 \\ -3 & -7 \end{pmatrix}(2 \ \ 5) \text{ does not exist;} \qquad \mathbf{BA} = \begin{pmatrix} 3 \\ -1 \end{pmatrix}\begin{pmatrix} -1 & 2 \\ -3 & -7 \end{pmatrix} \text{ does not exist;}$$

$$\mathbf{B}^2 = \begin{pmatrix} 3 \\ -1 \end{pmatrix}\begin{pmatrix} 3 \\ -1 \end{pmatrix} \text{ does not exist;} \qquad \mathbf{BC} = \begin{pmatrix} 3 \\ -1 \end{pmatrix}(2 \ \ 5) = \begin{pmatrix} 6 & 15 \\ -2 & -5 \end{pmatrix};$$

$$\mathbf{CA} = (2 \ \ 5)\begin{pmatrix} -1 & 2 \\ -3 & -7 \end{pmatrix} = (-17 \ \ -31); \qquad \mathbf{CB} = (2 \ \ 5)\begin{pmatrix} 3 \\ -1 \end{pmatrix} = (1);$$

$$\mathbf{C}^2 = (2 \ \ 5)(2 \ \ 5) \text{ does not exist.}$$

The product rule for multiplying matrices implies that you can only multiply two matrices if they are **conformable** for multiplication. That is, if $\mathbf{A}$ is an $m \times n$ matrix and $\mathbf{B}$ is a $p \times q$ matrix, then the product $\mathbf{AB}$ exists if, and only if, $n = p$. The size of the product is then $m \times q$.

Thus multiplying matrices of sizes $m \times n$ and $n \times q$ results in an $m \times q$ matrix.

Exercise 3A

1 Let $\mathbf{A} = \begin{pmatrix} 1 & 2 \\ 3 & 4 \end{pmatrix}$ and $\mathbf{B} = \begin{pmatrix} 2 & 3 \\ 4 & -1 \end{pmatrix}$. Calculate the matrices

   (a) $\mathbf{A} + \mathbf{B}$,   (b) $\mathbf{A} - \mathbf{B}$,   (c) $3\mathbf{A} + 2\mathbf{B}$,   (d) $4\mathbf{A} - 3\mathbf{B}$.

2 Solve for $\mathbf{X}$ the matrix equation $2\mathbf{X} + 3\mathbf{A} = 4\mathbf{X} - 3\mathbf{B}$. What do you need to assume about the sizes of $\mathbf{A}$, $\mathbf{B}$ and $\mathbf{X}$?

3 Prove that, for matrices $\mathbf{A}$, $\mathbf{B}$ and $\mathbf{C}$ of the same size, $\mathbf{A} + (\mathbf{B} + \mathbf{C}) = (\mathbf{A} + \mathbf{B}) + \mathbf{C}$.

4 Find the products $\mathbf{AB}$ and $\mathbf{BA}$ where $\mathbf{A} = \begin{pmatrix} 1 & 2 \\ 3 & 4 \end{pmatrix}$ and $\mathbf{B} = \begin{pmatrix} 2 & 3 \\ 4 & -1 \end{pmatrix}$.

5 Let $\mathbf{A} = \begin{pmatrix} 2 & 3 & -1 \\ 1 & 3 & 5 \\ -3 & -2 & 2 \end{pmatrix}$ and $\mathbf{B} = \begin{pmatrix} 4 & -2 & -3 \\ 5 & 1 & 2 \\ 2 & -4 & 1 \end{pmatrix}$. Calculate $\mathbf{AB}$ and $\mathbf{BA}$.

6 Let $\mathbf{A} = \begin{pmatrix} -3 & 2 & 6 \\ 2 & -1 & 2 \end{pmatrix}$ and $\mathbf{B} = \begin{pmatrix} 6 & 2 \\ 3 & 2 \\ 2 & -1 \end{pmatrix}$. Calculate $\mathbf{AB}$ and $\mathbf{BA}$.

7 Although in general, it is true that $\mathbf{AB} \neq \mathbf{BA}$, there are matrices $\mathbf{A}$ and $\mathbf{B}$ such that $\mathbf{AB} = \mathbf{BA}$. Find such a pair $\mathbf{A}$ and $\mathbf{B}$ in which none of the elements is 0.

8 Let $\mathbf{A} = \begin{pmatrix} 1 \\ -1 \\ 1 \end{pmatrix}$, $\mathbf{B} = \begin{pmatrix} -4 & 2 & 3 \\ -2 & 3 & -3 \end{pmatrix}$ and $\mathbf{C} = (2 \ \ 3 \ \ 1)$. Calculate those of the following matrix products which exist.

   (a) $\mathbf{AB}$ (b) $\mathbf{BA}$ (c) $\mathbf{AC}$ (d) $\mathbf{CA}$

   (e) $\mathbf{BC}$ (f) $\mathbf{CB}$ (g) $(\mathbf{CA})\mathbf{B}$ (h) $\mathbf{C}(\mathbf{AB})$

9 Find a matrix $\mathbf{X} = \begin{pmatrix} a & b \\ c & d \end{pmatrix}$ such that $\mathbf{X}\begin{pmatrix} 1 & 2 \\ 3 & 7 \end{pmatrix} = \begin{pmatrix} 1 & 0 \\ 0 & 1 \end{pmatrix}$. Calculate the product $\begin{pmatrix} 1 & 2 \\ 3 & 7 \end{pmatrix}\mathbf{X}$. Try to do the same calculations for $\begin{pmatrix} 1 & 2 \\ 3 & 6 \end{pmatrix}$.

10 Let $\mathbf{A} = \begin{pmatrix} a & b \\ c & d \end{pmatrix}$, $\mathbf{X} = \begin{pmatrix} x \\ y \end{pmatrix}$ and $\mathbf{P} = \begin{pmatrix} p \\ q \end{pmatrix}$. Show that solving the matrix equation $\mathbf{AX} = \mathbf{P}$ is equivalent to solving the simultaneous equations $\left.\begin{aligned} ax + by = p \\ cx + dy = q \end{aligned}\right\}$ and that this is equivalent to solving the matrix equation $x\begin{pmatrix} a \\ c \end{pmatrix} + y\begin{pmatrix} b \\ d \end{pmatrix} = \begin{pmatrix} p \\ q \end{pmatrix}$.

11 Find the matrix $\mathbf{X}$ such that $\begin{pmatrix} 1 & 2 & 2 \\ 1 & 3 & -1 \\ 2 & 4 & 5 \end{pmatrix}\mathbf{X} = \begin{pmatrix} 1 & 0 & 0 \\ 0 & 1 & 0 \\ 0 & 0 & 1 \end{pmatrix}$. Calculate $\mathbf{X}\begin{pmatrix} 1 & 2 & 2 \\ 1 & 3 & -1 \\ 2 & 4 & 5 \end{pmatrix}$.

12 Verify that $\mathbf{A}(\mathbf{B} + \mathbf{C}) = \mathbf{AB} + \mathbf{AC}$, $(\mathbf{B} + \mathbf{C})\mathbf{A} = \mathbf{BA} + \mathbf{CA}$ and $(\mathbf{AB})\mathbf{C} = \mathbf{A}(\mathbf{BC})$ for the following matrices:

$$\mathbf{A} = \begin{pmatrix} 3 & 2 \\ 6 & -2 \end{pmatrix}, \qquad \mathbf{B} = \begin{pmatrix} 1 & -1 \\ 2 & 0 \end{pmatrix} \quad \text{and} \quad \mathbf{C} = \begin{pmatrix} 2 & -1 \\ 1 & 3 \end{pmatrix}.$$

13 Let $\mathbf{A} = (2 \quad -3)$, $\mathbf{B} = \begin{pmatrix} 3 & 2 \\ -4 & 1 \end{pmatrix}$ and $\mathbf{C} = \begin{pmatrix} 4 \\ -1 \end{pmatrix}$. Verify that $(\mathbf{AB})\mathbf{C} = \mathbf{A}(\mathbf{BC})$.

14 Establish results for the products $\mathbf{AO}$ and $\mathbf{OA}$.

15 Prove for 2×2 matrices $\mathbf{A}$ and $\mathbf{B}$ and a scalar s that $(s\mathbf{A})\mathbf{B} = s(\mathbf{AB})$.

16 Prove that $\mathbf{A}(\mathbf{B} + \mathbf{C}) = \mathbf{AB} + \mathbf{AC}$ when $\mathbf{A}$, $\mathbf{B}$ and $\mathbf{C}$ are 2×2 matrices.

3.4 Rules for multiplication

To state the rules for multiplying two matrices, you need more notation.

The element in the ith row and jth column of a matrix $\mathbf{A}$ is denoted by a_{ij} using two suffixes i and j, the first for the row number and the second for the column number. This is called **double suffix notation**.

So, if $\mathbf{A}$ has m rows and n columns,

$$\mathbf{A} = \begin{pmatrix} a_{11} & a_{12} & \cdots & a_{1n} \\ a_{21} & a_{22} & \cdots & a_{2n} \\ \vdots & \vdots & & \vdots \\ a_{m1} & a_{m2} & \cdots & a_{mn} \end{pmatrix}.$$

Similarly, if $\mathbf{B}$ has n rows and p columns,

$$\mathbf{B} = \begin{pmatrix} b_{11} & b_{12} & \cdots & b_{1p} \\ b_{21} & b_{22} & \cdots & b_{2p} \\ \vdots & \vdots & & \vdots \\ b_{n1} & b_{n2} & \cdots & b_{np} \end{pmatrix}.$$

As the number of columns in **A** is equal to the number of rows in **B**, the product **AB** exists and the element in the ith row and jth column of **AB** is

$$a_{i1}b_{1j} + a_{i2}b_{2j} + \cdots + a_{in}b_{nj}.$$

AB is and $m \times p$ matrix.

From this it is possible to prove a number of rules, but it is not easy. However, Questions 12 to 16 in Exercise 3A suggest (correctly) that the following are true.

> For matrices **A**, **B** and **C**, and for scalars s:
>
> $$\mathbf{A(B+C) = AB + AC}, \qquad \mathbf{(B+C)A = BA + CA},$$
> $$\mathbf{A(BC) = (AB)C}, \qquad s\mathbf{(AB) = (sA)B = A(sB)},$$
> $$\mathbf{AO = O}, \qquad \mathbf{OA = O},$$
>
> provided that the various sums and products exist.
>
> In general, $\mathbf{AB \neq BA}$.

3.5 Division of matrices: stage one

Now that you can multiply matrices, what about division? How can you divide the matrix **B** by the matrix **A**?

With numbers, one way of approaching the division $b \div a$, which is really equivalent to solving the equation $ax = b$, is to begin by finding the reciprocal (or inverse) $\frac{1}{a}$, and then to notice that, if $x = \frac{1}{a} \times b$, then $ax = a \times \left(\frac{1}{a} \times b \right) = \left(a \times \frac{1}{a} \right) \times b = 1 \times b = b.$

The equivalent question for matrices is, given two matrices **A** and **B**, can you find a matrix **X** such that $\mathbf{AX = B}$ or $\mathbf{XA = B}$?

This question is more complicated for matrices than for numbers because, amongst other reasons, the answer depends on the sizes of **A** and **B**, and the fact that if $\mathbf{AX = B}$, **XA** may not be equal to **B**, or may not even exist. So it is best to approach the problem in stages.

Using the same approach as for numbers, the first step is to find the matrix equivalent of the number 1, with the property that $1 \times b = b$.

Example 3.5.1

Find the matrix $\begin{pmatrix} p & q \\ r & s \end{pmatrix}$ such that $\begin{pmatrix} p & q \\ r & s \end{pmatrix}\begin{pmatrix} 1 & 2 \\ 3 & 5 \end{pmatrix} = \begin{pmatrix} 1 & 2 \\ 3 & 5 \end{pmatrix}.$

If $\begin{pmatrix} p & q \\ r & s \end{pmatrix}\begin{pmatrix} 1 & 2 \\ 3 & 5 \end{pmatrix} = \begin{pmatrix} 1 & 2 \\ 3 & 5 \end{pmatrix}$, then $\begin{pmatrix} p+3q & 2p+5q \\ r+3s & 2r+5s \end{pmatrix} = \begin{pmatrix} 1 & 2 \\ 3 & 5 \end{pmatrix}.$

Looking at the elements in the top row, $p + 3q = 1$ and $2p + 5q = 2$.

Solving these equations simultaneously,

$$\left.\begin{array}{l} p + 3q = 1 \\ 2p + 5q = 2 \end{array}\right\} \quad \Leftrightarrow \quad \left.\begin{array}{l} p + 3q = 1 \\ -q = 0 \end{array}\right\} \quad r_2' = r_2 - 2r_1$$

The second equation gives $q = 0$, and substituting in the first equation, $p = 1$.

Looking at the second row elements, $r + 3s = 3$ and $2r + 5s = 5$. Then

$$\left.\begin{array}{l} r + 3s = 3 \\ 2r + 5s = 5 \end{array}\right\} \quad \Leftrightarrow \quad \left.\begin{array}{l} r + 3s = 3 \\ -s = -1 \end{array}\right\} \quad r_2' = r_2 - 2r_1$$

The second equation gives $s = 1$, and substituting in the first equation, $r = 0$.

So the matrix $\begin{pmatrix} p & q \\ r & s \end{pmatrix}$ is $\begin{pmatrix} 1 & 0 \\ 0 & 1 \end{pmatrix}$.

This matrix also has the property that $\begin{pmatrix} 1 & 0 \\ 0 & 1 \end{pmatrix}\begin{pmatrix} a & b \\ c & d \end{pmatrix} = \begin{pmatrix} a & b \\ c & d \end{pmatrix}$, for any matrix $\begin{pmatrix} a & b \\ c & d \end{pmatrix}$.

In addition, it also has the property that $\begin{pmatrix} a & b \\ c & d \end{pmatrix}\begin{pmatrix} 1 & 0 \\ 0 & 1 \end{pmatrix} = \begin{pmatrix} a & b \\ c & d \end{pmatrix}$.

The matrix $\begin{pmatrix} 1 & 0 \\ 0 & 1 \end{pmatrix}$ is called the **2 × 2 identity matrix**, and is denoted by **I**. Similarly the **3 × 3 identity matrix** is $\begin{pmatrix} 1 & 0 & 0 \\ 0 & 1 & 0 \\ 0 & 0 & 1 \end{pmatrix}$, and is also denoted by **I**. When you write a matrix statement such as

$$\mathbf{IX = XI = X}$$

then the size of the identity matrix **I** has to be the correct size for multiplication by **X**. This means that if **X** is 2 × 2 then **I** will be 2 × 2, and if **X** is 3 × 3 then **I** is 3 × 3. However, if **X** is not square, and is, say, $m \times n$, then the two **I**s in the equation $\mathbf{IX = XI = X}$ have different sizes. The left **I** will be $m \times m$ and the right **I** $n \times n$. This sounds horrendous, but it is never a problem in practice. If you wish to specify the size, then it is usual to write $\mathbf{I}_n$ for the $n \times n$ identity matrix.

A useful way of describing where the 1s occur in the identity matrix is to say that they appear on the **leading diagonal**, which, for a square matrix, runs from the top left corner to the bottom right.

> An **identity matrix** is a square matrix consisting of 1s on the leading diagonal and 0s everywhere else. The identity matrix with n rows and n columns is denoted by $\mathbf{I}_n$.
>
> If **X** is any matrix with m rows and n columns, then $\mathbf{I}_m\mathbf{X} = \mathbf{XI}_n = \mathbf{X}$.
>
> There is no such thing as a non-square identity matrix.

3.6   Division of matrices: stage two

The next step in the division problem is to find the equivalent of the reciprocal $\dfrac{1}{a}$. The key question is:

Given a matrix **A** is there a matrix **C** such that $\mathbf{AC} = \mathbf{CA} = \mathbf{I}$?

The answer to this question is 'sometimes' if **A** is a square matrix, and 'never' if **A** is not square. It is easy to give reasons for the answer 'never'.

Suppose **A** is an $m \times n$ matrix, where $m \neq n$. If the product **AC** is square and **A** is $m \times n$, then **C** must be $n \times m$, and the product **AC** is $m \times m$. However, similar reasoning shows that **CA** must be an $n \times n$ matrix. By supposition $m \neq n$, so $\mathbf{AC} \neq \mathbf{CA}$.

It is also easy to show, by taking some very special cases, that if **A** is square, the answer to the question is only 'sometimes'. If $\mathbf{A} = \mathbf{I}$, then take $\mathbf{C} = \mathbf{I}$, and the answer is 'yes'; and if $\mathbf{A} = \mathbf{O}$, then $\mathbf{AC} = \mathbf{CA} = \mathbf{O}$ for all matrices **C**, and the answer is 'no'.

> Given a square matrix **A** there is not always a matrix **C** such that $\mathbf{AC} = \mathbf{CA} = \mathbf{I}$.

However, if for a given matrix **A** there is a matrix **C** such that $\mathbf{AC} = \mathbf{CA} = \mathbf{I}$, then division becomes possible. For if $\mathbf{AX} = \mathbf{B}$, then multiplying by **C** on the left is, in effect, dividing by **A**.

$$
\begin{aligned}
\mathbf{AX} = \mathbf{B} \quad &\Rightarrow \quad \mathbf{C(AX)} = \mathbf{CB} \\
&\Rightarrow \quad \mathbf{(CA)X} = \mathbf{CB} \\
&\Rightarrow \quad \mathbf{IX} = \mathbf{CB} \\
&\Rightarrow \quad \mathbf{X} = \mathbf{CB}.
\end{aligned}
$$

Notice also that last line is reversible. If **C** exists, then

$$
\begin{aligned}
\mathbf{X} = \mathbf{CB} \quad &\Rightarrow \quad \mathbf{AX} = \mathbf{A(CB)} \\
&\Rightarrow \quad \mathbf{AX} = \mathbf{(AC)B} \\
&\Rightarrow \quad \mathbf{AX} = \mathbf{IB} \\
&\Rightarrow \quad \mathbf{AX} = \mathbf{B}.
\end{aligned}
$$

So if $\mathbf{AC} = \mathbf{CA} = \mathbf{I}$, then $\mathbf{AX} = \mathbf{B}$ is equivalent to $\mathbf{X} = \mathbf{CB}$.

A similar argument can be used if the order of multiplication is reversed, to obtain:

If $\mathbf{AC} = \mathbf{CA} = \mathbf{I}$, then $\mathbf{XA} = \mathbf{B}$ is equivalent to $\mathbf{X} = \mathbf{BC}$.

Try writing out the proof for yourself.

Given a square matrix **A**, a matrix **C** such that $\mathbf{AC} = \mathbf{CA} = \mathbf{I}$ is called the **inverse** of **A**, and written as $\mathbf{A}^{-1}$. If $\mathbf{A}^{-1}$ exists, the matrix **A** is said to be **non-singular**. If no such matrix exists, then the matrix **A** is said to be **singular**.

> A square matrix **A** has an inverse $\mathbf{A}^{-1}$ if, and only if, **A** is non-singular.

Notice also that if $\mathbf{AC} = \mathbf{CA} = \mathbf{I}$, then $\mathbf{CA} = \mathbf{AC} = \mathbf{I}$; so if $\mathbf{C}$ is the inverse of $\mathbf{A}$, $\mathbf{A}$ is also the inverse of $\mathbf{C}$. That is, $\mathbf{C} = \mathbf{A}^{-1}$ if and only if $\mathbf{A} = \mathbf{C}^{-1}$. So $\mathbf{A} = (\mathbf{A}^{-1})^{-1}$; that is, the inverse of $\mathbf{A}^{-1}$ is $\mathbf{A}$.

In Section 4.4, two important facts will be shown. You should assume them for now.

- If $\mathbf{A}$ is square and $\mathbf{CA} = \mathbf{I}$, then $\mathbf{AC} = \mathbf{I}$.
- Given $\mathbf{A}$, the matrix $\mathbf{C}$ such that $\mathbf{CA} = \mathbf{I}$, if it exists, is unique.

Example 3.6.1

Let $\mathbf{A} = \begin{pmatrix} 1 & 3 \\ 0 & 2 \end{pmatrix}$. Find a 2×2 matrix $\mathbf{C}$ such that $\mathbf{CA} = \mathbf{I}$. Verify that $\mathbf{AC} = \mathbf{I}$.

Let $\mathbf{C} = \begin{pmatrix} a & b \\ c & d \end{pmatrix}$.

Then if $\mathbf{CA} = \mathbf{I}$, $\begin{pmatrix} a & b \\ c & d \end{pmatrix}\begin{pmatrix} 1 & 3 \\ 0 & 2 \end{pmatrix} = \begin{pmatrix} 1 & 0 \\ 0 & 1 \end{pmatrix}$, so $\begin{pmatrix} a & 3a+2b \\ c & 3c+2d \end{pmatrix} = \begin{pmatrix} 1 & 0 \\ 0 & 1 \end{pmatrix}$.

Then, as the two matrices are equal, their elements are equal, so

$$a = 1, \; 3a + 2b = 0, \; c = 0 \; \text{ and } \; 3c + 2d = 1.$$

Solving these equations gives

$$a = 1, \quad b = -\tfrac{3}{2}, \quad c = 0 \quad \text{and} \quad d = \tfrac{1}{2}.$$

Therefore $\mathbf{C} = \begin{pmatrix} 1 & -\frac{3}{2} \\ 0 & \frac{1}{2} \end{pmatrix}$.

Then $\mathbf{AC} = \begin{pmatrix} 1 & 3 \\ 0 & 2 \end{pmatrix}\begin{pmatrix} 1 & -\frac{3}{2} \\ 0 & \frac{1}{2} \end{pmatrix} = \begin{pmatrix} 1 & -\frac{3}{2}+3\times\frac{1}{2} \\ 0 & 2\times\frac{1}{2} \end{pmatrix} = \begin{pmatrix} 1 & 0 \\ 0 & 1 \end{pmatrix} = \mathbf{I}$.

In Example 3.6.1, as $\mathbf{AC} = \mathbf{CA} = \mathbf{I}$, $\mathbf{C}$ is the inverse of $\mathbf{A}$, so $\mathbf{C} = \mathbf{A}^{-1}$.

So $\begin{pmatrix} 1 & 3 \\ 0 & 2 \end{pmatrix}^{-1} = \begin{pmatrix} 1 & -\frac{3}{2} \\ 0 & \frac{1}{2} \end{pmatrix}$.

You will see a better way of finding the inverse of a 2×2 matrix in Section 4.5.

Example 3.6.2

Multiply the matrices $\mathbf{A} = \begin{pmatrix} -1 & 2 & -3 \\ 2 & -7 & 1 \\ -1 & 3 & 2 \end{pmatrix}$ and $\mathbf{B} = \begin{pmatrix} -17 & -13 & -19 \\ -5 & -5 & -5 \\ -1 & 1 & 3 \end{pmatrix}$. Deduce that $\mathbf{A}$ is non-singular and find its inverse. Solve for $\mathbf{X}$ the matrix equation $\mathbf{AX} = \mathbf{B}$.

$$\mathbf{AB} = \begin{pmatrix} -1 & 2 & -3 \\ 2 & -7 & 1 \\ -1 & 3 & 2 \end{pmatrix}\begin{pmatrix} -17 & -13 & -19 \\ -5 & -5 & -5 \\ -1 & 1 & 3 \end{pmatrix} = \begin{pmatrix} 10 & 0 & 0 \\ 0 & 10 & 0 \\ 0 & 0 & 10 \end{pmatrix} = 10\mathbf{I}.$$

Therefore $\frac{1}{10}(\mathbf{AB}) = \mathbf{A}\left(\frac{1}{10}\mathbf{B}\right) = \mathbf{I}$, so the inverse of $\mathbf{A}$ is

$$\mathbf{A}^{-1} = \tfrac{1}{10}\mathbf{B} = \begin{pmatrix} -1.7 & -1.3 & -1.9 \\ -0.5 & -0.5 & -0.5 \\ -0.1 & 0.1 & 0.3 \end{pmatrix}; \text{ since } \mathbf{A}^{-1} \text{ exists, } \mathbf{A} \text{ is non-singular.}$$

If $\mathbf{AX} = \mathbf{B}$, then $\mathbf{X} = \mathbf{A}^{-1}\mathbf{B} = \frac{1}{10}\mathbf{BB} = \frac{1}{10}\mathbf{B}^2$, so

$$\mathbf{X} = \frac{1}{10}\begin{pmatrix} -17 & -13 & -19 \\ -5 & -5 & -5 \\ -1 & 1 & 3 \end{pmatrix}^2 = \frac{1}{10}\begin{pmatrix} 373 & 267 & 331 \\ 115 & 85 & 105 \\ 9 & 11 & 23 \end{pmatrix} = \begin{pmatrix} 37.3 & 26.7 & 33.1 \\ 11.5 & 8.5 & 10.5 \\ 0.9 & 1.1 & 2.3 \end{pmatrix}.$$

You will see a better way of finding the inverse of a 3×3 matrix in Section 10.7.

Exercise 3B

1 Find a matrix $\mathbf{X}$ such that $\mathbf{X}\begin{pmatrix} 5 & 3 \\ 3 & 2 \end{pmatrix} = \begin{pmatrix} 1 & 0 \\ 0 & 1 \end{pmatrix}$.

2 Find a matrix $\mathbf{X}$ such that $\mathbf{X}\begin{pmatrix} 5 & 2 \\ 7 & 3 \end{pmatrix} = \begin{pmatrix} 1 & 0 \\ 0 & 1 \end{pmatrix}$.

3 Find the inverse of the following 2×2 matrices.

(a) $\begin{pmatrix} 2 & 2 \\ 3 & 4 \end{pmatrix}$ (b) $\begin{pmatrix} -2 & -5 \\ 3 & 7 \end{pmatrix}$ (c) $\begin{pmatrix} a & b \\ c & d \end{pmatrix}$

4 Find the inverse of the matrix $\begin{pmatrix} -3 & -5 \\ 5 & 9 \end{pmatrix}$ and use it to find matrices $\mathbf{X}$ which satisfy the following equations:

(a) $\begin{pmatrix} -3 & -5 \\ 5 & 9 \end{pmatrix}\mathbf{X} = \begin{pmatrix} 4 \\ 8 \end{pmatrix}$,   (b) $\begin{pmatrix} -3 & -5 \\ 5 & 9 \end{pmatrix}\mathbf{X} = \begin{pmatrix} 4 & -4 \\ 8 & 12 \end{pmatrix}$.

5 Let $\mathbf{M} = \begin{pmatrix} 1 & 2 & -1 \\ 2 & 1 & 2 \\ 1 & 0 & 1 \end{pmatrix}$. Show that $\mathbf{M}^3 - 3\mathbf{M}^2 = 2\mathbf{I}$.

6 Find the inverse of $\begin{pmatrix} 2 & 3 \\ 4 & 5 \end{pmatrix}$ and use it to solve the equation $\begin{pmatrix} 2 & 3 \\ 4 & 5 \end{pmatrix}\begin{pmatrix} x \\ y \end{pmatrix} = \begin{pmatrix} 1 \\ 3 \end{pmatrix}$.

7 Find the matrix product $\begin{pmatrix} 1 & 4 & -5 \\ 1 & 5 & k \\ 1 & 3 & -7 \end{pmatrix}\begin{pmatrix} -29 & 13 & 17 \\ 5 & -2 & -3 \\ -2 & 1 & 1 \end{pmatrix}$, giving your answer in terms of k.

Hence find the inverse of the matrix $\begin{pmatrix} -29 & 13 & 17 \\ 5 & -2 & -3 \\ -2 & 1 & 1 \end{pmatrix}$.

8 Verify that $\mathbf{A}(\mathbf{BC}) = (\mathbf{AB})\mathbf{C}$ for the matrices $\mathbf{A} = (x \quad y)$, $\mathbf{B} = \begin{pmatrix} a & h \\ h & b \end{pmatrix}$ and $\mathbf{C} = \begin{pmatrix} x \\ y \end{pmatrix}$.

9 Verify that $\begin{pmatrix} 1 & -2 \\ -2 & 4 \end{pmatrix}\begin{pmatrix} 6 & 4 \\ 2 & 5 \end{pmatrix} = \begin{pmatrix} 1 & -2 \\ -2 & 4 \end{pmatrix}\begin{pmatrix} 2 & 2 \\ 0 & 4 \end{pmatrix}$. Note that in matrix algebra

$\mathbf{AB} = \mathbf{AC}$ does not imply that $\mathbf{B} = \mathbf{C}$ without extra information about the matrix $\mathbf{A}$. Show that, if $\mathbf{A}^{-1}$ exists, you can deduce from $\mathbf{AB} = \mathbf{AC}$ that $\mathbf{B} = \mathbf{C}$.

Miscellaneous exercise 3

1 The matrix $\mathbf{M}$ is given by $\mathbf{M} = \begin{pmatrix} 2 & 3 \\ 1 & 4 \end{pmatrix}$. Show that $\mathbf{M}^2 = 6\mathbf{M} - 5\mathbf{I}$.

2 Let $\mathbf{A} = \begin{pmatrix} 13 & -7 & 2 \\ 4 & -3 & 2 \\ 3 & -2 & 1 \end{pmatrix}$. Calculate the matrix $\mathbf{A}^3 - 11\mathbf{A}^2 - 3\mathbf{A}$.

3 Let $\mathbf{M}$ be the 2×2 matrix $\begin{pmatrix} a & b \\ c & d \end{pmatrix}$. Show that, for all values of a, b, c and d,

$$\mathbf{M}^2 - (a+d)\mathbf{M} + (ad - bc)\mathbf{I} = \mathbf{O}$$

where $\mathbf{I} = \begin{pmatrix} 1 & 0 \\ 0 & 1 \end{pmatrix}$ and $\mathbf{O} = \begin{pmatrix} 0 & 0 \\ 0 & 0 \end{pmatrix}$.

4 If $\mathbf{M} = \begin{pmatrix} 5 & 2 \\ 3 & 1 \end{pmatrix}$, find a matrix $\mathbf{P}$ of the form $\begin{pmatrix} a & b \\ 0 & d \end{pmatrix}$ such that $\mathbf{PM} = \begin{pmatrix} 1 & 0 \\ k & 1 \end{pmatrix}$, giving the values of a, b and d. Then find a matrix $\mathbf{Q}$ such that $\mathbf{QPM} = \begin{pmatrix} 1 & 0 \\ 0 & 1 \end{pmatrix}$. (OCR)

5 $\mathbf{M} = \begin{pmatrix} a & 1 \\ c & d \end{pmatrix}$ and $\mathbf{M}\begin{pmatrix} 5 \\ 2 \end{pmatrix} = \begin{pmatrix} -3 \\ 11 \end{pmatrix}$.

 (a) Find the value of a.

 (b) Given that $\mathbf{M}\left\{\begin{pmatrix} 5 \\ 2 \end{pmatrix} + \begin{pmatrix} 0 \\ 1 \end{pmatrix}\right\} = \begin{pmatrix} -2 \\ 14 \end{pmatrix}$, find $\mathbf{M}$.

6 If $\mathbf{M} = \begin{pmatrix} a & b \\ c & d \end{pmatrix}$, write down the products $\mathbf{M}\begin{pmatrix} p \\ r \end{pmatrix}$, $\mathbf{M}\begin{pmatrix} q \\ s \end{pmatrix}$ and $\mathbf{M}\begin{pmatrix} p & q \\ r & s \end{pmatrix}$. Deduce that,

 if $\mathbf{M}\begin{pmatrix} p \\ r \end{pmatrix} = \begin{pmatrix} w \\ y \end{pmatrix}$ and $\mathbf{M}\begin{pmatrix} q \\ s \end{pmatrix} = \begin{pmatrix} x \\ z \end{pmatrix}$, then $\mathbf{M}\begin{pmatrix} p & q \\ r & s \end{pmatrix} = \begin{pmatrix} w & x \\ y & z \end{pmatrix}$.

7 Let $\mathbf{A}$ be the matrix $\mathbf{A} = \begin{pmatrix} 1 & 2 & 3 \\ 4 & -1 & 2 \\ 2 & 3 & -2 \end{pmatrix}$.

 (a) For some real constant p, the matrix $\mathbf{B}$ is given by $\mathbf{B} = \begin{pmatrix} -4 & 13 & 7 \\ 12 & -8 & 10 \\ p & 1 & -9 \end{pmatrix}$. Find the product $\mathbf{AB}$, giving the elements (where appropriate) in terms of p.

 (b) (i) Given that $\mathbf{AB} = k\mathbf{I}$, where k is a scalar constant and $\mathbf{I}$ is the 3×3 identity matrix, determine the value of p, and state the value of k.

 (ii) Deduce the inverse matrix, $\mathbf{A}^{-1}$, of $\mathbf{A}$. (OCR)

4 Determinants and inverses of 2 × 2 matrices

This chapter takes a new look at linear equations with two equations and two unknowns, and finds, in terms of the coefficients, a way to tell whether or not the equations have a unique solution. When you have completed it, you should know

- that the equations can be written in matrix form
- that the equations have a unique solution if and only if the determinant of the associated matrix is non-zero
- how to evaluate determinants of 2 × 2 matrices
- how to find the inverses, if they exist, of 2 × 2 matrices
- how to find the inverse of a matrix product.

You should have studied Sections 1.3 and 1.4 before working on this chapter.

4.1 One equation and one unknown

Although this chapter is really about two linear equations with two unknowns, all the behaviour is also exhibited by one equation with one unknown. This short section will anticipate the situations which occur with two linear equations with two unknowns.

The simplest example of a linear equation is an equation of the type $ax = p$, where a and p are real numbers and you have to solve the equation to find x. Even in this simple case, there are three possibilities that you must consider.

Case 1 Suppose that $a \neq 0$. Then you can divide by a to get the single value $x = \dfrac{p}{a}$.

An example of this type of equation is $2x = 3$, so $x = \dfrac{3}{2} = 1\frac{1}{2}$.

Case 2a Suppose that $a = 0$ and $p \neq 0$. Then the equation reduces to $0x = p$, or $0 = p$. If $p \neq 0$, this is a contradiction. There is no value of x such that $0x = p$ when $p \neq 0$, so the equation has no solution.

An example of this type of equation is $0x = 1$.

Case 2b Suppose that $a = 0$ and $p = 0$. The equation now reduces to $0x = 0$, which is true for every value of $x \in \mathbb{R}$. So there are infinitely many values (all values!) of x which satisfy the equation.

This shows that equations of the form $ax = p$ are always one of three types.

In Chapter 1 you found that the solution of a pair of simultaneous equations involves three possible outcomes: a unique point; infinitely many points; and no points. This is also true for a single equation $ax = p$. You could regard $ax = p$ as a special case of a set of linear equations where there is just one equation and one unknown.

Example 4.1.1
Solve the equation $a(a - 1)x = a$ for all values of a.

If the coefficient of x is not 0, that is if $a \neq 0$ and $a \neq 1$, you can just divide both sides by $a(a - 1)$ to obtain $x = \dfrac{a}{a(a-1)} = \dfrac{1}{a-1}$. (Note that you can cancel the factor a since $a \neq 0$.)

If $a = 0$ the equation reduces to $0x = 0$, so every value of x satisfies the equation.

If $a = 1$ the equation reduces to $0x = 1$, so there is no solution.

Exercise 4A

1 Find the complete solution of each of the following equations where a and b are any real numbers.

(a) $ax = 2$ (b) $ax = a + 1$ (c) $bx = b^2$

4.2 Two equations and two unknowns

The purpose of this section is to find when the equations

$$\left. \begin{array}{l} ax + by = p \\ cx + dy = q \end{array} \right\}$$

are satisfied by a single set of values for x and y.

You will remember from Chapter 1 that a standard way of solving these equations is to find an equivalent pair of equations in triangular form,

$$\left. \begin{array}{l} kx + ly = r \\ \phantom{kx + {}} my = s \end{array} \right\}.$$

If $m \neq 0$ the second of these equations gives the single value $y = \dfrac{s}{m}$. Then, substituting in the first equation gives $kx = r - l\dfrac{s}{m}$. This equation gives a single value for x provided that $k \neq 0$.

So the solution of the simultaneous equations consists of a single set of values for x and y if, and only if, $k \neq 0$ and $m \neq 0$.

To deal with the problem with which this section began, you have to express these conditions in terms of a, b, c and d. There are various cases to consider.

Case 1 Suppose first that $a \neq 0$.

Then, multiplying the second equation by a and subtracting c times the first equation from it you get

$$\left. \begin{array}{l} ax + by = p \\ cx + dy = q \end{array} \right\} \quad \Leftrightarrow \quad \left. \begin{array}{l} ax + by = p \\ acx + ady = aq \end{array} \right\} \qquad r_2' = ar_2$$

$$\Leftrightarrow \quad \left. \begin{array}{l} ax + by = p \\ (ac - ac)\,x + (ad - bc)\,y = aq - cp \end{array} \right\} \quad r_2' = r_2 - cr_1$$

$$\Leftrightarrow \quad \left. \begin{array}{l} ax + by = p \\ (ad - bc)y = aq - cp \end{array} \right\}.$$

Can you see where the condition that $a \neq 0$ is used here? Notice that at the first step of the argument the second equation is multiplied by a. This, of course, is valid for any value of a. But to be able to use $\Leftrightarrow$ rather than merely $\Rightarrow$, you also have to be able to perform the reverse operation of division by a; and this is only valid if $a \neq 0$.

The second step, subtracting c times the first equation from the second, can be reversed for any value of c.

The original set of equations is therefore equivalent to a pair of equations in triangular form, with $k = a$ and $m = ad - bc$. So there is a unique solution if, and only if, $a \neq 0$ (which you know is true) and $ad - bc \neq 0$.

Case 2 If $a = 0$, find (if possible) a coefficient that isn't 0 and rearrange the equations and unknowns so that this coefficient comes in the top left corner. There are three possible layouts, with b, c or d in this position.

$$\left. \begin{array}{l} by + ax = p \\ dy + cx = q \end{array} \right\}, \quad \left. \begin{array}{l} cx + dy = q \\ ax + by = p \end{array} \right\}, \quad \left. \begin{array}{l} dy + cx = q \\ by + ax = p \end{array} \right\}.$$

You are now back to the situation in Case 1, but with different letters in each position. So instead of the condition $ad - bc \neq 0$ for the equations to have a unique solution, you will get one of

$$bc - ad \neq 0, \quad cb - da \neq 0 \quad \text{or} \quad da - cb \neq 0.$$

But all these are just the same condition as $ad - bc \neq 0$, written another way. So putting Case 1 and Case 2 together shows that, if any one of a, b, c or d is not 0, then the equations have a unique solution if, and only if, $ad - bc \neq 0$.

Case 3 The only other possibility is that all the coefficients are 0, so that the equations become

$$\left. \begin{array}{l} 0x + 0y = p \\ 0x + 0y = q \end{array} \right\}.$$

These equations are satisfied by all x and y if $p = q = 0$. Otherwise they are not satisfied by any x and y.

Putting all three cases together, if $ad - bc = 0$ (which always happens in case 3, and may happen in cases 1 and 2), the equations do not have a unique solution. But if $ad - bc \neq 0$ (which may happen in cases 1 and 2), they do. It follows that the equations have a unique solution if, and only if, $ad - bc \neq 0$.

Example 4.2.1

The sets of equations in Examples 1.2.1, 1.4.1 and 1.4.2 are $\left.\begin{array}{l} 2x + 3y = 1 \\ 4x - y = 9 \end{array}\right\}, \left.\begin{array}{l} -x + 2y = 0 \\ 2x - 4y = -4 \end{array}\right\}$

and $\left.\begin{array}{l} -2x + 4y = 1 \\ 4x - 8y = -2 \end{array}\right\}$. Calculate the value of '$ad - bc$' for each of these sets of equations, and

comment on its value in the light of the solutions to those examples.

For $\left.\begin{array}{l} 2x + 3y = 1 \\ 4x - y = 9 \end{array}\right\}$, $ad - bc = 2 \times (-1) - 3 \times 4 = -14$. Since this is not 0, the

equations are satisfied by a unique pair of values of x and y.

For $\left.\begin{array}{l} -x + 2y = 0 \\ 2x - 4y = -4 \end{array}\right\}$, $ad - bc = (-1) \times (-4) - 2 \times 2 = 0$. There are either no pairs of

values of x and y which satisfy these equations, or infinitely many such pairs.

For $\left.\begin{array}{l} -2x + 4y = 1 \\ 4x - 8y = -2 \end{array}\right\}$, $ad - bc = (-2) \times (-8) - 4 \times 4 = 0$. There are either no pairs of

values of x and y which satisfy these equations, or infinitely many such pairs.

4.3 Matrix notation for linear equations

In Section 4.2 you saw that

the solution of the equations $\left.\begin{array}{l} ax + by = p \\ cx + dy = q \end{array}\right\}$ is unique $\quad \Leftrightarrow \quad ad - bc \neq 0$.

So the value of $ad - bc$ is important as it gives information about the linear

equations $\left.\begin{array}{l} ax + by = p \\ cx + dy = q \end{array}\right\}$.

Note that the condition $ad - bc \neq 0$ refers only to the coefficients a, b, c and d, and not to p and q.

The set of equations $\left.\begin{array}{l} ax + by = p \\ cx + dy = q \end{array}\right\}$ can also be written as a single matrix equation in the

form $\begin{pmatrix} ax + by \\ cx + dy \end{pmatrix} = \begin{pmatrix} p \\ q \end{pmatrix}$. You will recognise the left side, $\begin{pmatrix} ax + by \\ cx + dy \end{pmatrix}$, as the matrix product

$\begin{pmatrix} a & b \\ c & d \end{pmatrix}\begin{pmatrix} x \\ y \end{pmatrix}$. So the set of linear equations $\left.\begin{array}{l} ax + by = p \\ cx + dy = q \end{array}\right\}$ is the same as the matrix equation

$$\begin{pmatrix} a & b \\ c & d \end{pmatrix}\begin{pmatrix} x \\ y \end{pmatrix} = \begin{pmatrix} p \\ q \end{pmatrix}.$$

The expression $ad - bc$ is called the **determinant** of the matrix $\begin{pmatrix} a & b \\ c & d \end{pmatrix}$, and is denoted by $\det \begin{pmatrix} a & b \\ c & d \end{pmatrix}$.

In some books you will find the notation $\begin{vmatrix} a & b \\ c & d \end{vmatrix}$ for the determinant.

The analysis of the simultaneous equations in Section 4.2 has shown that:

The set of linear equations $\left. \begin{array}{l} ax + by = p \\ cx + dy = q \end{array} \right\}$ can be written as the matrix equation $\begin{pmatrix} a & b \\ c & d \end{pmatrix} \begin{pmatrix} x \\ y \end{pmatrix} = \begin{pmatrix} p \\ q \end{pmatrix}$.

The solution of $\begin{pmatrix} a & b \\ c & d \end{pmatrix} \begin{pmatrix} x \\ y \end{pmatrix} = \begin{pmatrix} p \\ q \end{pmatrix}$ is unique $\Leftrightarrow$ $\det \begin{pmatrix} a & b \\ c & d \end{pmatrix} = ad - bc \neq 0$.

The Greek capital delta, Δ, is often used as a shorthand for the value of a determinant.

Notice that whether the solution of the equations $\left. \begin{array}{l} ax + by = p \\ cx + dy = q \end{array} \right\}$ is unique or not is independent of the values of p and q.

It is interesting to compare the determinant of a matrix with the discriminant of a quadratic. Both of them give important information about the solution of their associated equations.

Example 4.3.1

Find the values of (a) $\det \begin{pmatrix} 2 & 3 \\ 4 & 5 \end{pmatrix}$, (b) $\det \begin{pmatrix} 1 & 0 \\ 0 & 1 \end{pmatrix}$, (c) $\det \begin{pmatrix} 2 & -4 \\ -1 & 2 \end{pmatrix}$.

What do your results tell you about the following sets of equations?

(a) $\left. \begin{array}{l} 2x + 3y = p \\ 4x + 5y = q \end{array} \right\}$ (b) $\left. \begin{array}{l} x \quad\quad = p \\ \quad\quad y = q \end{array} \right\}$ (c) $\left. \begin{array}{l} 2x - 4y = p \\ -x + 2y = q \end{array} \right\}$

(a) $\det \begin{pmatrix} 2 & 3 \\ 4 & 5 \end{pmatrix} = 2 \times 5 - 3 \times 4 = 10 - 12 = -2$.

As $\det \begin{pmatrix} 2 & 3 \\ 4 & 5 \end{pmatrix} = -2 \neq 0$, the solution of the equations is unique.

(b) $\det \begin{pmatrix} 1 & 0 \\ 0 & 1 \end{pmatrix} = 1 \times 1 - 0 \times 0 = 1$.

As $\det \begin{pmatrix} 1 & 0 \\ 0 & 1 \end{pmatrix} = 1 \neq 0$, the solution of the equations is unique.

(c) $\det \begin{pmatrix} 2 & -4 \\ -1 & 2 \end{pmatrix} = 2 \times 2 - (-4) \times (-1) = 4 - 4 = 0.$

As $\det \begin{pmatrix} 2 & -4 \\ -1 & 2 \end{pmatrix} = 0$, the solution of the equations is not unique. There may be no values of x and y which satisfy the equations, or there may be infinitely many of them, depending on the values of p and q.

Example 4.3.2

Find the value of k such that the equations $\left.\begin{array}{l} 2x + 5y = 2 \\ -x + ky = -1 \end{array}\right\}$ do not have a unique solution.
For this value of k solve the equations completely.

From the result in the blue box, if the equations $\left.\begin{array}{l} 2x + 5y = 2 \\ -x + ky = -1 \end{array}\right\}$ do not have a

unique solution, $\det \begin{pmatrix} 2 & 5 \\ -1 & k \end{pmatrix} = 0$ giving $2k - 5 \times (-1) = 0$, or $k = -\frac{5}{2}$.

If $k = -\frac{5}{2}$ the equations $\left.\begin{array}{l} 2x + 5y = 2 \\ -x + ky = -1 \end{array}\right\}$ become $\left.\begin{array}{l} 2x + 5y = 2 \\ -x - \frac{5}{2}y = -1 \end{array}\right\}.$

Using the method of Section 1.2,

$$\left.\begin{array}{l} 2x + 5y = 2 \\ -x - \frac{5}{2}y = -1 \end{array}\right\} \quad \Leftrightarrow \quad \left.\begin{array}{l} 2x + 5y = 2 \\ 0y = 0 \end{array}\right\} \quad r'_2 = r_2 - \frac{1}{2}r_1.$$

The second equation is Case 2b of Section 4.1. It is satisfied by any value of y. So put $y = 2t$, where $t \in \mathbb{R}$. The first equation becomes $2x + 10t = 2$, giving $x = 1 - 5t$.

So the solution can be written as $\left.\begin{array}{l} x = 1 - 5t \\ y = \quad 2t \end{array}\right\}, \quad t \in \mathbb{R}.$

Example 4.3.3

Solve the equations $\left.\begin{array}{l} 3x + 2y = 5 \\ kx - 4y = 6 \end{array}\right\}$ for all possible values of k.

$\det \begin{pmatrix} 3 & 2 \\ k & -4 \end{pmatrix} = 3 \times (-4) - 2 \times k = -12 - 2k$, so if $\det \begin{pmatrix} 3 & 2 \\ k & -4 \end{pmatrix} = 0$ then $k = -6.$
In Case 1 the equations have been rewritten with y first; this allows the elimination to take place in the usual way without involving k.

Case 1   If $k \neq -6$,

$$\left.\begin{array}{l} 3x + 2y = 5 \\ kx - 4y = 6 \end{array}\right\} \quad \Leftrightarrow \quad \left.\begin{array}{l} 2y + 3x = 5 \\ -4y + kx = 6 \end{array}\right\} \quad \Leftrightarrow \quad \left.\begin{array}{l} 2y \quad + 3x = \quad 5 \\ (k+6)x = 16 \end{array}\right\} \quad r'_2 = r_2 + 2r_1.$$

So $x = \dfrac{16}{k+6}$. Substituting this value in the other equation gives $2y + \dfrac{3 \times 16}{k+6} = 5$

which reduces to $y = \dfrac{5k - 18}{2(k+6)}.$

Case 2   If $k = -6$, the equations become

$$\left.\begin{array}{r} 3x + 2y = 5 \\ -6x - 4y = 6 \end{array}\right\} \quad \Leftrightarrow \quad \left.\begin{array}{r} 3x + 2y = 5 \\ 0y = 16 \end{array}\right\} \quad r_2' = r_2 + 2r_1$$

and are inconsistent.

So when $k \neq -6$, $x = \dfrac{16}{k + 6}$ and $y = \dfrac{5k - 18}{2(k + 6)}$. Otherwise the equations are inconsistent.

Exercise 4B

1 Find the values of the following determinants.

(a) $\det \begin{pmatrix} 2 & 5 \\ 3 & 8 \end{pmatrix}$

(b) $\det \begin{pmatrix} 3 & -5 \\ 1 & 4 \end{pmatrix}$

(c) $\det \begin{pmatrix} 3 & -5 \\ -9 & 15 \end{pmatrix}$

(d) $\det \begin{pmatrix} \cos\theta & -\sin\theta \\ \sin\theta & \cos\theta \end{pmatrix}$

2 Find the values of k for which the following sets of equations have a unique solution. You are *not* required to solve the equations.

(a) $\left.\begin{array}{r} x + 2y = 2 \\ 3x + ky = 5 \end{array}\right\}$

(b) $\left.\begin{array}{r} 3x - 4y = 7 \\ kx - 3y = 8 \end{array}\right\}$

(c) $\left.\begin{array}{r} 2kx - 3y = 3 \\ x + 2y = -5 \end{array}\right\}$

(d) $\left.\begin{array}{r} kx + 8y = 2 \\ 2x + ky = 3 \end{array}\right\}$

(e) $\left.\begin{array}{r} (3 - k)x + 2y = 0 \\ -x - ky = 0 \end{array}\right\}$

(f) $\left.\begin{array}{r} x + 4y = kx \\ 5x + 2y = ky \end{array}\right\}$

3 Some of the following equations have unique solutions: others do not. Decide without attempting to solve them which is which; then solve them.

(a) $\left.\begin{array}{r} x + 2y = 2 \\ 3x + 4y = 8 \end{array}\right\}$

(b) $\left.\begin{array}{r} x + 2y = 1 \\ 3x + 5y = 4 \end{array}\right\}$

(c) $\left.\begin{array}{r} x + 2y = 3 \\ 3x + 6y = 8 \end{array}\right\}$

4 Find the value of k for which each of the following sets of equations do not have a unique solution. Solve the equations for this value of k.

(a) $\left.\begin{array}{r} x + y = 2 \\ -x + ky = -2 \end{array}\right\}$

(b) $\left.\begin{array}{r} 2x + 3y = 2 \\ -6x + ky = -8 \end{array}\right\}$

(c) $\left.\begin{array}{r} 4x + 3y = 2 \\ kx - 6y = -4 \end{array}\right\}$

5 Solve the following pairs of simultaneous equations for all possible values of a.

(a) $\left.\begin{array}{r} x + y = 2 \\ ax + y = a^2 - 3 \end{array}\right\}$

(b) $\left.\begin{array}{r} x + y = 2 \\ ax + y = a^2 + 1 \end{array}\right\}$

(c) $\left.\begin{array}{r} x + y = 2 \\ ax + y = 2a^2 \end{array}\right\}$

4.4   The inverse of a 2 × 2 matrix

Although in this section the method of finding inverses is shown only for a 2 × 2 matrix, it works for square matrices of all sizes.

Example 4.4.1

If $\mathbf{A}\begin{pmatrix} x \\ y \end{pmatrix} = \begin{pmatrix} p \\ q \end{pmatrix}$, where $\mathbf{A} = \begin{pmatrix} 1 & 2 \\ 3 & 4 \end{pmatrix}$, find a matrix $\mathbf{C}$ such that $\begin{pmatrix} x \\ y \end{pmatrix} = \mathbf{C}\begin{pmatrix} p \\ q \end{pmatrix}$.

Think of $\mathbf{A}\begin{pmatrix} x \\ y \end{pmatrix} = \begin{pmatrix} p \\ q \end{pmatrix}$ as the pair of simultaneous equations

$$\left. \begin{aligned} x + 2y &= p \\ 3x + 4y &= q \end{aligned} \right\}$$

where the coefficients on the left side of the equations are those of the matrix $\mathbf{A}$.

Now solve the equations in the usual way.

$$\left. \begin{aligned} x + 2y &= p \\ 3x + 4y &= q \end{aligned} \right\} \quad \Leftrightarrow \quad \left. \begin{aligned} x + 2y &= p \\ -2y &= -3p + q \end{aligned} \right\} \quad r_2' = r_2 - 3r_1.$$

The set of equations is now in triangular form and $y = \frac{3}{2}p - \frac{1}{2}q$.

If you substitute $y = \frac{3}{2}p - \frac{1}{2}q$ into the top equation to find x you get

$$x + 2\left(\tfrac{3}{2}p - \tfrac{1}{2}q\right) = p$$

which leads to $x = -2p + q$.

So the original equations $\left. \begin{aligned} x + 2y &= p \\ 3x + 4y &= q \end{aligned} \right\}$ are equivalent to $\left. \begin{aligned} x &= -2p + q \\ y &= \tfrac{3}{2}p - \tfrac{1}{2}q \end{aligned} \right\}$.

But if you write $\left. \begin{aligned} x &= -2p + q \\ y &= \tfrac{3}{2}p - \tfrac{1}{2}q \end{aligned} \right\}$ in matrix form, then

$$\begin{pmatrix} x \\ y \end{pmatrix} = \begin{pmatrix} -2 & 1 \\ \frac{3}{2} & -\frac{1}{2} \end{pmatrix}\begin{pmatrix} p \\ q \end{pmatrix},$$

and $\begin{pmatrix} x \\ y \end{pmatrix} = \mathbf{C}\begin{pmatrix} p \\ q \end{pmatrix}$ with $\mathbf{C} = \begin{pmatrix} -2 & 1 \\ \frac{3}{2} & -\frac{1}{2} \end{pmatrix}$. A number of things are going on here.

- First, the solution of $\mathbf{A}\begin{pmatrix} x \\ y \end{pmatrix} = \begin{pmatrix} p \\ q \end{pmatrix}$ is $\begin{pmatrix} x \\ y \end{pmatrix} = \mathbf{C}\begin{pmatrix} p \\ q \end{pmatrix}$.

- Secondly, if you substitute $\mathbf{C}\begin{pmatrix} p \\ q \end{pmatrix}$ for $\begin{pmatrix} x \\ y \end{pmatrix}$ in the equation $\mathbf{A}\begin{pmatrix} x \\ y \end{pmatrix} = \begin{pmatrix} p \\ q \end{pmatrix}$ you get

$\mathbf{AC}\begin{pmatrix} p \\ q \end{pmatrix} = \begin{pmatrix} p \\ q \end{pmatrix}$, which you can write as $(\mathbf{AC})\begin{pmatrix} p \\ q \end{pmatrix} = \begin{pmatrix} p \\ q \end{pmatrix}$. Since this is true for any p and q, $\mathbf{AC} = \mathbf{I}$.

- Substituting $\mathbf{A}\begin{pmatrix} x \\ y \end{pmatrix}$ for $\begin{pmatrix} p \\ q \end{pmatrix}$ in $\begin{pmatrix} x \\ y \end{pmatrix} = \mathbf{C}\begin{pmatrix} p \\ q \end{pmatrix}$ gives $\begin{pmatrix} x \\ y \end{pmatrix} = \mathbf{CA}\begin{pmatrix} x \\ y \end{pmatrix} = (\mathbf{CA})\begin{pmatrix} x \\ y \end{pmatrix}$ for any x and y, so $\mathbf{CA} = \mathbf{I}$.

Therefore $\mathbf{AC} = \mathbf{CA} = \mathbf{I}$.

From Section 3.6, $\mathbf{C}$ is the inverse of $\mathbf{A}$; that is, $\mathbf{C} = \mathbf{A}^{-1}$.

Therefore the inverse of $\mathbf{A} = \begin{pmatrix} 1 & 2 \\ 3 & 4 \end{pmatrix}$ is $\mathbf{A}^{-1} = \begin{pmatrix} -2 & 1 \\ \frac{3}{2} & -\frac{1}{2} \end{pmatrix}$.

- If you now recall Sections 4.2 and 4.3, the solution of the set of equations

$$\mathbf{A}\begin{pmatrix} x \\ y \end{pmatrix} = \begin{pmatrix} p \\ q \end{pmatrix}$$

is unique if $\det \mathbf{A}$ is not zero. In the equations above,

$$\det \begin{pmatrix} 1 & 2 \\ 3 & 4 \end{pmatrix} = 1 \times 4 - 2 \times 3 = -2 \neq 0.$$

Thus the solution $\begin{pmatrix} x \\ y \end{pmatrix} = \mathbf{A}^{-1}\begin{pmatrix} p \\ q \end{pmatrix}$ is unique, so the inverse, $\mathbf{A}^{-1}$, of $\mathbf{A}$ is unique.

Generalising from this example for all square matrices $\mathbf{A}$:

> If $\mathbf{A}$ is square and $\det \mathbf{A} \neq 0$, there exists a unique matrix $\mathbf{C}$ such that
> $\mathbf{AC} = \mathbf{CA} = \mathbf{I}$.

Alternatively you can say that the four following statements regarding a 2×2 matrix are equivalent. There are corresponding statements for other square matrices.

> $\det \mathbf{A} \neq 0$. $\mathbf{A}^{-1}$ exists and is unique.
>
> $\mathbf{A}$ is non-singular.   The equation $\mathbf{A}\begin{pmatrix} x \\ y \end{pmatrix} = \begin{pmatrix} p \\ q \end{pmatrix}$ has a unique solution.

Here is another set of four equivalent statements written in a different form.

> $\det \mathbf{A} = 0$. $\mathbf{A}^{-1}$ does not exist.
>
> $\mathbf{A}$ is singular.   The equation $\mathbf{A}\begin{pmatrix} x \\ y \end{pmatrix} = \begin{pmatrix} p \\ q \end{pmatrix}$ does not have a
> unique solution.

The results in the boxes apply for square matrices of all sizes.

4.5 Finding the inverse of a 2 × 2 matrix

If you are asked to find the inverse of a particular matrix it is time consuming if you have to solve a set of linear equations as in the previous section. It is helpful to have a general method.

Example 4.5.1

Find the matrix $\begin{pmatrix} p & q \\ r & s \end{pmatrix}$ such that $\begin{pmatrix} 2 & 3 \\ 5 & 4 \end{pmatrix}\begin{pmatrix} p & q \\ r & s \end{pmatrix} = \begin{pmatrix} 1 & 0 \\ 0 & 1 \end{pmatrix}$.

Since $\begin{pmatrix} 2 & 3 \\ 5 & 4 \end{pmatrix}\begin{pmatrix} p & q \\ r & s \end{pmatrix} = \begin{pmatrix} 1 & 0 \\ 0 & 1 \end{pmatrix}$, $\begin{pmatrix} 2p + 3r & 2q + 3s \\ 5p + 4r & 5q + 4s \end{pmatrix} = \begin{pmatrix} 1 & 0 \\ 0 & 1 \end{pmatrix}$.

You can see immediately that $2q + 3s = 0$, so put $q = 3t$, giving $s = -2t$, where t is any real number.

But since $5q + 4s = 1$, substituting for q and s gives

$$5(3t) + 4(-2t) = 1, \quad \text{so} \quad t = \tfrac{1}{7}. \quad \text{So} \quad q = \tfrac{3}{7} \quad \text{and} \quad s = -\tfrac{2}{7}.$$

But also $5p + 4r = 0$, so put $p = 4u$, giving $r = -5u$, where u is any real number.

But since $2p + 3r = 1$, substituting for p and r gives

$$2(4u) + 3(-5u) = 1, \quad \text{so} \quad u = -\tfrac{1}{7}. \quad \text{So} \quad p = -\tfrac{4}{7} \quad \text{and} \quad r = \tfrac{5}{7}.$$

The matrix $\begin{pmatrix} p & q \\ r & s \end{pmatrix}$ is $\begin{pmatrix} -\tfrac{4}{7} & \tfrac{3}{7} \\ \tfrac{5}{7} & -\tfrac{2}{7} \end{pmatrix}$, or $-\tfrac{1}{7}\begin{pmatrix} 4 & -1 \\ -5 & 2 \end{pmatrix}$.

In the general case, to find the inverse of a given matrix $\begin{pmatrix} a & b \\ c & d \end{pmatrix}$, where $ad - bc \neq 0$, you need to find a matrix $\begin{pmatrix} p & q \\ r & s \end{pmatrix}$ such that $\begin{pmatrix} a & b \\ c & d \end{pmatrix}\begin{pmatrix} p & q \\ r & s \end{pmatrix} = \begin{pmatrix} 1 & 0 \\ 0 & 1 \end{pmatrix}$. From the boxes at the end of the previous section, you know that if you find such a matrix it is the inverse, because the inverse is unique.

Since $\begin{pmatrix} a & b \\ c & d \end{pmatrix}\begin{pmatrix} p & q \\ r & s \end{pmatrix} = \begin{pmatrix} 1 & 0 \\ 0 & 1 \end{pmatrix}$, $\begin{pmatrix} ap + br & aq + bs \\ cp + dr & cq + ds \end{pmatrix} = \begin{pmatrix} 1 & 0 \\ 0 & 1 \end{pmatrix}$.

First look at the element in the first row and the second column of the product, which has to be 0. If you put $q = -tb$ and $s = ta$, where t is any real number, you find

$$aq + bs = a(-tb) + b(ta) = 0.$$

And now, looking at the element in the second row and second column of the product, you find that

$$cq + ds = c(-tb) + d(ta) = -bct + adt = t(ad - bc).$$

As this has to be 1, $t(ad - bc) = 1$, giving $t = \dfrac{1}{ad - bc}$, since $ad - bc \neq 0$.

Hence $q = \dfrac{-b}{ad - bc}$ and $s = \dfrac{a}{ad - bc}$.

Similarly, if you look at the element in the second row and first column of the product, and then the element in the first row and first column of the product, you find

$$p = \dfrac{d}{ad - bc} \quad \text{and} \quad r = \dfrac{-c}{ad - bc}.$$

So the matrix $\begin{pmatrix} p & q \\ r & s \end{pmatrix}$ is equal to $\begin{pmatrix} \dfrac{d}{ad-bc} & \dfrac{-b}{ad-bc} \\ \dfrac{-c}{ad-bc} & \dfrac{a}{ad-bc} \end{pmatrix} = \dfrac{1}{ad-bc}\begin{pmatrix} d & -b \\ -c & a \end{pmatrix}$.

So the inverse of $\begin{pmatrix} a & b \\ c & d \end{pmatrix}$ is $\dfrac{1}{ad - bc}\begin{pmatrix} d & -b \\ -c & a \end{pmatrix}$.

You can see from this result that there are difficulties when $ad - bc = 0$.

The inverse of the matrix $\mathbf{A} = \begin{pmatrix} a & b \\ c & d \end{pmatrix}$ is given by

$$\mathbf{A}^{-1} = \frac{1}{ad - bc} \begin{pmatrix} d & -b \\ -c & a \end{pmatrix}$$

$$= \frac{1}{\det \mathbf{A}} \begin{pmatrix} d & -b \\ -c & a \end{pmatrix}$$

provided that $\det \mathbf{A} \equiv ad - bc \neq 0$.

Always check your answer by calculating $\mathbf{A}\mathbf{A}^{-1}$ to see that it actually is $\mathbf{I}$.

Example 4.5.2

Find the inverse of $\begin{pmatrix} 4 & -5 \\ 3 & 7 \end{pmatrix}$, and use it to solve the equations $\left. \begin{matrix} 4x - 5y = 3 \\ 3x + 7y = 13 \end{matrix} \right\}$.

The inverse of $\begin{pmatrix} 4 & -5 \\ 3 & 7 \end{pmatrix}$ is $\frac{1}{43} \begin{pmatrix} 7 & 5 \\ -3 & 4 \end{pmatrix}$.

Writing the equations $\left. \begin{matrix} 4x - 5y = 3 \\ 3x + 7y = 13 \end{matrix} \right\}$ as $\begin{pmatrix} 4 & -5 \\ 3 & 7 \end{pmatrix}\begin{pmatrix} x \\ y \end{pmatrix} = \begin{pmatrix} 3 \\ 13 \end{pmatrix}$, the solution is

$$\begin{pmatrix} x \\ y \end{pmatrix} = \begin{pmatrix} 4 & -5 \\ 3 & 7 \end{pmatrix}^{-1} \begin{pmatrix} 3 \\ 13 \end{pmatrix} = \frac{1}{43} \begin{pmatrix} 7 & 5 \\ -3 & 4 \end{pmatrix}\begin{pmatrix} 3 \\ 13 \end{pmatrix} = \frac{1}{43} \begin{pmatrix} 21 + 65 \\ -9 + 52 \end{pmatrix} = \begin{pmatrix} 2 \\ 1 \end{pmatrix}.$$

Therefore the unique solution is $x = 2$, $y = 1$.

Whether this is a more effective way of solving the simultaneous equations than the usual elimination method is a matter of debate. Use whichever method suits you better.

Example 4.5.3

Solve for $\mathbf{M}$ the matrix equation $\mathbf{M}\begin{pmatrix} 2 & 1 \\ 1 & 1 \end{pmatrix} = \begin{pmatrix} 1 & 3 \\ 3 & 2 \end{pmatrix}$.

To solve, multiply on the right by $\begin{pmatrix} 2 & 1 \\ 1 & 1 \end{pmatrix}^{-1} = \frac{1}{1}\begin{pmatrix} 1 & -1 \\ -1 & 2 \end{pmatrix} = \begin{pmatrix} 1 & -1 \\ -1 & 2 \end{pmatrix}$.

Thus $\mathbf{M}\begin{pmatrix} 2 & 1 \\ 1 & 1 \end{pmatrix} = \begin{pmatrix} 1 & 3 \\ 3 & 2 \end{pmatrix} \Leftrightarrow \mathbf{M}\begin{pmatrix} 2 & 1 \\ 1 & 1 \end{pmatrix}\begin{pmatrix} 2 & 1 \\ 1 & 1 \end{pmatrix}^{-1} = \begin{pmatrix} 1 & 3 \\ 3 & 2 \end{pmatrix}\begin{pmatrix} 2 & 1 \\ 1 & 1 \end{pmatrix}^{-1}$

$$\Leftrightarrow \mathbf{MI} \qquad\qquad = \begin{pmatrix} 1 & 3 \\ 3 & 2 \end{pmatrix}\begin{pmatrix} 1 & -1 \\ -1 & 2 \end{pmatrix}$$

$$\Leftrightarrow \mathbf{M} \qquad\qquad = \begin{pmatrix} 1 & 3 \\ 3 & 2 \end{pmatrix}\begin{pmatrix} 1 & -1 \\ -1 & 2 \end{pmatrix} = \begin{pmatrix} -2 & 5 \\ 1 & 1 \end{pmatrix}.$$

Therefore $\mathbf{M} = \begin{pmatrix} -2 & 5 \\ 1 & 1 \end{pmatrix}$.

It is important in Example 4.5.3 to multiply by the inverse of $\begin{pmatrix} 2 & 1 \\ 1 & 1 \end{pmatrix}$ on the correct side of $\mathbf{M} \begin{pmatrix} 2 & 1 \\ 1 & 1 \end{pmatrix}$. The reason why the method works is that, when you multiply on the right by $\begin{pmatrix} 2 & 1 \\ 1 & 1 \end{pmatrix}^{-1}$, you get $\mathbf{M} \begin{pmatrix} 2 & 1 \\ 1 & 1 \end{pmatrix} \begin{pmatrix} 2 & 1 \\ 1 & 1 \end{pmatrix}^{-1}$, and the product of the last two factors is $\begin{pmatrix} 2 & 1 \\ 1 & 1 \end{pmatrix} \begin{pmatrix} 2 & 1 \\ 1 & 1 \end{pmatrix}^{-1} = \mathbf{I}$. If you multiply on the left, you get $\begin{pmatrix} 2 & 1 \\ 1 & 1 \end{pmatrix}^{-1} \mathbf{M} \begin{pmatrix} 2 & 1 \\ 1 & 1 \end{pmatrix}$ which you cannot simplify. This does not apply in the same way to Example 4.5.2, because you cannot multiply $\begin{pmatrix} 3 \\ 13 \end{pmatrix}$ on the right by the inverse of $\begin{pmatrix} 4 & -5 \\ 3 & 7 \end{pmatrix}$. Try it!

Example 4.5.4

Let $\mathbf{M} = \begin{pmatrix} 4 & 5 \\ 2 & 3 \end{pmatrix}$. Show that $\mathbf{M}^2 - 7\mathbf{M} + 2\mathbf{I} = \mathbf{O}$, and use this to find $\mathbf{M}^{-1}$.

$$\mathbf{M}^2 = \begin{pmatrix} 4 & 5 \\ 2 & 3 \end{pmatrix} \begin{pmatrix} 4 & 5 \\ 2 & 3 \end{pmatrix} = \begin{pmatrix} 4 \times 4 + 5 \times 2 & 4 \times 5 + 5 \times 3 \\ 2 \times 4 + 3 \times 2 & 2 \times 5 + 3 \times 3 \end{pmatrix} = \begin{pmatrix} 26 & 35 \\ 14 & 19 \end{pmatrix}, \text{ so}$$

$$\mathbf{M}^2 - 7\mathbf{M} + 2\mathbf{I} = \begin{pmatrix} 26 & 35 \\ 14 & 19 \end{pmatrix} - \begin{pmatrix} 28 & 35 \\ 14 & 21 \end{pmatrix} + \begin{pmatrix} 2 & 0 \\ 0 & 2 \end{pmatrix} = \begin{pmatrix} 0 & 0 \\ 0 & 0 \end{pmatrix}.$$

As $\mathbf{M}^2 - 7\mathbf{M} + 2\mathbf{I} = \mathbf{O}$,

$$2\mathbf{I} = 7\mathbf{M} - \mathbf{M}^2 = \mathbf{M}(7\mathbf{I} - \mathbf{M}),$$

so $\mathbf{I} = \mathbf{M} \left(\tfrac{1}{2}(7\mathbf{I} - \mathbf{M}) \right).$

As $\mathbf{MC} = \mathbf{I} \quad \Leftrightarrow \quad \mathbf{C} = \mathbf{M}^{-1}$, for a matrix $\mathbf{C}$,

$$\mathbf{M}^{-1} = \tfrac{1}{2}(7\mathbf{I} - \mathbf{M}).$$

Hence $\mathbf{M}^{-1} = \tfrac{1}{2} \left(\begin{pmatrix} 7 & 0 \\ 0 & 7 \end{pmatrix} - \begin{pmatrix} 4 & 5 \\ 2 & 3 \end{pmatrix} \right) = \tfrac{1}{2} \begin{pmatrix} 3 & -5 \\ -2 & 4 \end{pmatrix}.$

4.6 Inverse of a product

If you know that $\mathbf{A}$ and $\mathbf{B}$ are both square matrices, what can you say about the inverse of the matrix product $\mathbf{AB}$?

Suppose that both $\mathbf{A}$ or $\mathbf{B}$ are non-singular so that $\mathbf{A}^{-1}$ and $\mathbf{B}^{-1}$ both exist and are unique.

Then, if $\mathbf{X}$ is the inverse of $\mathbf{AB}$,

$$
\begin{aligned}
(\mathbf{AB})\mathbf{X} = \mathbf{I} \quad &\Leftrightarrow \quad \mathbf{A}(\mathbf{BX}) = \mathbf{I} \\
&\Leftrightarrow \quad \mathbf{BX} = \mathbf{A}^{-1} \\
&\Leftrightarrow \quad \mathbf{B}^{-1}\mathbf{BX} = \mathbf{B}^{-1}\mathbf{A}^{-1} \\
&\Leftrightarrow \quad \mathbf{IX} = \mathbf{B}^{-1}\mathbf{A}^{-1} \\
&\Leftrightarrow \quad \mathbf{X} = \mathbf{B}^{-1}\mathbf{A}^{-1}.
\end{aligned}
$$

so the inverse of $\mathbf{AB}$ is $\mathbf{B}^{-1}\mathbf{A}^{-1}$.

As a check, notice that, with this $\mathbf{X}$, $\mathbf{X}(\mathbf{AB}) = \mathbf{I}$, since $\mathbf{B}^{-1}\mathbf{A}^{-1}\mathbf{AB} = \mathbf{B}^{-1}\mathbf{IB} = \mathbf{B}^{-1}\mathbf{B} = \mathbf{I}$.

> For non-singular matrices $\mathbf{A}$ and $\mathbf{B}$,
> $$(\mathbf{AB})^{-1} = \mathbf{B}^{-1}\mathbf{A}^{-1}.$$

Example 4.6.1

You are given that $\mathbf{X}^{-1} = \begin{pmatrix} -1 & 2 & -3 \\ 2 & -7 & 1 \\ -1 & 3 & 2 \end{pmatrix}$ and $\mathbf{Y} = \begin{pmatrix} 2 & 1 & -4 \\ -2 & 3 & 5 \\ -1 & -3 & 2 \end{pmatrix}$. Find $(\mathbf{XY}^{-1})^{-1}$.

Since $(\mathbf{XY}^{-1})^{-1} = (\mathbf{Y}^{-1})^{-1}\mathbf{X}^{-1}$, and $(\mathbf{Y}^{-1})^{-1} = \mathbf{Y}$,

$$(\mathbf{XY}^{-1})^{-1} = \mathbf{YX}^{-1} = \begin{pmatrix} 2 & 1 & -4 \\ -2 & 3 & 5 \\ -1 & -3 & 2 \end{pmatrix} \begin{pmatrix} -1 & 2 & -3 \\ 2 & -7 & 1 \\ -1 & 3 & 2 \end{pmatrix} = \begin{pmatrix} 4 & -15 & -13 \\ 3 & -10 & 19 \\ -7 & 25 & 4 \end{pmatrix}.$$

Exercise 4C

1 Find the inverses (if they exist) of the following matrices.

(a) $\begin{pmatrix} 1 & -1 \\ 1 & 1 \end{pmatrix}$

(b) $\begin{pmatrix} 4 & 9 \\ 3 & 7 \end{pmatrix}$

(c) $\begin{pmatrix} 3 & -5 \\ -4 & 7 \end{pmatrix}$

(d) $\begin{pmatrix} 2 & -1 \\ -5 & 4 \end{pmatrix}$

(e) $\begin{pmatrix} 2 & -6 \\ -3 & 9 \end{pmatrix}$

(f) $\begin{pmatrix} 5 & -3 \\ 10 & -5 \end{pmatrix}$

2 By finding the appropriate inverse matrices, find the solutions of the following equations.

(a) $\left.\begin{array}{l} 2x + 3y = -1 \\ 3x - 2y = 18 \end{array}\right\}$

(b) $\left.\begin{array}{l} -3x + 2y = 13 \\ -5x + 4y = 23 \end{array}\right\}$

(c) $\left.\begin{array}{l} 2x + 5y = 9 \\ -5x + 2y = -8 \end{array}\right\}$

3 Solve for $\mathbf{X}$ the following matrix equations.

(a) $\begin{pmatrix} 1 & 3 \\ 2 & 4 \end{pmatrix} \mathbf{X} = \begin{pmatrix} -2 & 9 \\ -2 & 14 \end{pmatrix}$

(b) $\mathbf{X} \begin{pmatrix} 1 & 3 \\ 2 & 4 \end{pmatrix} = \begin{pmatrix} -2 & 9 \\ -2 & 14 \end{pmatrix}$

(c) $\begin{pmatrix} 1 & 3 \\ 2 & 4 \end{pmatrix} \mathbf{X}^{-1} = \begin{pmatrix} -2 & 9 \\ -2 & 14 \end{pmatrix}$

4 Let $\mathbf{X} = \dfrac{1}{\sqrt{2}} \begin{pmatrix} 1 & -1 \\ 1 & 1 \end{pmatrix}$. Calculate the matrix $\mathbf{A}$ where $\mathbf{X} \begin{pmatrix} 2 & 3 \\ 4 & 1 \end{pmatrix} \mathbf{X}^{-1} = \mathbf{A}$.

5 If $\mathbf{A}$ is the matrix $\begin{pmatrix} 7 & 4 \\ 6 & 3 \end{pmatrix}$, show that $\mathbf{A}^2 - 10\mathbf{A} - 3\mathbf{I} = \mathbf{O}$. Hence find $\mathbf{A}^{-1}$.

6 The matrices $\mathbf{A}$ and $\mathbf{B}$ are given by $\mathbf{A} = \begin{pmatrix} 4 & 7 \\ 2 & 3 \end{pmatrix}$ and $\mathbf{B} = \begin{pmatrix} 3 & 4 \\ 5 & 6 \end{pmatrix}$. Calculate $\mathbf{A}^{-1}$, $\mathbf{B}^{-1}$ and hence find $(\mathbf{BA})^{-1}$.

4.7 Simultaneous linear equations again

Here is a summary of the main results of this chapter.

> If a system of linear equations is written in the form $\mathbf{Ax} = \mathbf{p}$, where $\mathbf{A}$ is a square matrix and $\mathbf{x}$ and $\mathbf{p}$ are column matrices, then
>
> - if $\mathbf{A}$ is non-singular, then $\mathbf{x} = \mathbf{A}^{-1}\mathbf{p}$;
> - if $\mathbf{A}$ is singular, the equation may or may not have a solution, depending on the column matrix $\mathbf{p}$, but the solution (if it exists) is not unique.

You will notice that there is no mention in the box of $\mathbf{A}$ being a 2 × 2 matrix. In Chapter 10 you will find that the same statement is true if $\mathbf{A}$ is a 3 × 3 matrix. And in fact it is true for n equations with n unknowns, where $\mathbf{A}$ is an $n \times n$ matrix and $\mathbf{x}$ and $\mathbf{p}$ are $n \times 1$ column matrices.

Moreover, in Section 4.1, the solution of the equation $ax = p$, where $a, \ p \in \mathbb{R}$, was discussed, and the solution was given as $x = a^{-1}p$ provided that $a \neq 0$.

If $a = 0$, the equation may or may not have a solution, depending on the value of p.

If you are prepared to think of a as a 1 × 1 matrix, and to say that a being non-singular means that $a \neq 0$, then all these sets of equations fit into the same pattern.

Miscellaneous exercise 4

1 (a) Find the values of k for which $\det \begin{pmatrix} k & 2 \\ 2 & k \end{pmatrix} = 0$.

  (b) For each of these values of k solve the equations $\left. \begin{array}{r} 2x + ky = 2 \\ kx + 2y = 2 \end{array} \right\}$.

2 (a) Find the values of a for which the matrix $\begin{pmatrix} a & 3 \\ 2 & a-1 \end{pmatrix}$ is singular.

  (b) For these values of a solve the equations $\left. \begin{array}{r} ax + \ \ \ 3y = 2a \\ 2x + (a-1)y = a^2 \end{array} \right\}$.

3 (a) Find the values of λ for which the solution of the equations $\left. \begin{array}{r} 3x + 2y = \lambda x \\ 15x + 4y = \lambda y \end{array} \right\}$ is not unique.

  (b) For these values of λ, solve the equations $\left. \begin{array}{r} 3x + 2y = \lambda x \\ 15x + 4y = \lambda y \end{array} \right\}$ completely.

4 (a) Prove that the equations $\left. \begin{array}{r} x - y = \lambda x \\ x + y = \lambda y \end{array} \right\}$ have a unique solution for all possible values of the real constant λ.

  (b) Solve the equations for all values of λ.

5 Prove that the matrix $\begin{pmatrix} k+1 & k \\ -k & k+1 \end{pmatrix}$ is non-singular for all real values of k.

6 Let $\mathbf{X} = \dfrac{1}{\sqrt{2}} \begin{pmatrix} 1 & -1 \\ 1 & 1 \end{pmatrix}$. Calculate the matrix $\mathbf{A}^{-1}$ where $\mathbf{X} \begin{pmatrix} 2 & 1 \\ 4 & 3 \end{pmatrix} \mathbf{X}^{-1} = \mathbf{A}$.

7 The matrix $\mathbf{A} = \begin{pmatrix} 5 & -4 \\ -3 & 1 \end{pmatrix}$.

    (a) Show that $\mathbf{A}^2 = 6\mathbf{A} + 7\mathbf{I}$. Deduce that $\mathbf{A}^{-1} = \frac{1}{7}(\mathbf{A} - 6\mathbf{I})$.

    (b) Use your answer to part (a) to solve the equations $\left. \begin{array}{r} 5x - 4y = 25 \\ -3x + y = 6 \end{array} \right\}$.

8 The matrices $\mathbf{A}$ and $\mathbf{B}$ are given by $\mathbf{A} = \begin{pmatrix} 3 & -5 \\ 4 & 7 \end{pmatrix}$ and $\mathbf{B} = \begin{pmatrix} 7 & 5 \\ -4 & 3 \end{pmatrix}$.

    (a) Calculate the matrix $\mathbf{AB}$ and hence find $\mathbf{A}^{-1}$.

    (b) Use your answer to part (a) to solve the equations $\left. \begin{array}{r} 3x - 5y = 71 \\ 4x + 7y = 40 \end{array} \right\}$.

9* (a) Show that, for 2×2 matrices, $\det \mathbf{A} \det \mathbf{B} = \det(\mathbf{AB})$.

    (b) Hence find $\det(\mathbf{AB})$ where $\mathbf{A} = \begin{pmatrix} 14 & 15 \\ 13 & 14 \end{pmatrix}$ and $\mathbf{B} = \begin{pmatrix} 19 & 18 \\ 18 & 17 \end{pmatrix}$.

10* (a) Calculate the matrix product $(x \quad 1)\begin{pmatrix} a & b \\ b & c \end{pmatrix}\begin{pmatrix} x \\ 1 \end{pmatrix}$.

    (b) Show that the equation $(x \quad 1)\begin{pmatrix} a & b \\ b & c \end{pmatrix}\begin{pmatrix} x \\ 1 \end{pmatrix} = (0)$ has distinct real roots if, and only if,

    $\det \begin{pmatrix} a & b \\ b & c \end{pmatrix} < 0$.

5 Matrices and transformations

This chapter looks at matrices in a different way, as transformations of the plane. When you have completed it, you should

- understand how to use 2 × 2 matrices to represent geometrical transformations, including rotations, reflections, enlargements, stretches and shears
- know how to find the matrix which carries out a given transformation
- know that the matrix product **AB** represents the result of the matrix transformation carried out by **B** followed by the transformation carried out by **A**.

Before you start this chapter you should read C2 Sections 1.1 to 1.4 and 1.6 and you should be familiar with measuring angles in radians as explained in C2 Sections 9.1 and 9.3.

5.1 Points and column matrices

Consider the points $(3, 1)$ and $(1, 2)$ and the column matrices $\begin{pmatrix} 3 \\ 1 \end{pmatrix}$ and $\begin{pmatrix} 1 \\ 2 \end{pmatrix}$.

Fig. 5.1 shows the two points in the plane.

Suppose that you make a correspondence between points in the plane and column matrices such that the point (x, y) corresponds to the column matrix $\begin{pmatrix} x \\ y \end{pmatrix}$, and vice versa. You can see that to every point there corresponds just one column matrix and vice versa.

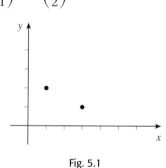

Fig. 5.1

You can't add points, but you can add column matrices. For instance

$$\begin{pmatrix} 3 \\ 1 \end{pmatrix} + \begin{pmatrix} 1 \\ 2 \end{pmatrix} = \begin{pmatrix} 1+3 \\ 2+1 \end{pmatrix} = \begin{pmatrix} 4 \\ 3 \end{pmatrix}.$$

If you now think of these column matrices as points, what relationship does the point $(4, 3)$ have to the original points $(3, 1)$ and $(1, 2)$?

The three points are shown in Fig. 5.2.

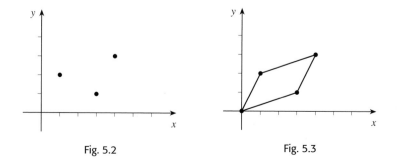

Fig. 5.2   Fig. 5.3

Fig. 5.3 shows the same points as Fig. 5.2, together with the origin. You can see that the four points form a parallelogram. So it appears that the operation of adding the column matrices corresponds to completing the parallelogram formed by the lines which join the two points to the origin.

Is this true in general? Fig. 5.4 shows the parallelogram $OPRQ$ made by the origin and the points $P(a, b)$ and $Q(c, d)$. What are the coordinates of R, the fourth vertex of the parallelogram $OPRQ$?

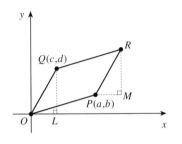

Fig. 5.4

Construct the triangles OLQ and PMR as shown in Fig. 5.4. If $OPRQ$ is a parallelogram the x- and y-steps from O to Q are the same as the x- and y-steps from P to R. The step is c in the x-direction and d in the y-direction. Thus the x- and y-coordinates of R are $a + c$ and $b + d$ respectively, so R is the point $(a + c, b + d)$. But since $\binom{a}{b} + \binom{c}{d} = \binom{a + c}{b + d}$, the point corresponding to $\binom{a + c}{b + d}$ is the fourth vertex R of the parallelogram.

> If the point P corresponds to the column matrix $\mathbf{p}$ and the point Q corresponds to the column matrix $\mathbf{q}$, then the point which corresponds to the column matrix $\mathbf{r} = \mathbf{p} + \mathbf{q}$ is R, the fourth vertex of the parallelogram $OPRQ$.

5.2 Multiplying by a number

Continuing the idea of the correspondence of the previous section, what happens to the points when you multiply a column matrix by a number?

Exercise 5A contains questions which look into this.

Exercise 5A

1 (a) What column matrix $\mathbf{p}$ corresponds to the point $P(3, 2)$?

   (b) What point Q corresponds to the column matrix $2\mathbf{p}$?

   (c) What is the geometric relationship between P and Q?

2 How would your answer to Question 1(c) change if $2\mathbf{p}$ is replaced by $\frac{1}{2}\mathbf{p}$?

3 How would your answer to Question 1(c) change if $2\mathbf{p}$ is replaced by $-\mathbf{p}$?

4 Let P be the point $(3, 1)$ and Q be the point $(1, 2)$, and let $\mathbf{p}$ and $\mathbf{q}$ be the corresponding column matrices. Find the coordinates of R, the point which corresponds to the column matrix $\mathbf{r}$, where $\mathbf{r} = 2\mathbf{p} + 3\mathbf{q}$. What geometric relationship does the point R have to the points P and Q?

5 Let P be the point (a, b) and Q be the point (c, d), and let $\mathbf{p}$ and $\mathbf{q}$ be the corresponding column matrices. Find the coordinates of R, the point which corresponds to the column matrix $\mathbf{r}$, where $\mathbf{r} = 2\mathbf{p} + 3\mathbf{q}$. What geometric relationship does the point R have to the points P and Q?

6 Let $\mathbf{p} = \begin{pmatrix} 1 \\ 1 \end{pmatrix}$ and $\mathbf{q} = \begin{pmatrix} 1 \\ -1 \end{pmatrix}$, and let P and Q be the points $(1, 1)$ and $(1, -1)$ respectively.

   (a) Describe the positions of the points given by $k\mathbf{p} + \mathbf{q}$ for $k = 0$, $k = 1$, $k = 2$ and $k = 3$.

   (b) Describe the positions of the points given by $k\mathbf{p} + \mathbf{q}$ for all possible integer values, positive and negative, of k.

   (c) Describe the positions of the points given by $k\mathbf{p} + l\mathbf{q}$ for all possible integer values, positive and negative, of k and l.

5.3 Matrices and transformations

Suppose that you multiply the column matrix $\begin{pmatrix} 2 \\ -1 \end{pmatrix}$ by the matrix $\mathbf{M} = \begin{pmatrix} 2 & -1 \\ 1 & 1 \end{pmatrix}$ to get the product $\begin{pmatrix} 2 & -1 \\ 1 & 1 \end{pmatrix}\begin{pmatrix} 2 \\ -1 \end{pmatrix} = \begin{pmatrix} 5 \\ 1 \end{pmatrix}$. You can think of this as the matrix $\mathbf{M}$ operating on the column matrix $\mathbf{v} = \begin{pmatrix} 2 \\ -1 \end{pmatrix}$ to give another column matrix $\mathbf{v}' = \begin{pmatrix} 5 \\ 1 \end{pmatrix}$. The matrix $\mathbf{M}$ can operate in the same way on any column matrix with two components to give another column matrix with two components. For example, $\mathbf{M}$ operates on $\mathbf{w} = \begin{pmatrix} -1 \\ 1 \end{pmatrix}$ to give $\mathbf{w}' = \begin{pmatrix} 2 & -1 \\ 1 & 1 \end{pmatrix}\begin{pmatrix} -1 \\ 1 \end{pmatrix} = \begin{pmatrix} -3 \\ 0 \end{pmatrix}$.

Using the correspondence of Section 5.1, you can also think of the matrix $\mathbf{M} = \begin{pmatrix} 2 & -1 \\ 1 & 1 \end{pmatrix}$ as transforming the point P corresponding to $\begin{pmatrix} 2 \\ -1 \end{pmatrix}$, that is $(2, -1)$, into the point P' corresponding to $\begin{pmatrix} 5 \\ 1 \end{pmatrix}$, that is $(5, 1)$. It also transforms the point Q corresponding to $\begin{pmatrix} -1 \\ 1 \end{pmatrix}$, that is $(-1, 1)$, into the point Q' corresponding to $\begin{pmatrix} -3 \\ 0 \end{pmatrix}$, that is $(-3, 0)$.

So you can think of the matrix $\mathbf{M} = \begin{pmatrix} 2 & -1 \\ 1 & 1 \end{pmatrix}$ as transforming $(2, -1)$ into $(5, 1)$, and $(-1, 1)$ into $(-3, 0)$. This is shown in Fig. 5.5.

In this sense, the matrix $\mathbf{M}$ is said to carry out a **transformation**, or a **mapping**, of each point into its **image**. In this book, the term 'transformation' will be used. Sometimes, if there is ambiguity, the term **image point** will be used. P' is said to be the image of P **under** the transformation.

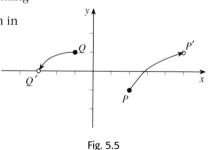

Fig. 5.5

If a diagram like the one in Fig. 5.5 gets too crowded, it can be helpful to draw the image points on a separate set of axes, as in Fig. 5.6.

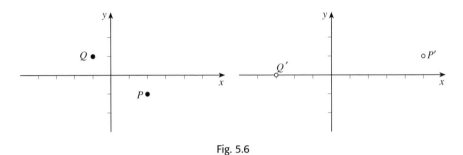

Fig. 5.6

A good way to understand matrix transformations is to consider their effect on the **unit square** $OABC$ formed by the origin and the points $A(1, 0)$, $B(1, 1)$ and $C(0, 1)$. The images of $\begin{pmatrix} 0 \\ 0 \end{pmatrix}$ and of the column matrices $\mathbf{a} = \begin{pmatrix} 1 \\ 0 \end{pmatrix}$, $\mathbf{b} = \begin{pmatrix} 1 \\ 1 \end{pmatrix}$, and $\mathbf{c} = \begin{pmatrix} 0 \\ 1 \end{pmatrix}$ when multiplied by the matrix $\mathbf{M} = \begin{pmatrix} 2 & -1 \\ 1 & 1 \end{pmatrix}$ are

$$\begin{pmatrix} 2 & -1 \\ 1 & 1 \end{pmatrix}\begin{pmatrix} 0 \\ 0 \end{pmatrix} = \begin{pmatrix} 0 \\ 0 \end{pmatrix}, \quad \mathbf{a}' = \begin{pmatrix} 2 & -1 \\ 1 & 1 \end{pmatrix}\begin{pmatrix} 1 \\ 0 \end{pmatrix} = \begin{pmatrix} 2 \\ 1 \end{pmatrix},$$

$$\mathbf{b}' = \begin{pmatrix} 2 & -1 \\ 1 & 1 \end{pmatrix}\begin{pmatrix} 1 \\ 1 \end{pmatrix} = \begin{pmatrix} 1 \\ 2 \end{pmatrix}, \quad \mathbf{c}' = \begin{pmatrix} 2 & -1 \\ 1 & 1 \end{pmatrix}\begin{pmatrix} 0 \\ 1 \end{pmatrix} = \begin{pmatrix} -1 \\ 1 \end{pmatrix}.$$

The origin O and the points A', B' and C', shown in Fig. 5.7, have coordinates $(0, 0)$, $(2, 1)$, $(1, 2)$ and $(-1, 1)$, and you will notice that $OA'B'C'$ is a parallelogram. $OA'B'C'$ is said to be the image of the unit square under the transformation.

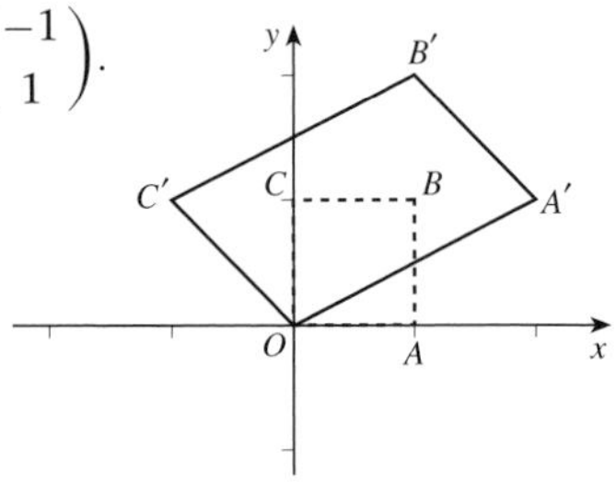

Fig. 5.7

In Fig. 5.8 the unit square and its image have been separated.

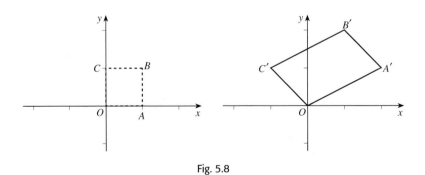

Fig. 5.8

Sometimes you may want to draw a diagram like Fig. 5.7. At other times, especially if the diagram becomes cluttered, a diagram like Fig. 5.8 may be more helpful.

Notice that all 2×2 matrices transform the origin to the origin. That is, the origin doesn't move. This will be assumed without further comment in all the examples which follow.

Example 5.3.1

Illustrate the matrix $\mathbf{R} = \begin{pmatrix} 0 & -1 \\ 1 & 0 \end{pmatrix}$ geometrically. Identify the geometric transformation carried out by $\mathbf{R}$.

Let the unit square be $OABC$ (see Fig. 5.9), and its image be $OA'B'C'$.

For A: $\begin{pmatrix} 0 & -1 \\ 1 & 0 \end{pmatrix}\begin{pmatrix} 1 \\ 0 \end{pmatrix} = \begin{pmatrix} 0 \\ 1 \end{pmatrix}$ so the image of $A(1, 0)$ is $A'(0, 1)$.

For C: $\begin{pmatrix} 0 & -1 \\ 1 & 0 \end{pmatrix}\begin{pmatrix} 0 \\ 1 \end{pmatrix} = \begin{pmatrix} -1 \\ 0 \end{pmatrix}$ so the image of $C(0, 1)$ is $C'(-1, 0)$.

For B: $\begin{pmatrix} 0 & -1 \\ 1 & 0 \end{pmatrix}\begin{pmatrix} 1 \\ 1 \end{pmatrix} = \begin{pmatrix} -1 \\ 1 \end{pmatrix}$ so the image of $B(1, 1)$ is $B'(-1, 1)$.

The image of the unit square $OABC$ (see Fig. 5.9) is the congruent square $OA'B'C'$. You will see that the matrix $\mathbf{R}$ has carried out a rotation about the origin through $\frac{1}{2}\pi$ (that is, 90°) anticlockwise.

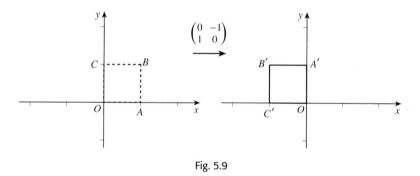

Fig. 5.9

Example 5.3.2

Illustrate the matrix $\mathbf{M} = \begin{pmatrix} -1 & 0 \\ 0 & 1 \end{pmatrix}$ geometrically. Identify the geometric transformation carried out by $\mathbf{M}$.

Let the unit square be $OABC$ (see Fig. 5.10), and its image be $OA'B'C'$.

For A: $\begin{pmatrix} -1 & 0 \\ 0 & 1 \end{pmatrix}\begin{pmatrix} 1 \\ 0 \end{pmatrix} = \begin{pmatrix} -1 \\ 0 \end{pmatrix}$ so the image of $A(1, 0)$ is $A'(-1, 0)$.

For C: $\begin{pmatrix} -1 & 0 \\ 0 & 1 \end{pmatrix}\begin{pmatrix} 0 \\ 1 \end{pmatrix} = \begin{pmatrix} 0 \\ 1 \end{pmatrix}$ so the image of $C(0, 1)$ is $C'(0, 1)$.

For B: $\begin{pmatrix} 0 & -1 \\ 1 & 0 \end{pmatrix}\begin{pmatrix} 1 \\ 1 \end{pmatrix} = \begin{pmatrix} -1 \\ 1 \end{pmatrix}$ so the image of $B(1, 1)$ is $B'(-1, 1)$.

The image of the unit square $OABC$, shown in Fig. 5.10, is the congruent square $OA'B'C'$. This shows that the matrix **M** has carried out a reflection in the y-axis.

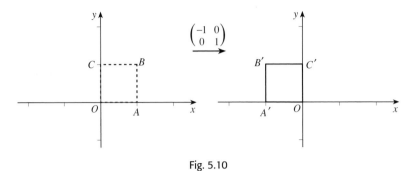

Fig. 5.10

Notice that the matrices in Examples 5.3.1 and 5.3.2 transform the unit square into the same square, but that the vertices are lettered differently. In Fig. 5.9, going round the image square in the order $OA'B'C'$, it is described in an anticlockwise direction; but in Fig. 5.10 it is described clockwise, because the square has been 'flipped over' by the transformation.

Exercise 5B

1 Draw diagrams of the unit square $OABC$ and its image $O'A'B'C'$ when the points are transformed by each of the following matrices. Identify the geometric transformation carried out by each of them.

(a) $\begin{pmatrix} 1 & 0 \\ 0 & -1 \end{pmatrix}$ (b) $\begin{pmatrix} 0 & 1 \\ 1 & 0 \end{pmatrix}$ (c) $\begin{pmatrix} 0 & 1 \\ -1 & 0 \end{pmatrix}$ (d) $\begin{pmatrix} 1 & 1 \\ 0 & 1 \end{pmatrix}$

(e) $\begin{pmatrix} -1 & 0 \\ 0 & -1 \end{pmatrix}$ (f) $\begin{pmatrix} 2 & 0 \\ 0 & 1 \end{pmatrix}$ (g) $\begin{pmatrix} -2 & 0 \\ 0 & -2 \end{pmatrix}$ (h) $\begin{pmatrix} 1 & 1 \\ 1 & 1 \end{pmatrix}$

2 Draw a diagram to show the points representing the column matrices $\begin{pmatrix} 0 \\ 0 \end{pmatrix}$, $\begin{pmatrix} 5 \\ 0 \end{pmatrix}$, $\begin{pmatrix} 5 \\ 5 \end{pmatrix}$ and $\begin{pmatrix} 0 \\ 5 \end{pmatrix}$ before and after they have been transformed by the matrix $\mathbf{M} = \begin{pmatrix} 0.8 & -0.6 \\ 0.6 & 0.8 \end{pmatrix}$.

Identify the geometric transformation carried out by **M**.

3 The single transformation carried out by $\begin{pmatrix} 3 & -4 \\ 4 & 3 \end{pmatrix}$ consists of two separate transformations, one followed by the other. Draw a diagram and then identify the two transformations.

4 Describe the geometric transformation carried out by $\begin{pmatrix} 0 & 0 \\ 0 & 0 \end{pmatrix}$.

5 Plot the points $(0, 0)$, $(1, 0)$, $(2, 0)$, $(3, 0)$, $(0, 1)$, $(1, 1)$, $(2, 1)$, $(3, 1)$, $(0, 2)$, $(1, 2)$, $(2, 2)$ and $(3, 2)$, and (on separate axes) their images after multiplication by the matrix $\mathbf{M} = \begin{pmatrix} 2 & -1 \\ 1 & 1 \end{pmatrix}$.

Describe the configuration of this set of points.

6 Use your results from Question 5 and some extra calculations to find and plot the images of the points $(0, 0)$, $(1, 0)$, $(2, 0)$, $(3, 0)$, $(1, 1)$, $(2, 1)$, $(3, 1)$, $(4, 1)$, $(2, 2)$, $(3, 2)$, $(4, 2)$ and $(5, 2)$ after multiplication by the matrix $\mathbf{M} = \begin{pmatrix} 2 & -1 \\ 1 & 1 \end{pmatrix}$. Describe the configurations of these sets of points.

7 Prove that, when points (p, q) are transformed by the matrix $\mathbf{M} = \begin{pmatrix} 0.36 & 0.48 \\ 0.48 & 0.64 \end{pmatrix}$, all the image points lie on a line. Find the equation of this line.

Show that the same property results when points (p, q) are transformed by the matrix $\mathbf{M} - \mathbf{I}$. State how the image line in this case is related to the first line.

5.4 Some generalisations

In Exercise 5B you discovered that the images of $(0, 0)$, $(1, 0)$, $(1, 1)$ and $(0, 1)$ always form a parallelogram. This is no coincidence. And Question 5 showed that the grid of squares was transformed to a grid of parallelograms. Question 6 showed that a grid of parallelograms is transformed into a grid of parallelograms.

These are general results which need proving. They follow from the rules of multiplication for matrices. The proofs are given below.

If you wish you can skip the proofs, but you should start reading again from the box which follows the proofs.

Theorem 1* The images of $(0, 0)$, $(1, 0)$, $(1, 1)$ and $(0, 1)$ form a parallelogram.

Proof Let $\mathbf{i} = \begin{pmatrix} 1 \\ 0 \end{pmatrix}$ and $\mathbf{j} = \begin{pmatrix} 0 \\ 1 \end{pmatrix}$. Then $\mathbf{i} + \mathbf{j} = \begin{pmatrix} 1 \\ 1 \end{pmatrix}$.

Let $\mathbf{M}$ be any 2×2 matrix and let the images of $(1, 0)$, $(1, 1)$ and $(0, 1)$ be U, V and W respectively, with corresponding column matrices $\mathbf{u}$, $\mathbf{v}$ and $\mathbf{w}$ respectively.

Then $\mathbf{v} = \mathbf{M}(\mathbf{i} + \mathbf{j})$ (definition of $\mathbf{v}$)

      $= \mathbf{M}\mathbf{i} + \mathbf{M}\mathbf{j}$ (using the distributive rule for matrices)

      $= \mathbf{u} + \mathbf{w}$ (definition of $\mathbf{u}$ and $\mathbf{w}$).

Therefore $\mathbf{v} = \mathbf{u} + \mathbf{w}$.

So the image of $\mathbf{i} + \mathbf{j}$ is the sum of the images of $\mathbf{i}$ and $\mathbf{j}$.

So, using the result in the box at the end of Section 5.1, the images of $(0, 0)$, $(1, 0)$, $(1, 1)$ and $(0, 1)$ form a parallelogram.

In fact there is a more general result than this. In Question 5 of Exercise 5B a grid of squares is transformed to a grid of parallelograms. And more generally still, in Question 6 a grid of parallelograms is transformed into a grid of parallelograms.

Theorem 2* If $OUVW$ is a parallelogram, then its image $OU'V'W'$ after being transformed by a 2×2 matrix $\mathbf{M}$ is also a parallelogram.

>**Proof**   Let $\mathbf{u}$, $\mathbf{v}$ and $\mathbf{w}$ be the column matrices representing U, V and W respectively and let $\mathbf{u}'$, $\mathbf{v}'$ and $\mathbf{w}'$ be the column matrices representing their images U', V' and W'.
>
>Since $OUVW$ is a parallelogram, $\mathbf{v} = \mathbf{u} + \mathbf{w}$.
>
>$$\begin{aligned} \text{Then } \mathbf{v}' &= \mathbf{Mv} && \text{(definition of } \mathbf{v}') \\ &= \mathbf{M(u + w)} && \text{(as } \mathbf{v} = \mathbf{u} + \mathbf{w}) \\ &= \mathbf{Mu} + \mathbf{Mw} \\ &= \mathbf{u}' + \mathbf{w}' && \text{(definition of } \mathbf{u}' \text{ and } \mathbf{w}'). \end{aligned}$$
>
>So $\mathbf{v}' = \mathbf{u}' + \mathbf{w}'$, and, using the result in the box at the end of Section 5.1, $OU'V'W'$ is a parallelogram.

Now take any point with coordinates (x, y). Its corresponding column matrix is

$$\begin{pmatrix} x \\ y \end{pmatrix} = \begin{pmatrix} x \\ 0 \end{pmatrix} + \begin{pmatrix} 0 \\ y \end{pmatrix} = x\mathbf{i} + y\mathbf{j}.$$

Then

$$\begin{aligned} \mathbf{M}(x\mathbf{i} + y\mathbf{j}) &= \mathbf{M}(x\mathbf{i}) + \mathbf{M}(y\mathbf{j}) \\ &= x\mathbf{M}(\mathbf{i}) + y\mathbf{M}(\mathbf{j}) \\ &= x\mathbf{u} + y\mathbf{v}. \end{aligned}$$

So the point corresponding to (x, y), that is the point which is x squares along and y squares up on the original grid, is transformed to the point (x, y), the point which is x parallelograms along and y up on the new grid.

>A 2×2 matrix $\mathbf{M}$ transforms parallelograms into parallelograms.
>
>In particular, $\mathbf{M}$ transforms a grid of squares into a grid of parallelograms, and the image of any point relative to the grid of squares is the corresponding point relative to the grid of parallelograms.

Fig. 5.11 illustrates this for the matrix $\mathbf{M} = \begin{pmatrix} 3 & -1 \\ 1 & 2 \end{pmatrix}$. The point (4, 2), that is, the point 4 along and 2 up on the left grid, has as its image the point which is '4 parallelograms along and 2 up' on the right grid.

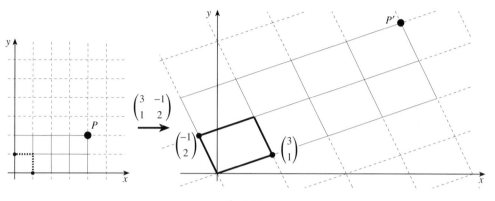

Fig. 5.11

Example 5.4.1

Draw and label the parallelogram into which the unit square $OABC$ is transformed by the matrix $\begin{pmatrix} 5 & 2 \\ 1 & 4 \end{pmatrix}$. On the diagram show the point which is the image of $P\left(\frac{1}{2}, 1\frac{1}{4}\right)$.

The images of $\begin{pmatrix} 1 \\ 0 \end{pmatrix}$, $\begin{pmatrix} 1 \\ 1 \end{pmatrix}$ and $\begin{pmatrix} 0 \\ 1 \end{pmatrix}$ are $\begin{pmatrix} 5 & 2 \\ 1 & 4 \end{pmatrix}\begin{pmatrix} 1 \\ 0 \end{pmatrix} = \begin{pmatrix} 5 \\ 1 \end{pmatrix}$, $\begin{pmatrix} 5 & 2 \\ 1 & 4 \end{pmatrix}\begin{pmatrix} 1 \\ 1 \end{pmatrix} = \begin{pmatrix} 7 \\ 5 \end{pmatrix}$ and $\begin{pmatrix} 5 & 2 \\ 1 & 4 \end{pmatrix}\begin{pmatrix} 0 \\ 1 \end{pmatrix} = \begin{pmatrix} 2 \\ 4 \end{pmatrix}$ respectively.

So the points (1, 0), (1, 1) and (0, 1) have images (5, 1), (7, 5) and (2, 4) respectively.

The image of $\left(\frac{1}{2}, 1\frac{1}{4}\right)$ is the point corresponding to $\begin{pmatrix} 5 & 2 \\ 1 & 4 \end{pmatrix}\begin{pmatrix} \frac{1}{2} \\ 1\frac{1}{4} \end{pmatrix} = \begin{pmatrix} 5 \\ 5\frac{1}{2} \end{pmatrix}$, that is $\left(5, 5\frac{1}{2}\right)$. This is shown in Fig. 5.12. To get from O to P' you go '$\frac{1}{2}$ a parallelogram along and $1\frac{1}{4}$ parallelograms up'.

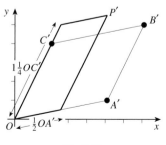

Fig. 5.12

Example 5.4.2

Illustrate the matrix $\mathbf{M} = \begin{pmatrix} 1.6 & 0.8 \\ 0.8 & 0.4 \end{pmatrix}$ geometrically.

Fig. 5.13 shows the image of the unit square. The 'parallelogram' with adjacent sides formed by the columns $\begin{pmatrix} 1.6 \\ 0.8 \end{pmatrix}$ and $\begin{pmatrix} 0.8 \\ 0.4 \end{pmatrix}$ of the matrix $\mathbf{M}$ has collapsed to a straight line because the points corresponding to $\begin{pmatrix} 1.6 \\ 0.8 \end{pmatrix}$ and $\begin{pmatrix} 0.8 \\ 0.4 \end{pmatrix}$ lie in the same direction from the origin.

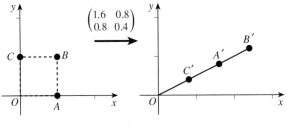

Fig. 5.13

Although strictly speaking the shape $OA'B'C'$ in Fig. 5.13 is not a parallelogram, it is useful to think of it as a collapsed parallelogram. The opposite 'sides' OA' and $C'B'$ are equal and parallel, and so are the opposite sides OC' and $A'B'$; so in this sense it satisfies the rules for a parallelogram. It will be convenient not to regard this as an exception to the rule that matrices transform parallelograms to parallelograms, but to recognise that sometimes parallelograms may collapse, so that all the vertices are in a straight line.

Exercise 5C

1 Draw and label the image of the unit square for the matrices $\begin{pmatrix} 1 & -1 \\ 1 & 1 \end{pmatrix}$ and $\begin{pmatrix} -1 & 1 \\ 1 & 1 \end{pmatrix}$.
Describe geometrically the transformations carried out by these matrices.

2 Draw and label the image of the unit square after transformation by the matrix $\begin{pmatrix} 1 & 2 \\ 0 & 1 \end{pmatrix}$.
Find the area of the image of the unit square.

3 The images of the column matrices $\begin{pmatrix} 1 \\ 0 \end{pmatrix}$ and $\begin{pmatrix} 0 \\ 1 \end{pmatrix}$ when multiplied by the matrix $\mathbf{M}$ are $\begin{pmatrix} 2 \\ 1 \end{pmatrix}$ and $\begin{pmatrix} -1 \\ 3 \end{pmatrix}$. Write down the points corresponding to the images of the column matrices

(a) $\begin{pmatrix} 2 \\ 0 \end{pmatrix}$ (b) $\begin{pmatrix} 1 \\ 1 \end{pmatrix}$ (c) $\begin{pmatrix} 3 \\ 1 \end{pmatrix}$

4 The matrix $\begin{pmatrix} 2 & 4 \\ 1 & 4 \end{pmatrix}$ transforms the unit square $OABC$ to $OA'B'C'$. Find the matrix which transforms the unit square to $OC'B'A'$.

5 (a) Let $\mathbf{M} = \begin{pmatrix} 5 & 3 \\ 3 & 2 \end{pmatrix}$. Write down the matrix $\mathbf{M}^{-1}$.

(b) Draw and label the image $OA'B'C'$ of the unit square $OABC$ after transformation by the matrix $\mathbf{M}$.

(c) What is the effect on $OA'B'C'$ of the matrix $\mathbf{M}^{-1}$?

5.5 Finding the matrix of a given transformation

Suppose that you know that a transformation can be carried out by a matrix. How can you find the matrix which carries out that transformation?

Let the matrix you are trying to find be $\begin{pmatrix} p & q \\ r & s \end{pmatrix}$.

First note that

$$\begin{pmatrix} p & q \\ r & s \end{pmatrix}\begin{pmatrix} 1 \\ 0 \end{pmatrix} = \begin{pmatrix} p \\ r \end{pmatrix} \quad \text{and} \quad \begin{pmatrix} p & q \\ r & s \end{pmatrix}\begin{pmatrix} 0 \\ 1 \end{pmatrix} = \begin{pmatrix} q \\ s \end{pmatrix}.$$

This shows that, if you can find the images of the column matrices $\begin{pmatrix} 1 \\ 0 \end{pmatrix}$ and $\begin{pmatrix} 0 \\ 1 \end{pmatrix}$ after the transformation, you can find the matrix $\begin{pmatrix} p & q \\ r & s \end{pmatrix}$ which carries it out. So the images of the points $(1, 0)$ and $(0, 1)$ are all that you need to know.

> To find the matrix $\mathbf{M}$ which carries out a given transformation, find the images of $(1, 0)$ and $(0, 1)$.
>
> If these are (p, r) and (q, s), then the image of $\begin{pmatrix} 1 \\ 0 \end{pmatrix}$ is $\begin{pmatrix} p \\ r \end{pmatrix}$ and the image of $\begin{pmatrix} 0 \\ 1 \end{pmatrix}$ is $\begin{pmatrix} q \\ s \end{pmatrix}$.
>
> Then $\mathbf{M} = \begin{pmatrix} p & q \\ r & s \end{pmatrix}$.

Example 5.5.1

Find the matrix which transforms the unit square into the parallelogram shown in Fig. 5.14, where the image of $(1, 0)$ is $(2, 1)$ and the image of $(0, 1)$ is $(1, 1)$.

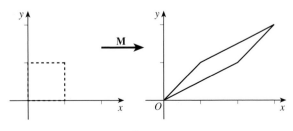

Fig. 5.14

As the image of (1, 0) is (2, 1), $\mathbf{M}\begin{pmatrix} 1 \\ 0 \end{pmatrix} = \begin{pmatrix} 2 \\ 1 \end{pmatrix}$.

The image of (0, 1) is (1, 1), so $\mathbf{M}\begin{pmatrix} 0 \\ 1 \end{pmatrix} = \begin{pmatrix} 1 \\ 1 \end{pmatrix}$.

So the matrix $\mathbf{M}$ is $\begin{pmatrix} 2 & 1 \\ 1 & 1 \end{pmatrix}$.

In this example it is important to specify which vertex of the parallelogram is the image of (1, 0), and which is the image of (0, 1). There are two matrices which transform the unit square into the parallelogram: the one in the example, and $\begin{pmatrix} 1 & 2 \\ 1 & 1 \end{pmatrix}$, for which the image of (1, 0) is (1, 1), and the image of (0, 1) is (2, 1).

In Examples 5.5.2 to 5.5.5 the matrices which carry out a number of standard transformations will be found. Don't learn these matrices. If you understand the general method, you can write them down very quickly.

Example 5.5.2
Find the matrix $\mathbf{R}_\theta$ which represents a rotation through an angle θ anticlockwise about the origin.

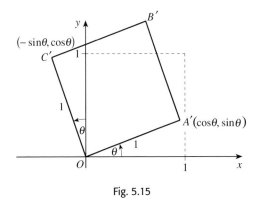

Fig. 5.15

In Fig. 5.15, the unit square, shown dashed, has been rotated about the origin through an angle θ anticlockwise. Since the side of the square is 1 unit, the coordinates of A' and C' are $(\cos\theta, \sin\theta)$ and $(-\sin\theta, \cos\theta)$ respectively.

These were the definitions of $\cos\theta$ and $\sin\theta$ in C2 Sections 1.1 and 1.2.

So the images of $\begin{pmatrix} 1 \\ 0 \end{pmatrix}$ and $\begin{pmatrix} 0 \\ 1 \end{pmatrix}$ are $\begin{pmatrix} \cos\theta \\ \sin\theta \end{pmatrix}$ and $\begin{pmatrix} -\sin\theta \\ \cos\theta \end{pmatrix}$.

The matrix which carries out the transformation is $\mathbf{R}_\theta = \begin{pmatrix} \cos\theta & -\sin\theta \\ \sin\theta & \cos\theta \end{pmatrix}$.

In Example 5.3.1, you saw that the matrix $\begin{pmatrix} 0 & -1 \\ 1 & 0 \end{pmatrix}$ represents a rotation of $\frac{1}{2}\pi$. This is a special case of $\mathbf{R}_\theta = \begin{pmatrix} \cos\theta & -\sin\theta \\ \sin\theta & \cos\theta \end{pmatrix}$ with $\theta = \frac{1}{2}\pi$.

Example 5.5.3

Find the matrix $\mathbf{M}_\theta$ which represents a reflection in the line at angle θ to the x-axis.

In Fig. 5.16, the mirror makes an angle θ with the x-axis. The image, A', of $(1, 0)$ is $(\cos 2\theta, \sin 2\theta)$.

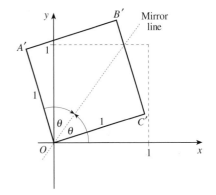

The line OC' makes an angle of $2\theta - \frac{1}{2}\pi$ with the x-axis, so the image, C', of $(0, 1)$ is $\left(\cos\left(2\theta - \frac{1}{2}\pi\right), \sin\left(2\theta - \frac{1}{2}\pi\right)\right)$.

It was shown in C2 Example 9.3.1 that $\cos\left(\theta - \frac{1}{2}\pi\right) \equiv \sin\theta$ and $\sin\left(\theta - \frac{1}{2}\pi\right) \equiv -\cos\theta$. Replacing θ by 2θ in these identities, the coordinates of C' are $(\sin 2\theta, -\cos 2\theta)$.

Fig. 5.16

So the images of $\begin{pmatrix} 1 \\ 0 \end{pmatrix}$ and $\begin{pmatrix} 0 \\ 1 \end{pmatrix}$ are $\begin{pmatrix} \cos 2\theta \\ \sin 2\theta \end{pmatrix}$ and $\begin{pmatrix} \sin 2\theta \\ -\cos 2\theta \end{pmatrix}$.

The matrix which carries out the transformation is $\mathbf{M}_\theta = \begin{pmatrix} \cos 2\theta & \sin 2\theta \\ \sin 2\theta & -\cos 2\theta \end{pmatrix}$.

In Example 5.3.2, you saw that the matrix $\begin{pmatrix} -1 & 0 \\ 0 & 1 \end{pmatrix}$ represents a reflection in the y-axis. This is a special case of $\mathbf{M}_\theta = \begin{pmatrix} \cos 2\theta & \sin 2\theta \\ \sin 2\theta & -\cos 2\theta \end{pmatrix}$ with $\theta = \frac{1}{2}\pi$.

Example 5.5.4

Find the matrices which represent stretches parallel to the axes.

Under a stretch in the x-direction with scale factor c, the image of $(1, 0)$ is $(c, 0)$ and the image of $(0, 1)$ is $(0, 1)$ (see Fig. 5.17).

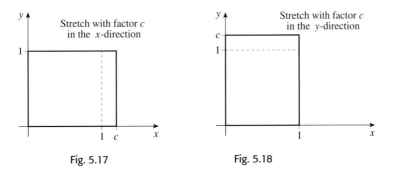

Fig. 5.17   Fig. 5.18

So the images of $\begin{pmatrix} 1 \\ 0 \end{pmatrix}$ and $\begin{pmatrix} 0 \\ 1 \end{pmatrix}$ are $\begin{pmatrix} c \\ 0 \end{pmatrix}$ and $\begin{pmatrix} 0 \\ 1 \end{pmatrix}$, and the matrix of a stretch in the x-direction with scale factor c is $\begin{pmatrix} c & 0 \\ 0 & 1 \end{pmatrix}$. Similarly, from Fig. 5.18, the matrix of a stretch in the y-direction with scale factor c is $\begin{pmatrix} 1 & 0 \\ 0 & c \end{pmatrix}$.

A transformation in which points on the x-axis stay fixed and points not on the x-axis move parallel to the x-axis in proportion to their distances from the x-axis (see Fig. 5.19) is called a **shear parallel to the x-axis.**

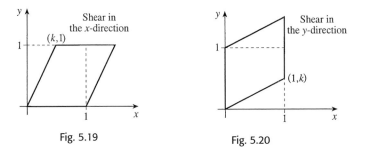

Fig. 5.19

Fig. 5.20

Similarly, a transformation in which points on the y-axis stay fixed and points not on the y-axis move parallel to the x-axis in proportion to their distances from the y-axis (see Fig. 5.20) is called a **shear parallel to the y-axis.**

Example 5.5.5
Find the matrix which represents a shear parallel to the x-axis.

From Fig. 5.19, the image of (1, 0) is (1, 0), and the image of (0, 1) is (k, 1).

So the images of $\begin{pmatrix} 1 \\ 0 \end{pmatrix}$ and $\begin{pmatrix} 0 \\ 1 \end{pmatrix}$ are $\begin{pmatrix} 1 \\ 0 \end{pmatrix}$ and $\begin{pmatrix} k \\ 1 \end{pmatrix}$, and the matrix $\mathbf{M}$ which represents a shear in the x- direction is given by $\mathbf{M} = \begin{pmatrix} 1 & k \\ 0 & 1 \end{pmatrix}$.

You can show for yourself, using Fig. 5.20, that the matrix which represents a shear parallel to the y-axis is given by $\mathbf{M} = \begin{pmatrix} 1 & 0 \\ k & 1 \end{pmatrix}$.

In the preceding examples the matrix has been found by using knowledge of the images of $\begin{pmatrix} 1 \\ 0 \end{pmatrix}$ and $\begin{pmatrix} 0 \\ 1 \end{pmatrix}$. The next example shows how the matrix can be found if you know the images of two other column matrices.

Example 5.5.6

Given that a 2×2 matrix $\mathbf{M}$ transforms $\begin{pmatrix} 2 \\ 1 \end{pmatrix}$ to $\begin{pmatrix} 1 \\ 3 \end{pmatrix}$ and $\begin{pmatrix} 1 \\ 1 \end{pmatrix}$ to $\begin{pmatrix} 3 \\ 2 \end{pmatrix}$, find $\mathbf{M}$.

Method 1   This is the 'brute force' method. Let $\mathbf{M} = \begin{pmatrix} a & b \\ c & d \end{pmatrix}$.

Then, since $\mathbf{M}\begin{pmatrix} 2 \\ 1 \end{pmatrix} = \begin{pmatrix} 1 \\ 3 \end{pmatrix}$, $\begin{pmatrix} a & b \\ c & d \end{pmatrix}\begin{pmatrix} 2 \\ 1 \end{pmatrix} = \begin{pmatrix} 1 \\ 3 \end{pmatrix}$ so $2a + b = 1$ and $2c + d = 3$.

Similarly, since $\begin{pmatrix} a & b \\ c & d \end{pmatrix}\begin{pmatrix} 1 \\ 1 \end{pmatrix} = \begin{pmatrix} 3 \\ 2 \end{pmatrix}$, $a + b = 3$ and $c + d = 2$. Solving these equations

gives $a = -2$, $b = 5$, $c = 1$ and $d = 1$. Therefore $\mathbf{M} = \begin{pmatrix} -2 & 5 \\ 1 & 1 \end{pmatrix}$.

Method 2   This method is subtler.

As $\begin{pmatrix} 2 \\ 1 \end{pmatrix} - \begin{pmatrix} 1 \\ 1 \end{pmatrix} = \begin{pmatrix} 1 \\ 0 \end{pmatrix}$,

$$\mathbf{M}\begin{pmatrix} 1 \\ 0 \end{pmatrix} = \mathbf{M}\left(\begin{pmatrix} 2 \\ 1 \end{pmatrix} - \begin{pmatrix} 1 \\ 1 \end{pmatrix}\right) = \mathbf{M}\begin{pmatrix} 2 \\ 1 \end{pmatrix} - \mathbf{M}\begin{pmatrix} 1 \\ 1 \end{pmatrix}$$
$$= \begin{pmatrix} 1 \\ 3 \end{pmatrix} - \begin{pmatrix} 3 \\ 2 \end{pmatrix} = \begin{pmatrix} -2 \\ 1 \end{pmatrix}.$$

And since $\begin{pmatrix} 0 \\ 1 \end{pmatrix} = 2\begin{pmatrix} 1 \\ 1 \end{pmatrix} - \begin{pmatrix} 2 \\ 1 \end{pmatrix}$,

$$\mathbf{M}\begin{pmatrix} 0 \\ 1 \end{pmatrix} = \mathbf{M}\left(2\begin{pmatrix} 1 \\ 1 \end{pmatrix} - \begin{pmatrix} 2 \\ 1 \end{pmatrix}\right) = 2\mathbf{M}\begin{pmatrix} 1 \\ 1 \end{pmatrix} - \mathbf{M}\begin{pmatrix} 2 \\ 1 \end{pmatrix}$$
$$= 2\begin{pmatrix} 3 \\ 2 \end{pmatrix} - \begin{pmatrix} 1 \\ 3 \end{pmatrix} = \begin{pmatrix} 5 \\ 1 \end{pmatrix}.$$

Finally, since the left column of $\mathbf{M}$ is the image of $\begin{pmatrix} 1 \\ 0 \end{pmatrix}$ and the right column is the

image of $\begin{pmatrix} 0 \\ 1 \end{pmatrix}$, $\mathbf{M} = \begin{pmatrix} -2 & 5 \\ 1 & 1 \end{pmatrix}$.

Method 3   This method uses inverse matrices.

Since $\mathbf{M}\begin{pmatrix} 2 \\ 1 \end{pmatrix} = \begin{pmatrix} 1 \\ 3 \end{pmatrix}$ and $\mathbf{M}\begin{pmatrix} 1 \\ 1 \end{pmatrix} = \begin{pmatrix} 3 \\ 2 \end{pmatrix}$, it follows that

$$\mathbf{M}\begin{pmatrix} 2 & 1 \\ 1 & 1 \end{pmatrix} = \begin{pmatrix} 1 & 3 \\ 3 & 2 \end{pmatrix}. \text{ (See Miscellaneous exercise 3 Question 6.)}$$

This is the equation which was solved in Example 4.5.3 using the inverse of the

matrix $\begin{pmatrix} 2 & 1 \\ 1 & 1 \end{pmatrix}$.

So $\mathbf{M} = \begin{pmatrix} 1 & 3 \\ 3 & 2 \end{pmatrix}\begin{pmatrix} 2 & 1 \\ 1 & 1 \end{pmatrix}^{-1} = \begin{pmatrix} 1 & 3 \\ 3 & 2 \end{pmatrix}\begin{pmatrix} 1 & -1 \\ -1 & 2 \end{pmatrix} = \begin{pmatrix} -2 & 5 \\ 1 & 1 \end{pmatrix}.$

Exercise 5D

1 Find the matrices corresponding to each of the following transformations:

   (a) a reflection in the y-axis,

   (b) a reflection in the line $y = -x$,

   (c) an enlargement with centre at the origin, and factor c, where $c \neq 0$,

   (d) a shear in which the point $(4, 3)$ is transformed to $(7, 3)$ and the x-axis remains fixed.

2 For each transformation in Question 1, describe the inverse transformation, and hence find the inverse matrix for each of those transformations. Verify algebraically that the inverse that you found using geometrical reasoning is correct.

3 Find the matrices which carry out an anticlockwise rotation about the origin through the following angles.

   (a) $\frac{1}{3}\pi = 60°$ (b) $-\frac{1}{3}\pi = -60°$ (c) $\frac{1}{4}\pi = 45°$ (d) $-\frac{1}{4}\pi = -45°$

   (e) θ, where $\tan\theta = \dfrac{b}{a}$, and where $a > 0$, $b > 0$ and $0 < \theta < \frac{1}{2}\pi$.

4 Find the matrix which carries out a clockwise rotation of θ about the origin.

5 Find the inverse of the matrix $\begin{pmatrix} 1 & k \\ 0 & 1 \end{pmatrix}$. Interpret your result geometrically.

6 Use geometrical reasoning to find the inverse of $\begin{pmatrix} c & 0 \\ 0 & 1 \end{pmatrix}$, where $c \neq 0$. Verify algebraically that your answer is correct.

7 Given that a 2×2 matrix $\mathbf{M}$ transforms $\begin{pmatrix} 3 \\ 2 \end{pmatrix}$ to $\begin{pmatrix} 12 \\ 1 \end{pmatrix}$ and $\begin{pmatrix} 1 \\ -1 \end{pmatrix}$ to $\begin{pmatrix} -1 \\ -3 \end{pmatrix}$, find $\mathbf{M}$.

8 Find the matrix which transforms $\begin{pmatrix} 4 \\ 3 \end{pmatrix}$ to $\begin{pmatrix} 9 \\ 10 \end{pmatrix}$ and $\begin{pmatrix} 2 \\ 1 \end{pmatrix}$ to $\begin{pmatrix} 5 \\ 6 \end{pmatrix}$.

9 Explain why you cannot find a matrix which transforms $\begin{pmatrix} 1 \\ -2 \end{pmatrix}$ to $\begin{pmatrix} 5 \\ 4 \end{pmatrix}$ and $\begin{pmatrix} -3 \\ 6 \end{pmatrix}$ to $\begin{pmatrix} 3 \\ -2 \end{pmatrix}$.

10* (a) Find the coordinates of the feet of the perpendiculars from $(1, 0)$ and $(0, 1)$ onto the line with equation $5y = 12x$.

   (b) Find the matrix $\mathbf{M}$ which carries out an orthogonal projection onto the line $5y = 12x$. (In an orthogonal projection the image of each point in the plane is the foot of the perpendicular from the point to the line.)

   (c) Verify that $\mathbf{M}^2 = \mathbf{M}$.

5.6   Area and magnification

Return to Example 5.5.1 in which you found that the matrix **M** which transforms the unit square to the parallelogram with vertices $(0, 0)$, $(2, 1)$, $(3, 2)$ and $(1, 1)$ is $\mathbf{M} = \begin{pmatrix} 2 & 1 \\ 1 & 1 \end{pmatrix}$. What does the matrix **M** tell you about the area of the image?

Fig. 5.21 shows the image of the unit square after the transformation.

You can find the area of the parallelogram by subtracting rectangles and triangles from the large rectangle formed by the dotted lines added to the diagram.

To get the area of the parallelogram, start with the rectangle with area $3 \times 2 = 6$, and subtract

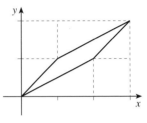

Fig. 5.21

> two squares of area $1 \times 1 = 1$,
>
> two triangles of area $\frac{1}{2} \times 2 \times 1 = 1$,
>
> two triangles of area $\frac{1}{2} \times 1 \times 1 = \frac{1}{2}$.

The area of the parallelogram is therefore

$$6 - 2 \times 1 - 2 \times 1 - 2 \times \tfrac{1}{2} = 1.$$

In the general case, the matrix $\mathbf{M} = \begin{pmatrix} a & b \\ c & d \end{pmatrix}$ transforms the unit square into the parallelogram $OPQR$ shown in Fig. 5.22. The vertices of the parallelogram have coordinates $(0, 0)$, (a, c), $(a + b, c + d)$ and (b, d).

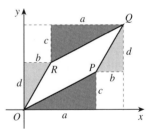

Fig. 5.22

To get the area of the parallelogram $OPQR$, start with the rectangle with area $(a + b)(c + d)$, and subtract

> two rectangles of area bc,
>
> two triangles of area $\frac{1}{2} \times a \times c = \frac{1}{2}ac$,
>
> two triangles of area $\frac{1}{2} \times b \times d = \frac{1}{2}bd$.

The area of the parallelogram is therefore

$$(a + b)(c + d) - 2bc - 2 \times \tfrac{1}{2}ac - 2 \times \tfrac{1}{2}bd = ac + bc + ad + bd - 2bc - ac - bd$$
$$= ad - bc.$$

You have met this expression before. It is the determinant of the matrix $\begin{pmatrix} a & b \\ c & d \end{pmatrix}$ which you met in Chapter 4.

So what has been shown is that, if the unit square is transformed into a parallelogram by a matrix **M**, the area of the parallelogram is $\det \mathbf{M}$.

The proof here only works if a, b, c and d are all positive, so that the parallelogram lies in the first quadrant. But the result holds whatever the signs of a, b, c and d.

Example 5.6.1

Fig. 5.7, repeated here as Fig. 5.23, shows the effect on the unit square of the matrix $\begin{pmatrix} 2 & -1 \\ 1 & 1 \end{pmatrix}$. Use the add and subtract method to find the area of the parallelogram image of the unit square.

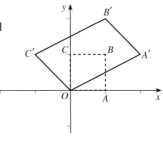

Fig. 5.23

To get the area of the parallelogram, start with the rectangle with area $3 \times 2 = 6$, and subtract

two triangles of area $\frac{1}{2} \times 2 \times 1 = 1$,

two triangles of area $\frac{1}{2} \times 1 \times 1 = \frac{1}{2}$.

The area of the parallelogram is therefore $6 - 2 \times 1 - 2 \times \frac{1}{2} = 3$.

Note that this result, 3, is given by $\det \begin{pmatrix} 2 & -1 \\ 1 & 1 \end{pmatrix} = 2 \times 1 - (-1 \times 1) = 3$ even though not all the elements of the matrix are positive.

However, all is not quite what it seems. For if the points (a, c) and (b, d) were located as in Fig. 5.24, the area of $ORQP$ would be

$$(a + b)(c + d) - 2ad - 2 \times \tfrac{1}{2}ac - 2 \times \tfrac{1}{2}bd = ab + bc + ad + bd - 2ad - ac - bd$$
$$= bc - ad,$$

which is $-\det \mathbf{M}$.

Thus the area the parallelogram is either $\det \mathbf{M}$ or $-\det \mathbf{M}$, whichever is positive. So in either case the area of the parallelogram is $|\det \mathbf{M}|$.

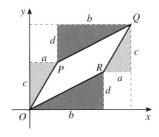

Fig. 5.24

But what is it that distinguishes Fig. 5.24 from Fig. 5.22? If you go round the perimeter of the parallelogram, taking the vertices in the order O, P, Q, R, then in Fig. 5.22 the sense is anticlockwise, which is the same as in the original unit square $OABC$; but in Fig. 5.24 the sense is clockwise.

In both cases the following rule holds.

When the unit square is transformed by the matrix $\mathbf{M} = \begin{pmatrix} a & b \\ c & d \end{pmatrix}$ into a parallelogram, the area of the parallelogram is given by

$$|\det \mathbf{M}| = |ad - bc|.$$

If $ad - bc > 0$ the sense in which the perimeter of the parallelogram is traced is unaltered by the transformation; if $ad - bc < 0$ the sense is reversed.

It is interesting to note that if the parallelogram $OPQR$ collapses to a straight line, then the area is zero and $|\det \mathbf{M}| = |ad - bc| = 0$. Thus $\det \mathbf{M} = 0$ is associated with a degenerate case, just as $\det \mathbf{M} = 0$ is associated with the solution of the

equations $\left.\begin{matrix} ax + by = p \\ cx + dy = q \end{matrix}\right\}$ not being unique.

Example 5.6.2

Use the add and subtract method to find the area of the parallelogram image of the unit square under the transformation carried out by $\begin{pmatrix} -1 & 2 \\ 1 & 1 \end{pmatrix}$.

The diagram for this problem is the same as Fig. 5.23 but with labels A' and C' interchanged. The calculation is exactly the same as that for Example 5.6.1. The area is 3. However, $\det \begin{pmatrix} -1 & 2 \\ 1 & 1 \end{pmatrix} = (-1 \times 1) - 2 \times 1 = -3$, so the area is $-\det \begin{pmatrix} -1 & 2 \\ 1 & 1 \end{pmatrix}$,

or $\left| \det \begin{pmatrix} -1 & 2 \\ 1 & 1 \end{pmatrix} \right|$.

Example 5.6.3

Find the determinants of

(a) the rotation matrix $\begin{pmatrix} \cos\theta & -\sin\theta \\ \sin\theta & \cos\theta \end{pmatrix}$,   (b) the reflection matrix $\begin{pmatrix} \cos 2\theta & \sin 2\theta \\ \sin 2\theta & -\cos 2\theta \end{pmatrix}$.

Interpret the results geometrically.

(a) $\det \begin{pmatrix} \cos\theta & -\sin\theta \\ \sin\theta & \cos\theta \end{pmatrix} = \cos\theta \times \cos\theta - (-\sin\theta) \times \sin\theta$

$$= \cos^2\theta + \sin^2\theta = 1.$$

The area of the image of the unit square is 1; also, rotation does not alter the sense in which the perimeter is traced.

(b) $\det \begin{pmatrix} \cos 2\theta & \sin 2\theta \\ \sin 2\theta & -\cos 2\theta \end{pmatrix} = \cos 2\theta(-\cos 2\theta) - \sin 2\theta \sin 2\theta$

$$= -\cos^2 2\theta - \sin^2 2\theta = -1.$$

The area of the image of the unit square is -1; but reflection alters the sense in which the perimeter is traced.

Example 5.6.4

Find the area of the parallelogram with vertices $O(0, 0)$, $A(2, 1)$, $B(1, 2)$ and $C(-1, 1)$. Find the image $OA'B'C'$ of this parallelogram when transformed by the matrix $\begin{pmatrix} a & b \\ c & d \end{pmatrix}$, and find the ratio of the areas $OA'B'C'$ and $OABC$.

In Example 5.6.1, the area of $OABC$ was found to be 3 units.

The area of $OA'B'C'$ is the area of the parallelogram with vertices $(0, 0)$, $(2a + b, 2c + d)$, $(a + 2b, c + 2d)$ and $(-a + b, -c + d)$ which is given by

$$\left| \det \begin{pmatrix} 2a + b & -a + b \\ 2c + d & -c + d \end{pmatrix} \right|.$$

Now $\det \begin{pmatrix} 2a + b & -a + b \\ 2c + d & -c + d \end{pmatrix} = (2a + b)(-c + d) - (-a + b)(2c + d)$

$$= -2ac - bc + 2ad + bd - (-2ac + 2bc - ad + bd)$$
$$= -2ac - bc + 2ad + bd + 2ac - 2bc + ad - bd$$
$$= 3ad - 3bc,$$

so $\left| \det \begin{pmatrix} 2a + b & -a + b \\ 2c + d & -c + d \end{pmatrix} \right| = |3ad - 3bc| = 3|ad - bc| = 3 \left| \det \begin{pmatrix} a & b \\ c & d \end{pmatrix} \right|.$

So the area of $OA'B'C'$ is $3 \left| \det \begin{pmatrix} a & b \\ c & d \end{pmatrix} \right|$, and the ratio of the areas is $\left| \det \begin{pmatrix} a & b \\ c & d \end{pmatrix} \right|$.

Example 5.6.4 shows that the area of the parallelogram $OABC$ is magnified by a factor of $|\det \mathbf{M}|$ when it is transformed by the matrix $\mathbf{M}$.

In fact it can be shown that the image of every shape is magnified in area by the factor $|\det \mathbf{M}|$. This shows that:

> When a shape is transformed by a matrix $\mathbf{M}$ the ratio of the area of the image shape to that of the original shape is $|\det \mathbf{M}|$.

Exercise 5E

1 Write down the matrices which represent shears in the x-direction and in the y-direction. Calculate the determinants of these matrices, and verify that shears do not alter area.

2 A parallelogram with one vertex at the origin has area 8. It is transformed by the matrix $\mathbf{A}$ where $\mathbf{A} = \begin{pmatrix} 4 & 2 \\ -4 & 3 \end{pmatrix}$. Write down the area of the image parallelogram.

3 Answer Question 2 with the matrix $\mathbf{B} = \begin{pmatrix} 2 & 4 \\ 3 & -4 \end{pmatrix}$.

4 The unit square is transformed to $OABC$ by the matrix $\begin{pmatrix} 6 & 5 \\ 8 & 7 \end{pmatrix}$, and $OABC$ is transformed to $OA'B'C'$ by the matrix $\begin{pmatrix} 8 & 10 \\ 7 & 9 \end{pmatrix}$. Calculate the area of the parallelogram $OA'B'C'$.

5 Here is another way to find the area of the dotted
   parallelogram in the diagram.

   (a) Find the matrix of the shear parallel to the y-axis which
       transforms the point (a, c) to the point $(a, 0)$.

   (b) Find the image of the point (b, d) under the same
       transformation.

   (c) Show how you can deduce that the area of the
       parallelogram is $ad - bc$, provided that $a \neq 0$.

   (d) How can you resolve the case when $a = 0$?

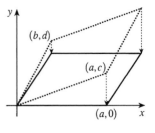

5.7 Successive transformations

It quite often happens that you want to find the effect of combining two transformations,
carried out one after the other. For example, if you have two mirrors set at an angle to each
other, what is the effect of looking at the reflection in the first mirror of the reflection of
yourself in the second mirror?

Suppose that you carry out a transformation on the unit square using the matrix **M**, and then
follow it with another transformation using the matrix **N**. What matrix carries out the
combined transformation?

This is illustrated in Fig. 5.25. The problem is to find the matrix which transforms the unit
square to the second parallelogram.

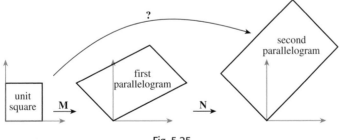

Fig. 5.25

Answering this question turns out to be much easier if you work generally.

Suppose that the point P, with corresponding column matrix $\begin{pmatrix} x \\ y \end{pmatrix}$, is transformed into P',
with corresponding matrix $\begin{pmatrix} x' \\ y' \end{pmatrix}$, using the matrix **M**. Then

$$\begin{pmatrix} x' \\ y' \end{pmatrix} = \mathbf{M} \begin{pmatrix} x \\ y \end{pmatrix}.$$

Now P', with corresponding matrix $\begin{pmatrix} x' \\ y' \end{pmatrix}$, is transformed into P'', with corresponding matrix $\begin{pmatrix} x'' \\ y'' \end{pmatrix}$, using the matrix $\mathbf{N}$. Then

$$\begin{pmatrix} x'' \\ y'' \end{pmatrix} = \mathbf{N} \begin{pmatrix} x' \\ y' \end{pmatrix}.$$

Substituting for $\begin{pmatrix} x' \\ y' \end{pmatrix}$ from the first equation into the second gives

$$\begin{pmatrix} x'' \\ y'' \end{pmatrix} = \mathbf{NM} \begin{pmatrix} x \\ y \end{pmatrix}.$$

So the matrix which transforms the point P to the point P'' in one move is $\mathbf{NM}$.

> The matrix product $\mathbf{NM}$ represents the matrix transformation $\mathbf{M}$ followed by the matrix transformation $\mathbf{N}$.

It is very important to get the matrices $\mathbf{N}$ and $\mathbf{M}$ in the right order. You have to read the product from right to left, as 'first $\mathbf{M}$, then $\mathbf{N}$'.

The product $\mathbf{MN}$ would mean 'first $\mathbf{N}$, then $\mathbf{M}$'. It will usually produce a different transformation from $\mathbf{NM}$.

Example 5.7.1

Find the matrix which carries out the transformation $\mathbf{M} = \begin{pmatrix} 3 & 1 \\ 0 & 2 \end{pmatrix}$ followed by $\mathbf{N} = \begin{pmatrix} 1 & 1 \\ -1 & 1 \end{pmatrix}$.

The matrix which carries out $\mathbf{M}$ followed by $\mathbf{N}$ is $\mathbf{NM}$.

$$\mathbf{NM} = \begin{pmatrix} 1 & 1 \\ -1 & 1 \end{pmatrix} \begin{pmatrix} 3 & 1 \\ 0 & 2 \end{pmatrix} = \begin{pmatrix} 3 & 3 \\ -3 & 1 \end{pmatrix}.$$

Example 5.7.2

(a) Find the matrix which carries out a shear with $k = 1$ in the y-direction followed by a shear with $k = 1$ in the x-direction.

(b) Find the matrix which carries out the transformations in part (a) in the reverse order.

(c) Illustrate your answers.

(a) The matrix $\mathbf{M}$ which carries out a shear with $k = 1$ in the y-direction is $\begin{pmatrix} 1 & 0 \\ 1 & 1 \end{pmatrix}$.

The matrix $\mathbf{N}$ which carries out a shear with $k = 1$ in the x-direction is $\begin{pmatrix} 1 & 1 \\ 0 & 1 \end{pmatrix}$.

So the matrix which carries out first **M** then **N** is **NM**, which is

$$\begin{pmatrix} 1 & 1 \\ 0 & 1 \end{pmatrix}\begin{pmatrix} 1 & 0 \\ 1 & 1 \end{pmatrix} = \begin{pmatrix} 2 & 1 \\ 1 & 1 \end{pmatrix}.$$

(b) The matrix which carries out this transformation is **MN**, which is

$$\begin{pmatrix} 1 & 0 \\ 1 & 1 \end{pmatrix}\begin{pmatrix} 1 & 1 \\ 0 & 1 \end{pmatrix} = \begin{pmatrix} 1 & 1 \\ 1 & 2 \end{pmatrix}.$$

(c)

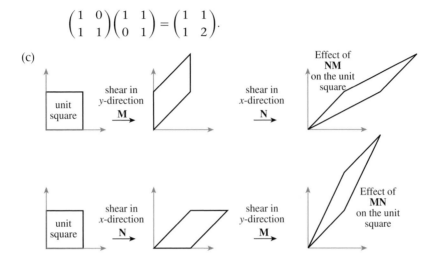

Example 5.7.3

Use the rotation matrices for the angles $\frac{1}{4}\pi$ and $\frac{1}{6}\pi$ to find exact expressions for $\cos\frac{5}{12}\pi$ and $\sin\frac{5}{12}\pi$.

The rotation matrix for a rotation of θ about the origin is $\begin{pmatrix} \cos\theta & -\sin\theta \\ \sin\theta & \cos\theta \end{pmatrix}$ so the rotation matrices for rotations of $\frac{1}{4}\pi$ and $\frac{1}{6}\pi$ (that is, $45°$ and $30°$) are respectively

$$\begin{pmatrix} \cos\frac{1}{4}\pi & -\sin\frac{1}{4}\pi \\ \sin\frac{1}{4}\pi & \cos\frac{1}{4}\pi \end{pmatrix} = \begin{pmatrix} \frac{1}{2}\sqrt{2} & -\frac{1}{2}\sqrt{2} \\ \frac{1}{2}\sqrt{2} & \frac{1}{2}\sqrt{2} \end{pmatrix} = \frac{1}{2}\sqrt{2}\begin{pmatrix} 1 & -1 \\ 1 & 1 \end{pmatrix}$$

and

$$\begin{pmatrix} \cos\frac{1}{6}\pi & -\sin\frac{1}{6}\pi \\ \sin\frac{1}{6}\pi & \cos\frac{1}{6}\pi \end{pmatrix} = \begin{pmatrix} \frac{1}{2}\sqrt{3} & -\frac{1}{2} \\ \frac{1}{2} & \frac{1}{2}\sqrt{3} \end{pmatrix} = \frac{1}{2}\begin{pmatrix} \sqrt{3} & -1 \\ 1 & \sqrt{3} \end{pmatrix}.$$

If you multiply these two matrices together, the transformation that results is a rotation of $\frac{1}{4}\pi$ followed by a rotation of $\frac{1}{6}\pi$ which is a rotation of $\frac{5}{12}\pi$.

So

$$\begin{pmatrix} \cos \frac{5}{12}\pi & -\sin \frac{5}{12}\pi \\ \sin \frac{5}{12}\pi & \cos \frac{5}{12}\pi \end{pmatrix} = \frac{1}{2}\begin{pmatrix} \sqrt{3} & -1 \\ 1 & \sqrt{3} \end{pmatrix} \times \frac{1}{2}\sqrt{2}\begin{pmatrix} 1 & -1 \\ 1 & 1 \end{pmatrix}$$

$$= \frac{1}{4}\sqrt{2}\begin{pmatrix} \sqrt{3} & -1 \\ 1 & \sqrt{3} \end{pmatrix}\begin{pmatrix} 1 & -1 \\ 1 & 1 \end{pmatrix}$$

$$= \frac{1}{4}\sqrt{2}\begin{pmatrix} \sqrt{3}-1 & -\sqrt{3}-1 \\ 1+\sqrt{3} & -1+\sqrt{3} \end{pmatrix}.$$

Therefore $\cos \frac{5}{12}\pi = \frac{1}{4}\sqrt{2}(\sqrt{3}-1)$ and $\sin \frac{5}{12}\pi = \frac{1}{4}\sqrt{2}(\sqrt{3}+1)$.

In this example, it doesn't matter in which order you multiply the matrices; a rotation of $\frac{1}{4}\pi$ followed by a rotation of $\frac{1}{6}\pi$ is the same as a rotation of $\frac{1}{6}\pi$ followed by a rotation of $\frac{1}{4}\pi$.

Example 5.7.4

Use the results that $\cos(\alpha + \pi) = -\cos\alpha$ and $\sin(\alpha + \pi) = -\sin\alpha$ for any angle α, and the matrices $\mathbf{M}_\theta$ and $\mathbf{M}_{\theta+\frac{1}{2}\pi}$, to prove that successive reflections in mirrors which are at right angles to each other are equivalent to a half-turn. (See Fig. 5.26.)

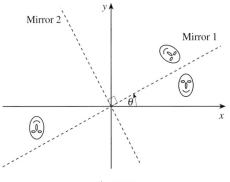

Fig. 5.26

From Example 5.5.3, $\mathbf{M}_\theta = \begin{pmatrix} \cos 2\theta & \sin 2\theta \\ \sin 2\theta & -\cos 2\theta \end{pmatrix}$. Replacing θ by $\theta + \frac{1}{2}\pi$ and using $\cos(\alpha + \pi) = -\cos\alpha$ and $\sin(\alpha + \pi) = -\sin\alpha$ for any angle α gives

$$\mathbf{M}_{\theta+\frac{1}{2}\pi} = \begin{pmatrix} \cos(2\theta + \pi) & \sin(2\theta + \pi) \\ \sin(2\theta + \pi) & -\cos(2\theta + \pi) \end{pmatrix} = \begin{pmatrix} -\cos 2\theta & -\sin 2\theta \\ -\sin 2\theta & \cos 2\theta \end{pmatrix}.$$

Then $\mathbf{M}_{\theta+\frac{1}{2}\pi}\mathbf{M}_\theta = \begin{pmatrix} -\cos 2\theta & -\sin 2\theta \\ -\sin 2\theta & \cos 2\theta \end{pmatrix}\begin{pmatrix} \cos 2\theta & \sin 2\theta \\ \sin 2\theta & -\cos 2\theta \end{pmatrix}$

$$= \begin{pmatrix} -\cos^2 2\theta - \sin^2 2\theta & -\cos 2\theta \sin 2\theta + \sin 2\theta \cos 2\theta \\ -\sin 2\theta \cos 2\theta + \cos 2\theta \sin 2\theta & -\sin^2 2\theta - \cos^2 2\theta \end{pmatrix}$$

$$= \begin{pmatrix} -1 & 0 \\ 0 & -1 \end{pmatrix}.$$

Since the last matrix represents a rotation of π, that is a half-turn, the product of successive reflections in mirrors that are at right angles to each other is equivalent to a half-turn.

Exercise 5F

1 The matrix $\begin{pmatrix} 1 & 3 \\ 2 & -4 \end{pmatrix}$ transforms the vertices of a parallelogram, and the new vertices are then transformed by the matrix $\begin{pmatrix} 3 & 1 \\ 0 & 1 \end{pmatrix}$. Find the matrix of the combined transformation.

2 The matrix $\begin{pmatrix} 9 & 7 \\ 5 & 4 \end{pmatrix}$ transforms a parallelogram, which is itself then transformed by $\begin{pmatrix} 4 & -7 \\ -5 & 9 \end{pmatrix}$. Find the matrix of the combined transformation. What can you deduce from your answer?

3 When the transformation carried out by $\begin{pmatrix} 4 & 1 \\ 2 & -1 \end{pmatrix}$ is followed by another transformation carried out by $\mathbf{M}$, the final result is the same as that carried out by $\begin{pmatrix} 10 & -2 \\ -12 & -6 \end{pmatrix}$. Find $\mathbf{M}$.

4 Write down the matrices $\mathbf{A}$ and $\mathbf{B}$ which represent rotations of $\frac{1}{6}\pi$ and $\frac{1}{3}\pi$ anticlockwise about the origin. Verify that $\mathbf{B} = \mathbf{A}^2$, and that $\mathbf{AB} = \mathbf{BA}$, and interpret these geometrically.

5 A, B and C are three points. Two matrices $\mathbf{P}$ and $\mathbf{Q}$ are given by $\mathbf{P} = \begin{pmatrix} 0 & -1 \\ 1 & 0 \end{pmatrix}$ and $\mathbf{Q} = \begin{pmatrix} 1 & 0 \\ 0 & -1 \end{pmatrix}$. The images of A, B and C under $\mathbf{P}$ are A_1, B_1 and C_1, and the images of A_1, B_1 and C_1 under $\mathbf{Q}$ are A_2, B_2 and C_2. What single matrix transforms ABC to $A_2 B_2 C_2$? If $\mathbf{M} = \begin{pmatrix} 0 & 1 \\ -1 & 1 \end{pmatrix}$, verify that $\mathbf{M}^3 = \mathbf{P}^2$. State, with a reason, the smallest number of successive multiplications by $\mathbf{M}$ that need to be applied to ABC to restore it to its original position.

6 (a) Let $\mathbf{A} = \begin{pmatrix} 0.6 & -0.8 \\ 0.8 & 0.6 \end{pmatrix}$ and $\mathbf{B} = \begin{pmatrix} 5 & 0 \\ 0 & 5 \end{pmatrix}$. Identify the geometric transformations carried out by $\mathbf{A}$, $\mathbf{B}$, $\mathbf{AB}$ and $\mathbf{BA}$.

 (b) Let $\mathbf{M} = \begin{pmatrix} a & -b \\ b & a \end{pmatrix}$ where a, $b \in \mathbb{R}$ and $a > 0$. Find the geometric transformation carried out by this matrix, and interpret your result as a combination of two simpler transformations.

7 Do similar calculations to those in Example 5.7.3 to find exact values for $\cos \frac{\pi}{12}$ and $\sin \frac{\pi}{12}$.

8 Let $\mathbf{M} = \begin{pmatrix} a & b \\ c & d \end{pmatrix}$ and $\mathbf{N} = \begin{pmatrix} p & q \\ r & s \end{pmatrix}$. Show that $\det(\mathbf{NM}) = \det \mathbf{N} \times \det \mathbf{M}$.

 (a) by considering the area factors of the transformations carried out by $\mathbf{N}$ and $\mathbf{M}$,

 (b) by finding the product $\mathbf{NM}$ and calculating $\det(\mathbf{NM})$ by brute force.

9 (a) Use the matrices $\mathbf{R}_\theta$ and $\mathbf{R}_{-\phi}$ to calculate $\mathbf{R}_\theta \mathbf{R}_{-\phi}$.
Hence derive formulae for $\sin(\theta - \phi)$ and $\cos(\theta - \phi)$
in terms of $\cos\theta$, $\cos\phi$, $\sin\theta$ and $\sin\phi$.

(b) Show that the area of the parallelogram in the diagram is
$rs\sin(\theta - \phi)$. Use your formula for $\sin(\theta - \phi)$ to show that
$rs\sin(\theta - \phi) = ad - bc$.

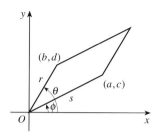

Miscellaneous exercise 5

1 By thinking geometrically, find a matrix $\mathbf{M}$ other than the identity matrix such that $\mathbf{M}^3 = \mathbf{I}$.

2 Let $\mathbf{A}$ be the matrix $\begin{pmatrix} \cos\theta & \sin\theta \\ \sin\theta & -\cos\theta \end{pmatrix}$.

(a) Interpret $\mathbf{A}$ geometrically.

(b) Interpret the matrix $\mathbf{A}^2$ geometrically, and use this to show that $\cos^2\theta + \sin^2\theta = 1$.

3 $\mathbf{S}$ is the matrix $\begin{pmatrix} 1 & 0 \\ 2 & 1 \end{pmatrix}$. Draw a sketch showing the unit square $OABC$, where O is the
origin, A is $(1, 0)$, B is $(1, 1)$ and C is $(0, 1)$, and its image $OA'B'C'$ when the column matrices
representing the points are multiplied by $\mathbf{S}$. Describe the geometrical transformation
involved. If a point P is known to lie on the line $y = -x$, what can you say about its image
under the transformation represented by $\mathbf{S}$?

$\mathbf{R}$ is the matrix $\begin{pmatrix} 0 & -1 \\ -1 & 0 \end{pmatrix}$. State the geometrical transformation represented by $\mathbf{R}$.

Calculate the matrix $\mathbf{X}$ given by $\mathbf{X} = \mathbf{RSR}$, and state what geometrical transformation $\mathbf{X}$
represents.

4 The matrix $\mathbf{A}$ is $\begin{pmatrix} \frac{1}{\sqrt2} & -\frac{1}{\sqrt2} \\ \frac{1}{\sqrt2} & \frac{1}{\sqrt2} \end{pmatrix}$. By considering the effect on the unit square, or otherwise,

describe the geometrical transformation represented by $\mathbf{A}$.

The matrix $\mathbf{C}$ is $\begin{pmatrix} 1 & -1 \\ \frac{1}{\sqrt2} & \frac{1}{\sqrt2} \end{pmatrix}$ and represents the combined effect of the transformation

represented by $\mathbf{A}$ followed by the transformation represented by a matrix $\mathbf{B}$.

(a) Find $\mathbf{B}$.

(b) Describe fully the transformation represented by $\mathbf{B}$.   (OCR)

5 The matrix $\begin{pmatrix} 5 & 10 \\ -3 & -8 \end{pmatrix}$ transforms the point (x, y) to the point (x', y'), where

$\begin{pmatrix} x' \\ y' \end{pmatrix} = \begin{pmatrix} 5 & 10 \\ -3 & -8 \end{pmatrix}\begin{pmatrix} x \\ y \end{pmatrix}$. Find the values of m such that all points on the line $y = mx$

transform to points which are also on the line $y = mx$.   (MEI, adapted)

6 A geometric transformation in the xy-plane is represented by the 2×2 matrix $\mathbf{R}$. The transformation may be considered as an anticlockwise rotation about the origin through $\frac{1}{3}\pi$ followed by a stretch in the x-direction with scale factor 2.

(a) Write down the matrix $\mathbf{P}$ which represents the rotation.

(b) Write down the matrix $\mathbf{Q}$ which represents the stretch.

(c) Hence find $\mathbf{R}$.

(d) Calculate $\det \mathbf{R}$.　　　　　　　　　　　　　　　　　(OCR, adapted)

7 The matrix $\mathbf{C}$ is $\begin{pmatrix} -1 & 0 \\ 0 & 2 \end{pmatrix}$. The geometrical transformation represented by $\mathbf{C}$ may be considered as the result of a reflection followed by a stretch. By considering the effect on the unit square, or otherwise, describe fully the reflection and the stretch.

Find matrices $\mathbf{A}$ and $\mathbf{B}$ which represent the reflection and the stretch respectively.　　(OCR)

8 The matrix $\mathbf{M}$ is given by $\mathbf{M} = \begin{pmatrix} 1 & -1 \\ 0 & 1 \end{pmatrix}$.

Describe fully the geometrical transformation represented by $\mathbf{M}$.

The matrix $\mathbf{C}$ is given by $\mathbf{C} = \begin{pmatrix} \frac{1}{2} & \frac{1}{2}(\sqrt{3} - 1) \\ -\frac{1}{2}\sqrt{3} & \frac{1}{2}(\sqrt{3} + 1) \end{pmatrix}$.

$\mathbf{C}$ represents the combined effect of the transformation represented by $\mathbf{M}$ followed by the transformation represented by a matrix $\mathbf{B}$.

(a) Find the matrix $\mathbf{B}$.

(b) Describe fully the geometrical transformation represented by $\mathbf{B}$.　　　　(OCR)

9 The matrix $\mathbf{P}$ is given by $\mathbf{P} = \begin{pmatrix} 2 & 0 \\ 1 & 2 \end{pmatrix}$.

(a) Describe fully a set of geometrical transformations carried out by $\mathbf{P}$.

The matrix $\mathbf{Q}$ is given by $\mathbf{Q} = \begin{pmatrix} a & b \\ c & d \end{pmatrix}$.

The combined effect of the transformation represented by $\mathbf{P}$ followed by the transformation represented by $\mathbf{Q}$ is a rotation of $\dfrac{\pi}{2}$ anticlockwise.

(b) Find a, b, c and d.

1 The matrix $\mathbf{C}$ is given by $\mathbf{C} = \mathbf{AB}$, where $\mathbf{A} = \begin{pmatrix} 0 & 1 \\ 1 & 0 \end{pmatrix}$, $\mathbf{B} = \begin{pmatrix} 3 & -4 \\ 4 & 3 \end{pmatrix}$.

   (a) Evaluate $\mathbf{C}$.

   (b) Find the point of the xy-plane which, under the transformation represented by $\mathbf{C}$, becomes the point with coordinates $(50, -100)$.   (OCR, adapted)

2 The matrices $\mathbf{A}$, $\mathbf{B}$ and $\mathbf{C}$ are defined as follows:

$$\mathbf{A} = \begin{pmatrix} \frac{1}{2}\sqrt{3} & \frac{1}{2} \\ -\frac{1}{2} & \frac{1}{2}\sqrt{3} \end{pmatrix}, \quad \mathbf{B} = \begin{pmatrix} 1 & 0 \\ 0 & -1 \end{pmatrix}, \quad \mathbf{C} = \mathbf{A}^{-1}\mathbf{BA}.$$

   In either order,

   (a) evaluate $\mathbf{C}$,

   (b) describe the single geometrical transformation represented by $\mathbf{C}$.   (OCR)

3 The matrices $\mathbf{A}$ and $\mathbf{B}$ are given by $\mathbf{A} = \begin{pmatrix} 3 & -4 \\ 4 & 3 \end{pmatrix}$, $\mathbf{B} = \begin{pmatrix} 1 & 0 \\ 0 & -1 \end{pmatrix}$.

   Under the transformation represented by $\mathbf{AB}$, a triangle P transforms to the triangle Q whose vertices are $(0, 0)$, $(9, 12)$ and $(22, -4)$.

   (a) Find the coordinates of the vertices of P.

   (b) State the area of P and hence find the area of Q.

   (c) Find the area of the image of P under the transformation represented by $\mathbf{ABA}^{-1}$.   (OCR)

4 For each of the following series, the sum of the first n terms is given. In each case, state whether the series is convergent or not, and find the sum to infinity when it is convergent.

   (a) $\displaystyle\sum_{r=1}^{n} u_r = \frac{1}{3} + \frac{1}{n+1}$ (b) $\displaystyle\sum_{r=1}^{n} u_r = \frac{1}{2} + \frac{n(n+1)}{n+2}$ (c) $\displaystyle\sum_{r=1}^{n} u_r = \frac{3n^2 + 1}{4n^2 + 2}$ (OCR)

5 Find the single matrix which carries out the transformation of a stretch in the y-direction with factor k, followed by a reflection in the line $y = x$.

6 (a) Show that $\dfrac{1}{r!} - \dfrac{1}{(r+1)!} \equiv \dfrac{r}{(r+1)!}$.

   (b) Hence find the sum of the first n terms of the series $\dfrac{1}{2!} + \dfrac{2}{3!} + \cdots + \dfrac{r}{(r+1)!} + \cdots$.   (OCR)

7 Show that $\displaystyle\sum_{r=1}^{n} (2r-1)^2 = \tfrac{1}{3}n(2n+1)(2n-1)$.   (OCR)

8 Let $\mathbf{P}$ be the matrix which carries out a stretch with factor 3 in the x-direction and let $\mathbf{R}$ be the matrix of a rotation of $\tfrac{1}{2}\pi$ anticlockwise about the origin.

   (a) Find the matrices $\mathbf{P}$ and $\mathbf{R}$.

   (b) Calculate the matrix $\mathbf{RPR}^{-1}$.

   (c) What single transformation is carried out by $\mathbf{RPR}^{-1}$?

9 (a) Show that $\dfrac{1}{r^2} - \dfrac{1}{(r+1)^2} = \dfrac{2r+1}{r^2(r+1)^2}$.

   (b) Hence find the sum of the first n terms of the series

   $$\frac{3}{1^2 \cdot 2^2} + \frac{5}{2^2 \cdot 3^2} + \frac{7}{3^2 \cdot 4^2} + \cdots + \frac{2r+1}{r^2(r+1)^2} + \cdots$$

   (c) Show that the series is convergent and state the sum to infinity.   (OCR)

10 The matrix $\mathbf{A}$ is given by $\mathbf{A} = \begin{pmatrix} 1 & -\sqrt{3} \\ \sqrt{3} & 1 \end{pmatrix}$.

   (a) Describe fully a sequence of two geometrical transformations represented by $\mathbf{A}$.

   (b) The triangle PQR is mapped by the transformation represented by $\mathbf{A}$ onto the triangle $P'Q'R'$. Given that the area of PQR is 8, find the area of $P'Q'R'$.   (OCR)

11 The matrices $\mathbf{M}$ and $\mathbf{I}$ are given by $\mathbf{M} = \begin{pmatrix} 2 & -3 \\ -1 & 2 \end{pmatrix}$ and $\mathbf{I} = \begin{pmatrix} 1 & 0 \\ 0 & 1 \end{pmatrix}$.

   (a) Verify that $\mathbf{M}^2 = 4\mathbf{M} - \mathbf{I}$.

   (b) Hence obtain an expression for $\mathbf{M}^4$ in the form $a\mathbf{M} + b\mathbf{I}$

   (c) Obtain also an expression for $\mathbf{M}^{-1}$ in the form $c\mathbf{M} + d\mathbf{I}$.   (OCR)

12 Prove that the sum of the first n terms of the series

   $$1^2 + 2 \times 2^2 + 3^2 + 2 \times 4^2 + 5^2 + 2 \times 6^2 + \ldots$$

   is $\frac{1}{2}n(n+1)^2$ when n is even. Find a similar formula for the sum when n is odd.

13 Find the sum $n^2 + ((n-1)^2 - 1^2) + ((n-2)^2 - 2^2) + \cdots + ((n-r)^2 - r^2)$, when r is an integer which is less than $\frac{1}{2}n$.

   How does your answer differ, if at all, if r is an integer which can be greater than or equal to $\frac{1}{2}n$?

14 Let $\mathrm{f}(r) = \dfrac{1}{k+1}r(r+1)(r+2)\cdots(r+k)$, where r and k are positive integers.

   (a) Find and simplify an expression for $\mathrm{f}(r+1) - \mathrm{f}(r)$.

   (b) Find the sum of the series

   $$1 \times 2 \times 3 \times 4 + 2 \times 3 \times 4 \times 5 + \cdots + n(n+1)(n+2)(n+3).$$

15 (a) By thinking geometrically, write down the effect on the point $(\cos\theta, \sin\theta)$ of a rotation about the origin through an angle θ clockwise followed by a reflection in the x-axis, followed by a rotation about the origin through an angle θ anticlockwise.

   (b) Repeat part (a) with the point $(-\sin\theta, \cos\theta)$.

   (c) What single transformation is carried out by the combination of the three transformations in part (a) and (b).

(d) Write down the matrices which carry out the three transformations, and, using these three matrices, find the single matrix which carries out the single transformation in part (c).

(e) By using one of the results in Section 5.5, deduce that $\sin 2\theta \equiv 2\sin\theta\cos\theta$, and write down an expression for $\cos 2\theta$ in terms of $\cos\theta$ and $\sin\theta$.

6 Mathematical induction

This chapter introduces a powerful method of proof called mathematical induction which is used to prove statements which involve positive integers. When you have completed the chapter, you should

- understand and be able to use the method of mathematical induction
- understand the terms 'proposition', 'basis case', and 'inductive step'
- be able to guess results, in simple cases, and prove them by mathematical induction.

6.1 The principle of mathematical induction

In this chapter you will meet a method of proof which can be applied to a number of widely differing situations.

The idea behind this method of proof is very straightforward. Imagine an infinite set of dominoes, each standing on its end, and placed close enough to the next domino so that if it falls over, it also knocks over the next domino. See Fig. 6.1.

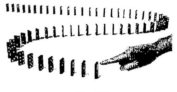

Fig. 6.1

Push the first domino over. The second domino falls over, and pushes the third domino over, and so on. Eventually all the dominoes fall over!

Suppose now that you have a set S of positive integers. You are given that if any positive integer k belongs to S then $k + 1$ also belongs to S. You are also given that 1 belongs to S. What can you say about the set S?

The answer is that, since $1 \in S$, $2 \in S$. And since $2 \in S$, $3 \in S$. And so on, until eventually every positive integer belongs to S. That is, S is the complete set of positive integers, $\mathbb{N}$.

Notice the analogy between the integers and the dominoes. The statement

$$1 \in S$$

corresponds to the fact that the first domino is pushed over.

And the statement

$$\text{if } k \in S \text{ then } (k + 1) \in S$$

corresponds to the statement that if one domino falls over, so does the next.

Example 6.1.1
For each of the following sets, explain why the set does not satisfy the 'domino conditions'.

(a) $\{1, 2, 3, 4, 5, 6\}$,   (b) $\{1, 3, 5, 7, 9, \ldots\}$,   (c) $\{10, 11, 12, 13, 14, \ldots\}$.

(a) One of the members of the set, $k = 6$, has $k + 1 = 7$, which is not in the set. So the condition 'if $k \in S$ then $(k + 1) \in S$' is not satisfied when $k = 6$.

(b) This set consists of all the odd natural numbers. If k is any one of these numbers, then $k + 1$ is an even number, so $k + 1$ is not a member of the set. The condition 'if $k \in S$ then $(k + 1) \in S$' is not satisfied for any number in the set.

(c) For every number in the set the condition 'if $k \in S$ then $(k + 1) \in S$' is satisfied. But 1 is not a member of the set.

The two statements, '$1 \in S$' and 'if $k \in S$ then $(k + 1) \in S$' together imply that S is the set of positive integers, which corresponds to the conclusion that all the dominoes fall over.

The discussion before Example 6.1.1 can be summarised in the following way, and is called the **principle of mathematical induction**.

> The **principle of mathematical induction** states that
>
> if S is a set of positive integers, and
>
> - if $1 \in S$,
> - $k \in S \Rightarrow (k + 1) \in S$,
>
> then S is the complete set of positive integers.

You cannot *prove* the principle of mathematical induction. The statement in the box is essentially an assumption about the positive integers, that is, a fundamental property of the positive integers.

Notice also that both conditions are necessary if all the dominoes are to fall over in the way described. If the first domino is not pushed over, none of them will fall over. And if the connecting link between any pair of dominoes is broken, the falling process will stop, and not all the dominoes will fall over.

Showing that $1 \in S$ is called the **basis case**.

The linking mechanism between k and $k + 1$, that is $k \in S \Rightarrow (k + 1) \in S$, is called the **inductive step**.

6.2   Using the principle of mathematical induction

Mathematical induction is used to establish the truth of statements about positive integers. In this context, a statement about a number n, which stands for a positive integer, is called a **proposition**.

Here are some examples of propositions involving positive integers.

$$\sum_{r=1}^{n} r^2 = \tfrac{1}{6}n(n+1)(2n+1).$$

$2^n > n.$

The sum of the angles in a convex n-sided polygon is $180(n-2)$ degrees.

$7^{2n-1} + 3^{2n}$ is divisible by 8.

In a set of n positive integers there is a smallest member.

To emphasise that the proposition is about positive integers, it is often denoted by $P(n)$, which you can think of as a proposition about n.

> Notice that the second proposition still makes sense (and is in fact true) if n stands for any number, not necessarily an integer. But induction can only be used to prove it when n is a positive integer.

Example 6.2.1 shows clearly how the method of proof by induction is linked to the principle of mathematical induction. In practice, the proofs are more usually laid out as in Section 6.3.

Example 6.2.1
Prove that $1 + 3 + \cdots + (2n-1) = n^2$ is true for all integers $n \geqslant 1$.

Proposition   Let $P(n)$ be the proposition that

$$1 + 3 + \cdots + (2n-1) = n^2.$$

Let T be the set of positive integers for which $P(n)$ is true.

> The letter T is used for this set because it is the first letter of 'true'.
>
> The proof will involve showing that T has the properties $1 \in T$ and $k \in T \Rightarrow (k+1) \in T$, and so, from the principle of mathematical induction, T will be the set of positive integers, showing that $P(n)$ is true for all positive integers.
>
> Notice that to say that T is the set of positive integers for which $P(n)$ is true does not imply that the proposition is actually true. For all we know at the moment, T may have no members.

Basis case   To show that $1 \in T$, that is the proposition is true for $n = 1$, substitute $n = 1$ in the proposition. When $n = 1$ the left side is 1; when $n = 1$ the right side is $1^2 = 1$. Therefore $P(1)$ is true, so $1 \in T$.

Inductive step   You have to establish that $k \in T \Rightarrow (k+1) \in T$.

Suppose that $k \in T$, that is $P(k)$ is true. This means that

$$1 + 3 + \cdots + (2k-1) = k^2.$$

You now have to prove that $k \in T \Rightarrow (k+1) \in T$; that is, if P($k$) is true, then P($k+1$) is true. This is the same as proving that if the statement $1 + 3 + \cdots + (2k - 1) = k^2$ is true, then $1 + 3 + \cdots + (2k - 1) + (2k + 1) = (k + 1)^2$ is true.

Starting with the left side, $1 + 3 + \cdots + (2k - 1) + (2k + 1)$,

$$
\begin{aligned}
1 + 3 + \cdots + (2k - 1) + (2k + 1) &= (1 + 3 + \cdots + (2k - 1)) + (2k + 1) \\
&= k^2 + (2k + 1) \qquad \text{(assuming P(k))} \\
&= k^2 + 2k + 1 \\
&= (k + 1)^2.
\end{aligned}
$$

Therefore, if $k \in T$, then $k + 1 \in T$,   or $k \in T \Rightarrow (k + 1) \in T$.

Completion   As $1 \in T$ and $k \in T \Rightarrow (k + 1) \in T$ the principle of mathematical induction shows that T is the set of positive integers. So P(n) is true for all positive integers; that is $1 + 3 + \cdots + (2n - 1) = n^2$ is true for all positive integers.

Notice where in the inductive step the supposition that $1 + 3 + \cdots + (2k - 1) = k^2$ is true was used. Some people find this the most difficult part of proof by mathematical induction.

In practice, this detailed form of writing out an induction proof is streamlined by leaving out some of the detail. This is taken up in the next section.

6.3   Examples of proof by induction

This section consists almost wholly of examples to show the wide variety of situations in which you can use proof by mathematical induction.

The usual method of writing out an induction proof involves interpreting the box in Section 6.1 in the following way.

If P(n) is a proposition about a positive integer n, and

- P(1) is true,

- P(k) $\Rightarrow$ P($k + 1$)

then P(n) is true for all positive integers.

Every proof by mathematical induction consists of four parts:

- a statement of the proposition, P(n),

- a proof of the basis case, P(1) is true,

- a proof of the inductive step, P(k) $\Rightarrow$ P($k + 1$), that is, if P(k) is true then P($k + 1$) is true,

- the completion of the proof.

The first example is like Example 6.2.1, and is the proof of the formula for the sum of the squares of the first n positive integers, $\sum_{r=1}^{n} r^2 = \frac{1}{6}n(n+1)(2n+1)$, which was derived, but not proved, in Section 2.1.

Example 6.3.1

Prove that $\sum_{r=1}^{n} r^2 = \frac{1}{6}n(n+1)(2n+1)$ is true for all positive integers n.

Proposition   Let P(n) be the proposition that $\sum_{r=1}^{n} r^2 = \frac{1}{6}n(n+1)(2n+1)$.

Basis case   When $n = 1$:

the left side is $\sum_{r=1}^{1} r^2 = 1^2 = 1$;

the right side is $\frac{1}{6} \times 1 \times (1+1) \times (2+1) = \frac{1}{6} \times 2 \times 3 = 1$.

Therefore P(1) is true.

Inductive step   Suppose that P(k) is true. Then $\sum_{r=1}^{k} r^2 = \frac{1}{6}k(k+1)(2k+1)$.

With $(k+1)$ terms the sum on the left is

$$\sum_{r=1}^{k+1} r^2 = (1^2 + 2^2 + \cdots + k^2) + (k+1)^2$$

$$= \sum_{r=1}^{k} r^2 + (k+1)^2$$

$$= \frac{1}{6}k(k+1)(2k+1) + (k+1)^2 \qquad \text{(assuming P(k))}$$

$$= \frac{1}{6}(k+1)(k(2k+1) + 6(k+1))$$

$$= \frac{1}{6}(k+1)(2k^2 + k + 6k + 6)$$

$$= \frac{1}{6}(k+1)(2k^2 + 7k + 6)$$

$$= \frac{1}{6}(k+1)((k+2)(2k+3))$$

$$= \frac{1}{6}(k+1)(k+2)(2k+3).$$

This is P(n) with $n = k+1$. Therefore, if P(k) is true, then P($k+1$) is true.

Completion   P(1) is true and if P(k) is true, then P($k+1$) is true.

Using the principle of mathematical induction, P(n) is true for all positive integers.

That is, $\sum_{r=1}^{n} r^2 = \frac{1}{6}n(n+1)(2n+1)$ is true for all positive integers n.

Example 6.3.2

Prove that $2^n > n$ for all natural numbers n.

Proposition   Let P(n) be the proposition that $2^n > n$.

Basis case   When $n = 1$:

the left side is $2^1 = 2$;

the right side is 1.

As $2 > 1$, P(1) is true.

Inductive step   Suppose that P(k) is true. Then $2^k > k$.

$$2^{k+1} = 2 \times 2^k$$
$$\geqslant 2 \times k \qquad \text{(assuming P(k))}$$
$$= k + k$$
$$\geqslant k + 1 \qquad \text{(since $k \geqslant 1$).}$$

Therefore, if P(k) is true, then P($k + 1$) is true.

Completion   P(1) is true and if P(k) is true, then P($k + 1$) is true.

Using the principle of mathematical induction, P(n) is true for all positive integers.

That is, $2^n > n$ for all natural numbers n.

Example 6.3.3
Prove that the sum of the angles in a convex n-sided polygon is $180(n - 2)$ degrees.

Note that the statement to be proved does not place any conditions on n, but the idea is meaningless unless $n \geqslant 3$. So take the basis case to be $n = 3$, and use mathematical induction to prove the statement for $n \geqslant 3$.

Proposition   For $n \geqslant 3$, let P(n) be the proposition that the sum of the angles in a convex n-sided polygon is $180(n - 2)$ degrees.

Basis case   The basis case is $n = 3$.

When $n = 3$, the polygon is a triangle and the sum of the angles is 180 degrees;

when $n = 3$, $180(n - 2) = 180$.

So P(3) is true.

Inductive step   Suppose that P(k) is true, where $k \geqslant 3$.

Then the angle sum of a k-sided polygon is $180(k - 2)$ degrees.

Now consider the convex ($k + 1$)-sided polygon, $A_1 A_2 \ldots A_{k-1} A_k A_{k+1}$ (see Fig. 6.2). As the polygon is convex, you can join A_k to A_1 to form a convex k-sided polygon, together with a triangle.

Fig. 6.2

Therefore the sum of the angles is the sum of the angles in a convex k-sided polygon, together with a triangle.

So, assuming P(k), the sum of the angles in a convex k-sided polygon is $(180(k - 2) + 180)$ degrees, or $180((k + 1) - 2)$ degrees.

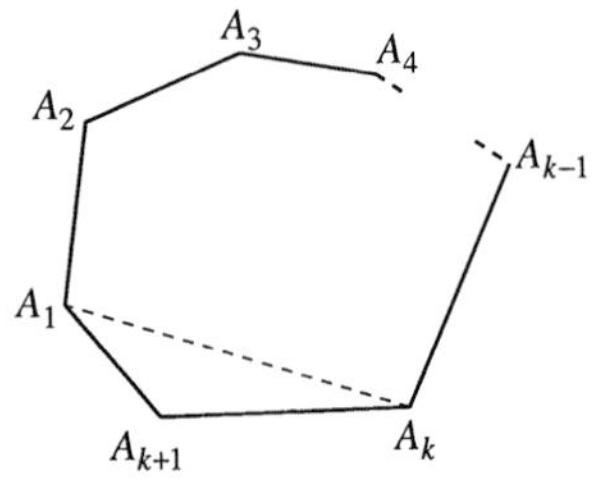

Therefore, if P(k) is true, then P($k + 1$) is true.

Completion P(3) is true and if P(k) is true, then P(k + 1) is true.

Using the principle of mathematical induction, P(n) is true for all positive integers $\geqslant 3$.

That is, the sum of the angles in a convex n-sided polygon is $180(n - 2)$ degrees.

The method of mathematical induction can sometimes be used to prove a property which you discover by observation. Here is an example.

Example 6.3.4
Find the values of $2^{n+2} + 3^{2n+1}$ when $n = 0, 1, 2$ and 3. Make a conjecture about a number which divides $2^{n+2} + 3^{2n+1}$, and prove your conjecture by induction.

When $n = 0$, $2^{n+2} + 3^{2n+1} = 2^2 + 3 = 4 + 3 = 7$.

When $n = 1$, $2^{n+2} + 3^{2n+1} = 2^3 + 3^3 = 8 + 27 = 35$.

When $n = 2$, $2^{n+2} + 3^{2n+1} = 2^4 + 3^5 = 16 + 243 = 259$.

When $n = 3$, $2^{n+2} + 3^{2n+1} = 2^5 + 3^7 = 32 + 2187 = 2219$.

As $7 \times 5 = 35$, $7 \times 37 = 259$ and $7 \times 317 = 2219$, the conjecture is that 7 divides $2^{n+2} + 3^{2n+1}$ for all values of n.

Proposition Let P(n) be the proposition that for all positive integers n, $2^{n+2} + 3^{2n+1}$ is divisible by 7.

Basis case When $n = 1$, the earlier part of the question shows that P(1) is true.

Inductive step Let $f(k) = 2^{k+2} + 3^{2k+1}$, so if P(k) is true, 7 divides $f(k)$.

Also, if $f(k) = 2^{k+2} + 3^{2k+1}$, then

$$\begin{aligned}
f(k + 1) &= 2^{(k+1)+2} + 3^{2(k+1)+1} \\
&= 2^{k+3} + 3^{2k+3} \\
&= 2 \times 2^{k+2} + 3^2 \times 3^{2k+1} \\
&= 2 \times 2^{k+2} + 9 \times 3^{2k+1}.
\end{aligned}$$

Eliminate 2^{k+2} between the equations for $f(k)$ and $f(k + 1)$ by considering $f(k + 1) - 2f(k)$.

$$\begin{aligned}
f(k + 1) - 2f(k) &= \left(2^{k+3} + 9 \times 3^{2k+1}\right) - 2 \times \left(2^{k+2} + 3^{2k+1}\right) \\
&= 2^{k+3} + 9 \times 3^{2k+1} - 2 \times 2^{k+2} - 2 \times 3^{2k+1} \\
&= 7 \times 3^{2k+1}.
\end{aligned}$$

so $f(k + 1) = 2f(k) + 7 \times 3^{2k+1}$.

Now suppose that P(k) is true, so that $f(k)$ is divisible by 7. Then as the expression $7 \times 3^{2k+1}$ is obviously divisible by 7, the whole of the right side is divisible by 7. Therefore the expression on the left is also divisible by 7; that is, P(k + 1) is true.

Therefore 7 divides the left side, that is, 7 divides $f(k + 1)$.

Therefore if P(k) is true, then P($k + 1$) is true.

Completion   P(1) is true and if P(k) is true, then P($k + 1$) is true.

Using the principle of mathematical induction, P(n) is true for all positive integers.

That is, 7 divides $2^{n+2} + 3^{2n+1}$ for all positive integers n.

Example 6.3.5
Prove that in any set of n numbers there is a smallest member.

Proposition   Let P(n) be the proposition that in a collection of n numbers there is a smallest member.

Basis case   When $n = 1$, the set consists of just one number. Therefore P(1) is true.

Inductive step   Suppose that P(k) is true. Then every set of k numbers has a smallest member. Now consider a set of $k + 1$ numbers, and split it into a set of k numbers, and one number. Assuming P(k), the set of k numbers has a smallest member r. Suppose the single number is s. Then the smaller of r and s will be the smallest member for the set of $k + 1$ numbers.

Therefore if P(k) is true, then P($k + 1$) is true.

Completion   P(1) is true and if P(k) is true, then P($k + 1$) is true.

Using the principle of mathematical induction, P(n) is true for all positive integers.

That is, in any set of numbers there is a smallest member.

This result, which appears obvious, will be used in FP3.

You may wonder whether there is any way of proving results about real numbers (as opposed to integers) using the principle of induction. The answer is 'no'. The problem with real numbers is that there is no next number in the same way that there is with integers. In fact, the analogy with a row of dominoes at the beginning of the chapter has no parallel in dealing with real numbers.

Exercise 6

1 Use the method of mathematical induction to prove that, for all positive integers n,

$$2 + 4 + 6 + \cdots + (2n) = n(n + 1).$$

2 Use the method of mathematical induction to prove that, for $n \in \mathbb{N}$,

$$1^3 + 2^3 + 3^3 + \cdots + n^3 = \tfrac{1}{4}n^2(n + 1)^2.$$

3 Use the method of mathematical induction to prove that, for all positive integers n,

$$1 \times 4 + 2 \times 5 + 3 \times 6 + \cdots + n(n + 3) = \tfrac{1}{3}n(n + 1)(n + 5).$$

4 Use the principle of mathematical induction to prove that, for $n \in \mathbb{N}$,

$$1 \times 2 + 2 \times 3 + \cdots + n(n + 1) = \tfrac{1}{3}n(n + 1)(n + 2).$$

5 Use the method of mathematical induction to prove that, for all positive integers n,

$$(n + 1) + (n + 2) + (n + 3) + \cdots + 2n = \tfrac{1}{2}n(3n + 1).$$

6 Use the principle of mathematical induction to prove that, for integers $n > 2$,

$$\sum_{r=2}^{n} (r - 1)r = \tfrac{1}{3}n(n^2 - 1).$$

7 By calculating $\sum_{r=1}^{n} (3r(r + 1) + 1)$ for the first few values of n, make a conjecture about the value of the sum, and prove it by mathematical induction.

8 Prove that if $u_{n+1} = u_n + 2$ for $n \in \mathbb{N}$, and $u_1 = 3$, then $u_n = 2n + 1$.

9 Prove that if $u_{n+1} = 3u_n + 4$ for $n \in \mathbb{N}$, and $u_1 = 2$, then $u_n = 4 \times 3^{n-1} - 2$.

10 Prove that if $u_{n+2} = 3u_{n+1} - 2u_n$ for $n \in \mathbb{N}$, and $u_1 = 1$, $u_2 = 3$, then $u_n = 2^n - 1$.

11 Prove that if $u_{n+2} = 5u_{n+1} - 6u_n$ for $n \in \mathbb{N}$, and $u_0 = u_1 = -1$, then $u_n = 3^n - 2^{n+1}$.

12 Consider the sequence $u_{n+1} = u_n + (2n + 1)$, with $u_1 = 1$. Calculate the values of u_2, u_3 and u_4, and use your results to guess at the form of u_n. Prove your guess by mathematical induction.

13 Prove by mathematical induction that $\sum_{r=1}^{n} 2r > n^2$.

14 Prove by mathematical induction that $\sum_{r=1}^{n} r^2 > \tfrac{1}{3}n^3$ for $n \in \mathbb{N}$.

15 Prove by mathematical induction that $\tfrac{1}{4}n^4 < \sum_{r=1}^{n} r^3 \leqslant n^4$.

16 A sequence is defined by $a_{n+1} = \sqrt{2 + a_n}$ and $a_1 = 3$. Prove by mathematical induction that $a_n > 2$ for all positive integers.

17 Prove that $(1 + x)^n > 1 + nx$ for all $x > 0$ and for integers $n > 1$.

18 The nth member a_n of a sequence is defined by $a_n = 5^n + 12n - 1$. By considering $a_{k+1} - 5a_k$ prove that a_n is divisible by 16.

19 A sequence is defined by $u_n = 2^{n+1} + 9 \times 13^n$ for $n \geqslant 1$. By considering $13u_k - u_{k+1}$ prove that u_n is divisible by 11.

20 Calculate the values of $3 \times 5^{2n+1} + 2^{3n+1}$ for $n = 0$, 1 and 2. Make a conjecture about a number which divides $3 \times 5^{2n+1} + 2^{3n+1}$ for every positive integer. Prove your conjecture by induction.

21 Make a conjecture about the sum of the series

$$1 \times 1! + 2 \times 2! + 3 \times 3! + \cdots + n \times n!$$

and prove it by mathematical induction.

22 Let $\mathbf{A} = \begin{pmatrix} 1 & 1 \\ 0 & 1 \end{pmatrix}$. Calculate the matrices $\mathbf{A}^2$ and $\mathbf{A}^3$. Make a conjecture about the matrix $\mathbf{A}^n$ and prove it by induction.

23 Calculate the sums of three consecutive cubes in a number of cases, and make a conjecture about a factor of the sum of three consecutive cubes. Prove your conjecture.

24* Make a conjecture about a number which divides $3^{2n+1} + 2^{4n+2}$, and prove it.

Miscellaneous exercise 6

1 Let $f(n+1) = 3f(n) + 8$, with $f(1) = 11$. Prove by induction that $f(n) = 5 \times 3^n - 4$.

2 Prove by induction that the sum of the series $(1 \times 3) + (2 \times 4) + (3 \times 5) + \cdots + n(n+2)$ is $\frac{1}{6}n(n+1)(2n+7)$. (OCR)

3 Prove by mathematical induction that, for all positive integers n,

$$\frac{1}{2} + \frac{1}{4} + \frac{1}{8} + \frac{1}{16} + \cdots + \frac{1}{2^n} = 1 - \frac{1}{2^n}.$$ (OCR)

4 If $S_n = 1 \times n + 2(n-1) + 3(n-2) + \cdots + (n-1) \times 2 + n \times 1$, where n is a positive integer, prove that $S_{n+1} - S_n = \frac{1}{2}(n+1)(n+2)$.

Use induction to prove that $S_n = \frac{1}{6}n(n+1)(n+2)$. (OCR)

5 Let $f(n) = 13^n + 6^{n-1}$. By considering $f(n+1) + f(n)$, or otherwise, prove that $13^n + 6^{n-1}$ is divisible by 7.

6 Prove that, if n is a positive integer, $f(n) = 5^{2n} + 12^{n-1}$ is divisible by 13. (Hint: consider $f(k+1) + f(k)$.)

7 Prove that, if n is a positive integer, $5^{2n+2} - 24n - 25$ is divisible by 576. (OCR)

8 Show that, if you were trying to prove the false proposition

$$1 + 2 + 3 + \cdots + n = \frac{1}{2}(n-1)(n+2),$$

the inductive step works perfectly but the basis case does not.

9 (a) An arithmetic progression is such that the sum of the first 12 terms is 270 and the sum of the first 17 terms is 510. Find the first term and the common difference.

(b) A geometric progression is such that the sum of the first two terms is 1 and the sum of the first four terms is 5. Given that all the terms are positive, find the first term and the common ratio.

(c) A new series is formed as follows. The kth term of the new series is the product of the kth term of the arithmetic progression in (a) and the kth term of the geometric progression in (b). Show that the kth term of the new series is $(k+1)2^{k-1}$.

Prove by induction that $\sum_{k=1}^{n} (k+1)2^{k-1} = n2^n$. (OCR)

10* An emerging currency has two kinds of bank note, one for 5 schenkels and one for 9 schenkels. Prove that every account greater than 31 schenkels can be paid without change by using the 5 schenkel and 9 schenkel notes.

7 Complex numbers

In this chapter the concept of number is extended so that all numbers have square roots. When you have completed it, you should

- understand that new number systems can be created, provided that the definitions are algebraically consistent
- appreciate that complex number algebra excludes inequalities
- be able to do calculations with complex numbers
- know the meaning of conjugate complex numbers, and that non-real roots of equations with real coefficients occur in conjugate pairs
- know how to represent complex numbers as points in an Argand diagram and as translations
- be able to solve simple equations with complex coefficients.

7.1 Extending the number system

Before negative numbers were developed, it was impossible to subtract a from b if $a > b$. If only positive numbers exist, then there is no number x such that $a + x = b$.

This was a serious drawback for mathematics and science, so a new kind of number was invented which could be either positive or negative. It was found that this results in a consistent system of numbers in which the ordinary rules of algebra apply, provided that you also make up the right rules for combining numbers, such as $b - a = -(a - b)$ and $(-a) \times (-b) = +(ab)$.

There is a similar problem with real numbers, that square roots only exist for positive numbers and zero. That is, if $a < 0$, there is no real number x such that $x^2 = a$.

The mathematical response to this is to invent a new kind of number, called a **complex number**. It turns out that this can be done very simply, by introducing just one new number, usually denoted by i, whose square is -1. If you also require that this number combines with the real numbers by the usual rules of algebra, this creates a whole new system of numbers.

Notice first that you don't need a separate symbol for the square root of -2, since the rules of algebra require that $\sqrt{-2} = \sqrt{2} \times \sqrt{-1}$, so that $\sqrt{-2}$ is just $\sqrt{2}\,$i. Similarly for any other negative number; if $a > 0$, then $\sqrt{-a} = \sqrt{a}\,$i.

Since you must be able to combine i with all the real numbers, the complex numbers must include all the products bi where b is any real number. They must also include all the sums $a + b$i, where a is any real number.

The **complex numbers** consist of numbers of the form $a + b$i, where a and b are real numbers and $i^2 = -1$.

Complex numbers of the form $a + 0$i are called **real numbers**; complex numbers of the form $0 + b$i are called **imaginary numbers**.

In a general complex number $a + b$i, a is called the **real part** and b the **imaginary part**. This is written $\text{Re}(a + b\text{i}) = a$, $\text{Im}(a + b\text{i}) = b$.

Some people prefer to use j rather than i for the square root of -1. Also, some books define the imaginary part of $a + b$i as bi rather than b.

Two questions need to be asked before going further: is algebra with complex numbers consistent, and are complex numbers useful? The answers are 'yes, but . . .' and 'yes, very'. Complex numbers have an important place in modern physics and electronics.

The reason for the 'but' is that with complex numbers you cannot use the inequality symbols > and <. To see why, recall that one of the rules for inequalities is that

if $a > b$ and $c > 0$, then $ac > bc$.

So, taking $b = 0$ and $c = a$,

if $a > 0$ and $a > 0$, then $aa > 0a$.

That is, if $a > 0$, $a^2 > 0$.

What about the number i? Is $i > 0$ or $i < 0$?

Try following through the consequences of each assumption in turn:

$$
\begin{aligned}
i > 0 \quad &\Rightarrow \quad i^2 > 0 \qquad \text{(putting } a = i) \\
&\Leftrightarrow \quad -1 > 0; \\
i < 0 \quad &\Leftrightarrow \quad i + (-i) < 0 + (-i) \qquad \text{(adding } -i \text{ to both sides)} \\
&\Leftrightarrow \quad 0 < -i \\
&\Leftrightarrow \quad -i > 0 \\
&\Rightarrow \quad (-i)^2 > 0 \qquad \text{(putting } a = -i) \\
&\Leftrightarrow \quad -1 > 0.
\end{aligned}
$$

Either assumption leads to the conclusion that $-1 > 0$, which you know to be false. The way out of the dilemma is to make the rule:

The relations > and < cannot be used to compare pairs of complex numbers.

Example 7.1.1
Solve the equation $x^2 = -16$.

Since $4^2 = 16$ and $i^2 = -1$, one root is $4i$.

Another is $-4i$, because

$$(-4i) \times (-4i) = +16i^2 = -16.$$

The roots of the equation are $+4i$ and $-4i$. But you can't say that $+4i$ is the positive root and $-4i$ is the negative root, because the words 'positive' and 'negative' have no meaning with complex numbers.

7.2 Operations with complex numbers

It is remarkable, and not at all obvious, that when you add, subtract, multiply or divide two complex numbers $a + bi$, $c + di$, the result is another complex number.

Addition and subtraction   By the usual rules of algebra,

$$(a + bi) + (c + di) = a + bi + c + di = a + c + bi + di = (a + c) + (b + d)i,$$
$$(a + bi) - (c + di) = a + bi - c - di = a - c + bi - di = (a - c) + (b - d)i.$$

Since a, b, c, d are real numbers, so are $a \pm c$ and $b \pm d$. The expressions at the end of each line therefore have the form $p + qi$ where p and q are real.

Example 7.2.1
If $r = 3 + 5i$ and $s = 1 - 4i$, find $r + s$ and $r - s$.

$$
\begin{aligned}
r + s &= (3 + 5i) + (1 - 4i) \\
&= 3 + 5i + 1 - 4i \\
&= (3 + 1) + (5i - 4i) \\
&= 4 + i. \\
r - s &= (3 + 5i) - (1 - 4i) \\
&= 3 + 5i - 1 + 4i \\
&= (3 - 1) + (5i + 4i) \\
&= 2 + 9i.
\end{aligned}
$$

Uniqueness   If $a + bi = 0$, then $a = -bi$, so that

$$a^2 = (-bi)^2 = -b^2.$$

Now a and b are real, so that

$$a^2 \geqslant 0 \text{ and } -b^2 \leqslant 0.$$

They can only be equal if

$$a^2 = 0 \text{ and } b^2 = 0.$$

That is,

$$a = 0 \text{ and } b = 0.$$

So if a complex number is zero, its real and imaginary parts are both zero.

Combining this with the rule for subtraction shows that

$$(a + b\,\mathrm{i}) = (c + d\,\mathrm{i}) \quad \Leftrightarrow \quad (a + b\,\mathrm{i}) - (c + d\,\mathrm{i}) = 0$$
$$\Leftrightarrow \quad (a - c) + (b - d)\,\mathrm{i} = 0$$
$$\Leftrightarrow \quad a - c = 0 \quad \text{and} \quad b - d = 0$$
$$\Leftrightarrow \quad a = c \quad \text{and} \quad b = d.$$

That is:

> If two complex numbers are equal, their real parts are equal and their imaginary parts are equal.

Multiplication   By the usual rules for multiplying out brackets,

$$(a + b\,\mathrm{i}) \times (c + d\,\mathrm{i}) = ac + a\,(d\,\mathrm{i}) + (b\,\mathrm{i})\,c + (b\,\mathrm{i})\,(d\,\mathrm{i})$$
$$= ac + ad\,\mathrm{i} + bc\,\mathrm{i} + bd\,\mathrm{i}^2$$
$$= ac + ad\,\mathrm{i} + bc\,\mathrm{i} - bd \qquad (\text{since } \mathrm{i}^2 = -1)$$
$$= (ac - bd) + (ad + bc)\,\mathrm{i}.$$

Since a, b, c, d are real numbers, so are $ac - bd$ and $ad + bc$. The product is therefore of the form $p + q\,\mathrm{i}$ where p and q are real.

Example 7.2.2
With $r = 3 + 5\,\mathrm{i}$ and $s = 1 - 4\,\mathrm{i}$, find $r \times s$.

$$r \times s = (3 + 5\,\mathrm{i}) \times (1 - 4\,\mathrm{i})$$
$$= 3 - 12\,\mathrm{i} + 5\,\mathrm{i} - 20\,\mathrm{i}^2$$
$$= 3 - 12\,\mathrm{i} + 5\,\mathrm{i} + 20 \qquad (\text{since } \mathrm{i}^2 = -1)$$
$$= 23 - 7\,\mathrm{i}.$$

An important special case of the multiplication rule is

$$(a + b\,\mathrm{i}) \times (a - b\,\mathrm{i}) = (aa - b(-b)) + (a(-b) + ba)\,\mathrm{i} = (a^2 + b^2) + 0\,\mathrm{i},$$

which is a real number. It follows that:

> In complex number algebra, the sum of two squares $a^2 + b^2$ can be factorised as $(a + b\,\mathrm{i})\,(a - b\,\mathrm{i})$.

Division   First, there are two special cases to consider, when the denominator of $\dfrac{a + b\,\mathrm{i}}{c + d\,\mathrm{i}}$ is either a real number or an imaginary number.

If the denominator is real, so that $d = 0$, then

$$\frac{a + b\,\mathrm{i}}{c + 0\,\mathrm{i}} = \frac{a + b\,\mathrm{i}}{c} = \frac{a}{c} + \frac{b}{c}\,\mathrm{i}.$$

If the denominator is imaginary, so that $c = 0$, you can simplify the expression by multiplying numerator and denominator by i:

$$\frac{a+b\,\mathrm{i}}{0+d\,\mathrm{i}} = \frac{a+b\,\mathrm{i}}{d\,\mathrm{i}} = \frac{(a+b\,\mathrm{i})\,\mathrm{i}}{(d\,\mathrm{i})\,\mathrm{i}} = \frac{a\,\mathrm{i}+b\,\mathrm{i}^2}{d\,\mathrm{i}^2}$$

$$= \frac{a\,\mathrm{i}-b}{-d} = \frac{-b}{-d} + \left(\frac{a\,\mathrm{i}}{-d}\right) = \frac{b}{d} - \frac{a}{d}\,\mathrm{i}.$$

Example 7.2.3

Write as complex numbers, in the form $p + q\,\mathrm{i}$,   (a) $\dfrac{1}{\mathrm{i}}$,   (b) $\dfrac{1+4\,\mathrm{i}}{2\,\mathrm{i}}$.

(a) $\dfrac{1}{\mathrm{i}} = \dfrac{\mathrm{i}}{\mathrm{i}\times\mathrm{i}} = \dfrac{\mathrm{i}}{-1} = -\mathrm{i}.$

(b) **Method 1**

$$\frac{1+4\,\mathrm{i}}{2\,\mathrm{i}} = \frac{(1+4\,\mathrm{i})\times\mathrm{i}}{2\,\mathrm{i}\times\mathrm{i}}$$

$$= \frac{\mathrm{i}+4\,\mathrm{i}^2}{2\,\mathrm{i}^2}$$

$$= \frac{\mathrm{i}-4}{-2}$$

$$= -\tfrac{1}{2}\mathrm{i}+2 = 2 - \tfrac{1}{2}\mathrm{i}.$$

Method 2

$$\frac{1+4\,\mathrm{i}}{2\,\mathrm{i}} = \frac{1}{2\,\mathrm{i}} + \frac{4\,\mathrm{i}}{2\,\mathrm{i}}$$

$$= \tfrac{1}{2}\times(-\mathrm{i})+2 \qquad \text{(using the result of part (a))}$$

$$= -\tfrac{1}{2}\mathrm{i}+2 = 2 - \tfrac{1}{2}\,\mathrm{i}.$$

In the general case $\dfrac{a+b\,\mathrm{i}}{c+d\,\mathrm{i}}$ the trick is to multiply numerator and denominator by $c - d\,\mathrm{i}$, and to use the result in the box above, in the form $(c+d\,\mathrm{i})\,(c-d\,\mathrm{i}) = c^2 + d^2$.

$$\frac{a+b\,\mathrm{i}}{c+d\,\mathrm{i}} = \frac{(a+b\,\mathrm{i})\,(c-d\,\mathrm{i})}{(c+d\,\mathrm{i})\,(c-d\,\mathrm{i})}$$

$$= \frac{(ac+bd)+(-ad+bc)\,\mathrm{i}}{c^2+d^2}$$

$$= \frac{ac+bd}{c^2+d^2} + \left(\frac{bc-ad}{c^2+d^2}\right)\mathrm{i}.$$

In every case the result has the form $p + q\,\mathrm{i}$ where p and q are real numbers. The only exception is when $c^2 + d^2 = 0$; since c and d are both real this can only occur if c and d are both 0, so that $c + d\,\mathrm{i} = 0 + 0\,\mathrm{i} = 0$. With complex numbers, as with real numbers, you cannot divide by zero.

> Do not try to remember the formulae for $(a+b\,\mathrm{i})\,(c+d\,\mathrm{i})$ and $\dfrac{a+b\,\mathrm{i}}{c+d\,\mathrm{i}}$ in this section. As long as you understand the method, it is simple to apply it when you need it.

Example 7.2.4

If $r = 1 + 2i$ and $s = 2 + i$, express rs and $\dfrac{r}{s}$ in the form $(a + bi)$.

$$rs = (1 + 2i)(2 + i) = 2 + i + 4i + 2i^2 = 2 + i + 4i - 2 = 5i.$$

To find $\dfrac{r}{s}$, multiply both numerator and denominator by $2 - i$.

$$\frac{r}{s} = \frac{1 + 2i}{2 + i} = \frac{(1 + 2i)(2 - i)}{(2 + i)(2 - i)} = \frac{2 - i + 4i - 2i^2}{4 - 2i + 2i - i^2} = \frac{2 - i + 4i + 2}{4 - 2i + 2i + 1} = \frac{4 + 3i}{5} = \tfrac{4}{5} + \tfrac{3}{5}i.$$

Exercise 7A

1   If $p = 2 + 3i$ and $q = 2 - 3i$, express the following in the form $a + bi$, where a and b are real numbers.

   (a) $p + q$ (b) $p - q$ (c) pq (d) $(p + q)(p - q)$
   (e) $p^2 - q^2$ (f) $p^2 + q^2$ (g) $(p + q)^2$ (h) $(p - q)^2$

2   If $r = 3 + i$ and $s = 1 - 2i$, express the following in the form $a + bi$, where a and b are real numbers.

   (a) $r + s$ (b) $r - s$ (c) $2r + s$ (d) $r + si$

   (e) rs (f) r^2 (g) $\dfrac{r}{s}$ (h) $\dfrac{s}{r}$

   (i) $\dfrac{r}{i}$ (j) $\dfrac{1}{r} + \dfrac{1}{s}$ (k) $\dfrac{s}{1 + i}$ (l) $\dfrac{1 - i}{s}$

3   If $(2 + i)(x + yi) = 1 + 3i$, where x and y are real numbers, write two equations connecting x and y, and solve them.

   Compare your answer with that given by dividing $1 + 3i$ by $2 + i$ using the method described in the text.

4   Evaluate the following.

   (a) $\text{Re}(3 + 4i)$ (b) $\text{Im}(4 - 3i)$ (c) $\text{Re}(2 + i)^2$

   (d) $\text{Im}(3 - i)^2$ (e) $\text{Re}\dfrac{1}{1 + i}$ (f) $\text{Im}\dfrac{1}{i}$

5   If $s = a + bi$ and $t = c + di$ are complex numbers, which of the following are always true?

   (a) $\text{Re}\,s + \text{Re}\,t = \text{Re}(s + t)$ (b) $\text{Re}\,3s = 3\text{Re}\,s$ (c) $\text{Re}(is) = \text{Im}\,s$
   (d) $\text{Im}(is) = \text{Re}\,s$ (e) $\text{Re}\,s \times \text{Re}\,t = \text{Re}(st)$ (f) $\dfrac{\text{Im}\,s}{\text{Im}\,t} = \text{Im}\left(\dfrac{s}{t}\right)$

7.3   Solving equations

Now that $a + bi$ is recognised as a number in its own right, there is no need to go on writing it out in full. You can use a single letter, such as s (or any other letter you like, except i), to represent it. If you write $s = a + b\mathrm{i}$, it is understood that s is a complex number and that a and b are real numbers.

Just as x is often used to stand for a general real number, it is conventional to use z for a general complex number, and to write $z = x + y\mathrm{i}$, where x and y are real numbers. When you see z as the unknown in an equation, you know that there is a possibility that at least some of the roots may be complex numbers. (But if you see some other letter, don't assume that the solution is not complex.) If a second unknown is introduced, $w = u + v\mathrm{i}$ is often used.

Example 7.3.1

If $p = 1 + \mathrm{i}, q = 3 - 4\mathrm{i}$ and $r = 5 + 6\mathrm{i}$, solve the equation $pz + q = r$.

You proceed in just the same way as you would with real numbers. Begin by subtracting q from both sides, giving $pz = r - q$. That is,

$$\begin{aligned}(1 + \mathrm{i})z &= (5 + 6\mathrm{i}) - (3 - 4\mathrm{i}) \\ &= (5 - 3) + (6\mathrm{i} - (-4\mathrm{i})) \\ &= 2 + 10\mathrm{i}.\end{aligned}$$

Now divide both sides by p, giving $z = \dfrac{r - q}{p}$. That is,

$$\begin{aligned}z &= \frac{2 + 10\mathrm{i}}{1 + \mathrm{i}} \\ &= \frac{(2 + 10\mathrm{i})(1 - \mathrm{i})}{(1 + \mathrm{i})(1 - \mathrm{i})} \\ &= \frac{2 + 8\mathrm{i} - 10\mathrm{i}^2}{1 - \mathrm{i}^2} = \frac{2 + 8\mathrm{i} + 10}{1 + 1} \\ &= \frac{12 + 8\mathrm{i}}{2} = 6 + 4\mathrm{i}.\end{aligned}$$

In a similar way you can solve simultaneous equations in which the coefficients and the solutions are complex.

Example 7.3.2

Find the complex numbers z and w which satisfy the simultaneous equations

$$\left.\begin{aligned}\mathrm{i}z + (1 + 2\mathrm{i})w &= 2 + 3\mathrm{i} \\ (1 + \mathrm{i})z + \qquad \mathrm{i}w &= 2 + 4\mathrm{i}\end{aligned}\right\}.$$

Begin by multiplying the first equation by a number so that the coefficients of z in the two equations are the same. The multiplier must be $\dfrac{1 + \mathrm{i}}{\mathrm{i}}$, which is

$$\frac{1 + \mathrm{i}}{\mathrm{i}} = \frac{(1 + \mathrm{i}) \times \mathrm{i}}{\mathrm{i} \times \mathrm{i}} = \frac{\mathrm{i} + \mathrm{i}^2}{\mathrm{i}^2} = \frac{\mathrm{i} - 1}{-1} = 1 - \mathrm{i}.$$

So subtract $1 - \mathrm{i}$ times the first equation from the second equation. (In the notation of Section 1.2, $r_2' = r_2 - (1 - \mathrm{i})r_1$.) The effect of this on coefficients in the second equation will then be as follows.

$$\text{Coefficient of } z: \quad (1+i) - (1-i) \times i = 1 + i - i - 1 = 0.$$
$$\text{Coefficient of } w: \quad i - (1-i) \times (1+2i) = i - (1+i+2) = -3.$$
$$\text{Right side}: \quad (2+4i) - (1-i) \times (2+3i) = 2 + 4i - (2+i+3) = -3 + 3i.$$

The equations are now

$$\left. \begin{array}{r} iz + (1+2i)w = 2 + 3i \\ 0z - \quad 3w = -3 + 3i \end{array} \right\}.$$

From the second equation,

$$w = \frac{-3+3i}{-3} = 1 - i.$$

Substituting $w = 1 - i$ in the first equation gives

$$iz + (1+2i)(1-i) = 2 + 3i,$$
$$iz + (1 + i + 2) = 2 + 3i,$$
$$iz = -1 + 2i,$$

so

$$z = \frac{-1+2i}{i} = \frac{(-1+2i) \times i}{i \times i} = \frac{-i-2}{-1} = 2 + i.$$

The solution is $z = 2 + i$, $w = 1 - i$.

The roots of quadratic equations can also be complex numbers.

Example 7.3.3
Solve the quadratic equation $z^2 + 4z + 13 = 0$.

Method 1   In the usual notation $a = 1$, $b = 4$ and $c = 13$, so that $b^2 - 4ac = 16 - 52 = -36$. Previously you would have said that there are no roots, but you can now write $\sqrt{-36} = 6i$. Using the formula,

$$z = \frac{-b \pm \sqrt{b^2 - 4ac}}{2a} = \frac{-4 \pm 6i}{2} = -2 \pm 3i.$$

Method 2   In completed square form, $z^2 + 4z + 13 = (z+2)^2 + 9$. This is the sum of two squares, which you can now factorise, as

$$((z+2) - 3i)((z+2) + 3i).$$

So you can write the equation as

$$(z + 2 - 3i)(z + 2 + 3i) = 0,$$

with roots $z = -2 + 3i$ and $-2 - 3i$.

You can use a similar method with any quadratic equation, $az^2 + bz + c = 0$, where the coefficients a, b and c are real. If $b^2 - 4ac > 0$ there are two roots, both real numbers. But if

$b^2 - 4ac < 0$, you can write $b^2 - 4ac$ as $-(4ac - b^2)$, one of whose square roots is $\sqrt{4ac - b^2}\,i$, so that the roots of the equation are $\dfrac{-b \pm \sqrt{4ac - b^2}\,i}{2a}$, both complex numbers.

Notice that, if the roots are complex numbers, then they have the form $x \pm y\,i$ with the same real parts but opposite imaginary parts. Pairs of numbers like this are called **conjugate complex numbers**. If $x + y\,i$ is written as z, then the conjugate $x - y\,i$ is denoted by z^* (which is read as 'z-star').

> Complex numbers $z = x + y\,i$, $z^* = x - y\,i$ are conjugate complex numbers.
>
> Their sum $z + z^* = 2x$ and product $zz^* = x^2 + y^2$ are real numbers, and their difference $z - z^* = 2y\,i$ is an imaginary number.
>
> If a quadratic equation with real coefficients has two complex roots, these roots are conjugate.

You have already used conjugate complex numbers once in this chapter. The method used in Section 7.2 to divide $s = a + b\,i$ by $t = c + d\,i$ is to multiply numerator and denominator by $c - d\,i$, which is t^*.

That is,

$$\frac{s}{t} = \frac{st^*}{tt^*},$$

and $tt^* = c^2 + d^2$, which is a real number.

Exercise 7B

1 If $p = 3 + 4\,i$, $q = 1 - i$ and $r = -2 + 3\,i$, solve the following equations for the complex number z.

(a) $p + z = q$ (b) $2r + 3z = p$ (c) $qz = r$ (d) $pz + q = r$

2 Solve these pairs of simultaneous equations for the complex numbers z and w.

(a) $(1 + i)z + (2 - i)\,w = 3 + 4\,i$
    $i\,z + (3 + i)\,w = -1 + 5\,i$

(b) $5z - (3 + i)\,w = 7 - i$
    $(2 - i)\,z + 2\,iw = -1 + i$

3 Solve the following quadratic equations, giving answers in the form $a + b\,i$, where a and b are real numbers.

(a) $z^2 + 9 = 0$ (b) $z^2 + 4z + 5 = 0$ (c) $z^2 - 6z + 25 = 0$ (d) $2z^2 + 2z + 13 = 0$

4 Write down the conjugates of the following.

(a) $1 + 7\,i$ (b) $-2 + i$ (c) 5 (d) $3\,i$

For each of these complex numbers z find the values of

(i) $z + z^*$,   (ii) $z - z^*$,   (iii) zz^*,   (iv) $\dfrac{z}{z^*}$.

7.4   Properties of conjugate complex numbers

Conjugate complex numbers have some important properties. Suppose, for example, that $s = a + b\,i$ and $t = c + d\,i$ are two complex numbers, so that $s^* = a - b\,i$ and $t^* = c - d\,i$. Using the results in the Section 7.2 and replacing b by $-b$ and d by $-d$, you get

$$s + t = (a + c) + (b + d)\,i \quad \text{and} \quad s^* + t^* = (a + c) - (b + d)\,i;$$

$$s - t = (a - c) + (b - d)\,i \quad \text{and} \quad s^* - t^* = (a - c) - (b - d)\,i;$$

$$st = (ac - bd) + (ad + bc)\,i \quad \text{and} \quad s^* t^* = (ac - bd) - (ad + bc)\,i;$$

$$\frac{s}{t} = \frac{ac + bd + (bc - ad)\,i}{c^2 + d^2} \quad \text{and} \quad \frac{s^*}{t^*} = \frac{ac + bd - (bc - ad)\,i}{c^2 + d^2}.$$

You can see that the outcomes in each case are conjugate pairs.

> If s and t are complex numbers, then
>
> $$(s + t)^* = s^* + t^*, \quad (s - t)^* = s^* - t^*, \quad (st)^* = s^* t^*, \quad \left(\frac{s}{t}\right)^* = \frac{s^*}{t^*}.$$
>
> That is,
>
> the conjugate of the $\begin{cases} \text{sum} \\ \text{difference} \\ \text{product} \\ \text{quotient} \end{cases}$ of two complex numbers
>
> is the $\begin{cases} \text{sum} \\ \text{difference} \\ \text{product} \\ \text{quotient} \end{cases}$ of their conjugates.

Example 7.4.1

If $s = 1 + 2\,i$, show that   (a) $(s^2)^* = (s^*)^2$,   (b) $\left(\dfrac{1}{s}\right)^* = \dfrac{1}{s^*}$.

(a) $s^2 = (1 + 2\,i)^2 = 1 + 4\,i - 4 = -3 + 4\,i$,

so its conjugate is

$$(s^2)^* = -3 - 4\,i.$$

Also $s^* = 1 - 2\,i$, so

$$(s^*)^2 = (1 - 2\,i)^2 = 1 - 4\,i - 4 = -3 - 4\,i.$$

Therefore $(s^2)^* = (s^*)^2$.

(b) $\dfrac{1}{s} = \dfrac{1}{1+2\,\mathrm{i}} = \dfrac{1-2\,\mathrm{i}}{(1+2\,\mathrm{i})\,(1-2\,\mathrm{i})} = \dfrac{1-2\,\mathrm{i}}{1+4} = \tfrac{1}{5} - \tfrac{2}{5}\,\mathrm{i},$

so its conjugate is $\left(\dfrac{1}{s}\right)^{*} = \tfrac{1}{5} + \tfrac{2}{5}\,\mathrm{i}.$

Also $\dfrac{1}{s^{*}} = \dfrac{1}{1-2\,\mathrm{i}} = \dfrac{1+2\,\mathrm{i}}{(1-2\,\mathrm{i})\,(1+2\,\mathrm{i})} = \dfrac{1+2\,\mathrm{i}}{1+4} = \tfrac{1}{5} + \tfrac{2}{5}\,\mathrm{i}.$

Therefore $\left(\dfrac{1}{s}\right)^{*} = \dfrac{1}{s^{*}}.$

If in the rule $(st)^{*} = s^{*}t^{*}$ you set both s and t equal to z, you get

$$(zz)^{*} = z^{*}z^{*},$$

that is

$$(z^{2})^{*} = (z^{*})^{2}.$$

Then, setting $s = z^{2}$ and $t = z$, it follows that

$$(z^{2}z)^{*} = (z^{2})^{*}z^{*} = (z^{*})^{2}z^{*},$$

that is

$$(z^{3})^{*} = (z^{*})^{3};$$

and so on.

This suggests a general result about powers of conjugate complex numbers.

> If z is a complex number and n is a positive integer,
> $$(z^{n})^{*} = (z^{*})^{n}.$$

You know from Chapter 6 that results like this are proved by mathematical induction. You are asked to do this in Exercise 7C Question 10.

It is useful to extend this result by introducing a real number a and considering the conjugate of az^{n}. Using $(st)^{*} = s^{*}t^{*}$ again,

$$(az^{n})^{*} = a^{*}(z^{n})^{*}.$$

Since a is real, $a^{*} = a$. Also $(z^{n})^{*} = (z^{*})^{n}$. So

$$(az^{n})^{*} = a(z^{*})^{n}.$$

> If z is a complex number, a is a real number and n is a positive integer,
> $$(az^{n})^{*} = a(z^{*})^{n}.$$

Example 7.4.2

If $a = 2$, $z = 1 + 3i$ and $n = 4$, calculate $(az^n)^*$ and $a(z^*)^n$, and verify that $(az^n)^* = a(z^*)^n$.

A simple way of calculating z^4 is to use $z^4 = (z^2)^2$. The details of the working have been left for you to check for yourself.

If $z = 1 + 3i$,

$$z^2 = (1 + 3i)^2 = -8 + 6i$$

so $$z^4 = (-8 + 6i)^2 = 28 - 96i$$

and $$az^4 = 2(28 - 96i) = 56 - 192i.$$

This gives $$(az^n)^* = 56 + 192i.$$

The conjugate $z^* = 1 - 3i$

so $$(z^*)^2 = (1 - 3i)^2 = -8 - 6i$$

and $$(z^*)^4 = (-8 - 6i)^2 = 28 + 96i$$

giving $$a(z^*)^4 = 2(28 + 96i) = 56 + 192i.$$

Therefore, for these values of a, z and n, $(az^n)^* = a(z^*)^n$.

It is important, though, that a is a real number. For example, if you carry out the calculations in Example 7.4.2 with $a = 2 + i$ you get

$$az^4 = (2 + i)(28 - 96i) = 152 - 164i$$

giving $(az^4)^* = 152 + 164i$;

but $$a(z^*)^4 = (2 + i)(28 + 96i) = 220i - 40,$$

so that $(az^4)^* \neq a(z^*)^4$.

Where does the proof that $(az^n)^* = a(z^*)^n$ use the fact that a is real?

7.5 Polynomial equations

The results of the previous section have applications to equations of the form $p(z) = 0$, where $p(z)$ stands for a polynomial in which the variable z is complex.

Example 7.5.1

If $p(z) = z^3 + 3z + 4$ and $s = 1 + i$, calculate $p(s)$ and $p(s^*)$, and show that $p(s^*) = (p(s))^*$.

Now $$s^2 = (1 + i)^2 = 1 + 2i - 1 = 2i$$

and $$(s^*)^2 = (1 - i)^2 = 1 - 2i - 1 = -2i,$$

$$s^3 = (1 + i) \times 2i = 2i - 2 = -2 + 2i$$

and $$(s^*)^3 = (1 - i) \times (-2i) = -2i - 2 = -2 - 2i,$$

so $$p(s) = (-2 + 2i) + (3 + 3i) + 4 = 5 + 5i$$

and $$p(s^*) = (-2 - 2i) + (3 - 3i) + 4 = 5 - 5i.$$

The conjugate of $p(s)$ is $(5 + 5i)^* = 5 - 5i$, so $p(s^*) = (p(s))^*$.

You don't in fact need to know the particular value of s to show that $p(s^*)$ is the conjugate of $p(s)$. If $p(z) = z^3 + 3z + 4$ and s is any complex number,

$$p(s^*) = (s^*)^3 + 3s^* + 4.$$

You know that $(s^*)^3 = (s^3)^*$, that $3s^* = (3s)^*$ and that $4 = 4^*$. So

$$\begin{aligned} p(s^*) &= (s^3)^* + (3s)^* + 4^* \\ &= (s^3 + 3s + 4)^* \quad \text{(the sum of the conjugates is the conjugate of the sum)} \\ &= (p(s))^*. \end{aligned}$$

This argument could obviously be used with any polynomial provided that the coefficients are real. Suppose that you have a polynomial of degree n,

$$p(z) = a_n z^n + a_{n-1} z^{n-1} + \cdots + a_2 z^2 + a_1 z + a_0,$$

whose coefficients $a_n, a_{n-1}, \ldots a_2, a_1$ and a_0 are all real numbers. Then $p(z^*)$ is the sum of $n + 1$ terms of the form $a_r(z^*)^r$, which you can write as $(a_r z^r)^*$. So each term is the conjugate of the corresponding term in $p(z)$. Since the sum of conjugate numbers is the conjugate of the sum, it follows that $p(z^*)$ is the conjugate of $p(z)$.

> If $p(z)$ is a polynomial with real coefficients,
> $$p(z^*) = (p(z))^*.$$

It is only a short step from this last theorem to an important result about equations of the form $p(z) = 0$. Suppose that $z = s$ is a non-real root of this equation. Then, by the factor theorem for polynomials (C2 Section 8.3), $p(s) = 0$, so

$$p(s^*) = (p(s))^* = 0^* = 0,$$

which means that $z = s^*$ is also a root of the equation.

You saw an example of this result in Example 7.3.3 for a quadratic equation. You can now see that this was a special case of a far more general result, for polynomial equations of any degree.

> If s is a non-real root of the equation $p(z) = 0$, then s^* is also a root; that is, the non-real roots of the equation $p(z) = 0$ occur as conjugate pairs.

Example 7.5.2
Solve the equation $z^3 + z - 10 = 0$.

> Every cubic equation has at least one real root. To show this for the given equation, display the graph of $y = x^3 + x - 10$ on a graphic calculator. You will see that one end of the graph is in the third quadrant and that the other end is in the first quadrant. So the graph must cross the x-axis at least once. The x-coordinate of any point where it does so is a real root of the equation.

Denote the polynomial $z^3 + z - 10$ by p(z). and use the factor theorem. (See C2 Chapter 8. The theory about polynomials and factors in that chapter holds equally well with complex numbers as with real numbers.) If p(z) has a factor $z - a$, where a is an integer, then a can only be $\pm 1, \pm 2, \pm 5$ or ± 10. Trial substitution of these values shows that p(2) = 0. So, by the factor theorem, $z - 2$ is a factor of p(z). Then, using the usual division procedure,

$$z^3 + z - 10 \equiv (z - 2)(z^2 + 2z + 5).$$

Therefore, if $z^3 + z - 10 = 0$, either $z - 2 = 0$ or $z^2 + 2z + 5 = 0$.

The quadratic equation can be written in completed square form as

$$(z + 1)^2 = -4,$$

which gives $z = -1 \pm 2i$.

The roots of $z^3 + z - 10 = 0$ are therefore 2, $-1 + 2i$ and $-1 - 2i$. There is one real root and a pair of conjugate complex roots.

Example 7.5.3
Show that $(1 + i)^4 = -4$. Hence find all the roots of the equation $z^4 + 4 = 0$.

$$(1 + i)^2 = 1 + 2i + i^2 = 1 + 2i - 1 = 2i, \text{ so } (1 + i)^4 = (2i)^2 = 4i^2 = -4.$$

This shows that $1 + i$ is a root of the equation $z^4 + 4 = 0$, so another root must be its conjugate $1 - i$. You can deduce that $z - 1 - i$ and $z - (1 - i) = z - 1 + i$ are both factors of $z^4 + 4$.

Now $(z - 1 - i)(z - 1 + i) \equiv (z - 1)^2 - i^2 \equiv z^2 - 2z + 2$. This means that $z^4 + 4$ must be the product of $z^2 - 2z + 2$ and another quadratic factor. Denoting this second factor by $Az^2 + Bz + C$,

$$z^4 + 4 \equiv (z^2 - 2z + 2)(Az^2 + Bz + C)$$
$$\equiv Az^4 + (B - 2A) z^3 + (C - 2B + 2A) z^2 + (-2C + 2B) z + 2C.$$

Equating coefficients of these two quartic expressions (see C2 Section 8.4) gives the five equations

$$A = 1, B - 2A = 0, C - 2B + 2A = 0, -2C + 2B = 0, 2C = 4.$$

From the first three equations $A = 1$, $B = 2$, $C = 2 \times 2 - 2 \times 1 = 2$. (Check that these satisfy the other two equations.) So the second quadratic factor is $z^2 + 2z + 2$.

The other two roots are therefore the roots of the quadratic equation $z^2 + 2z + 2 = 0$, that is

$$z = \frac{-2 \pm \sqrt{4 - 4 \times 1 \times 2}}{2} = \frac{-2 \pm \sqrt{-4}}{2} = \frac{-2 \pm 2i}{2} = -1 \pm i.$$

There are two conjugate pairs of roots: $1 + i$, $1 - i$, and $-1 + i$, $-1 - i$.

With hindsight, and a great deal of ingenuity, you might spot that if $z^4 + 4$ is written as $(z^4 + 4z^2 + 4) - 4z^2 = (z^2 + 2)^2 - (2z)^2$, then this is the difference of two squares, with factors $(z^2 + 2 - 2z)(z^2 + 2 + 2z)$.

Example 7.5.4
Solve the equation $z^5 - 6z^3 - 2z^2 + 17z - 10 = 0$.

Denote the left side by p(z) and begin by trying to find some real factors, using the factor theorem.

Try $z = 1$: p(1) $= 1 - 6 - 2 + 17 - 10 = 0$, so $z - 1$ is a factor of p(z). Write p(z) $= (z - 1)$q(z), where q(z) $= Az^4 + Bz^3 + Cz^2 + Dz + E$. Then

$$z^5 - 6z^3 - 2z^2 + 17z - 10$$
$$\equiv (z - 1)(Az^4 + Bz^3 + Cz^2 + Dz + E)$$
$$\equiv Az^5 + (B - A)z^4 + (C - B)\, z^3 + (D - C)\, z^2 + (E - D)\, z - E.$$

Equating coefficients gives the equations

$$A = 1,\ B - A = 0,\ C - B = -6,\ D - C = -2,\ E - D = 17,\ -E = -10,$$

with solution $A = 1,\ B = 1,\ C = -5,\ D = -7,\ E = 10$. So

$$q(z) = z^4 + z^3 - 5z^2 - 7z + 10.$$

The same method can now be used to factorise q(z). Again try $z = 1$: q(1) $= 0$ so q(z) $= (z - 1)$r(z). You can check for yourself that r(z) $= z^3 + 2z^2 - 3z - 10$.

Continuing in the same way, try to factorise r(z). This time r(1) $\neq 0$, but r(2) $= 0$, so r(z) $= (z - 2)$s(z). You can check that s(z) $= z^2 + 4z + 5$.

Finally, completing the square,

$$z^2 + 4z + 5 = (z + 2)^2 + 1 = (z + 2 - i)(z + 2 + i).$$

Thus p(z) $= (z - 1)^2(z - 2)(z + 2 - i)(z + 2 + i)$, and the roots are 1 (a repeated root, counted twice), 2 and the conjugate complex pair $-2 \pm i$.

Exercise 7C

1 If s and t are complex numbers, simplify

(a) $(s^*)^*$,   (b) $(s^* + t)^*$,   (c) $(st^*)^*$,

(d) $\left(\dfrac{5}{s^*}\right)^*$,   (e) $(s - it)^*$,   (f) $(as^* + bt)^*$, where a and b are real.

2 If a and b are real numbers and z is complex, simplify

(a) $\left(\dfrac{a + z}{1 + bz}\right)^*$,   (b) $\left(\dfrac{ai + z}{1 + biz}\right)^*$.

Check your answers by substituting $a = 3, b = 2$ and $z = -1 + i$ in the original expression and in your simplified form.

3 (a) If $p(z) = 2z^3 - 3z^2 + 4$, evaluate p(2 + i) and p(2 − i), and verify that
   $p(2 - i) = (p(2 + i))^*$.
   (b) If $q(z) = 2z^3 - 3iz^2 + 4$, evaluate q(2 + i) and q(2 − i), and show that
   $q(2 - i) \neq (q(2 + i))^*$.

4 Write the following polynomials as products of linear factors.
   (a) $z^2 + 25$ (b) $9z^2 - 6z + 5$ (c) $4z^2 + 12z + 13$ (d) $z^4 - 16$
   (e) $z^4 - 8z^2 - 9$ (f) $z^3 + z - 10$ (g) $z^3 - 3z^2 + z + 5$ (h) $z^4 - z^2 - 2z + 2$

5 Prove that $1 + i$ is a root of the equation $z^4 + 3z^2 - 6z + 10 = 0$. Find the other roots.

6 Prove that $-2 + i$ is a root of the equation $z^4 + 24z + 55 = 0$. Find the other roots.

7 Let $z = a + bi$, where a and b are real numbers. If $\dfrac{z}{z^*} = c + di$, where c and d are real, prove that $c^2 + d^2 = 1$.

8 Prove that, for any complex number z, $zz^* = (\text{Re } z)^2 + (\text{Im } z)^2$.

9 If $z = a + bi$, where a and b are real, use the binomial theorem to find the real and imaginary parts of z^5 and $(z^*)^5$.

10 Use mathematical induction to prove that, if z is a complex number and n is a positive integer, $(z^*)^n = (z^n)^*$.
   Is it true that $(z^*)^n = (z^n)^*$ if n is a negative integer? Justify your answer.

7.6   Geometrical representation

You are used to the idea of representing real numbers by points on a number line, as in Fig. 7.1. Is there a corresponding representation for complex numbers?

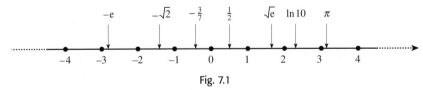

Fig. 7.1

The real numbers take up the whole number line, so to represent complex numbers you need a plane rather than a line. There is a simple way of doing this, by showing the number $s = a + bi$ as the point S with coordinates (a, b), as in Fig. 7.2.

Fig. 7.3 shows that, when you do this, all the real numbers (with $b = 0$) are placed on the horizontal axis. This axis is in fact just the same as the real number line in Fig. 7.1; it is usually called the **real axis**. All purely imaginary numbers (with $a = 0$) lie on the vertical axis, called the **imaginary axis**. Other complex numbers, with neither a nor b zero, occupy the rest of the plane.

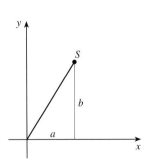

Fig. 7.2

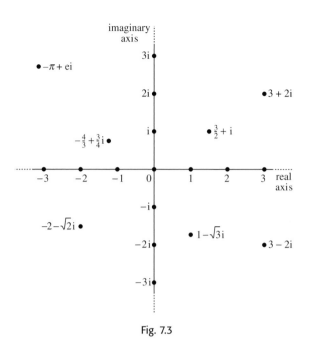

Fig. 7.3

One important property is that the points representing pairs of conjugate complex numbers, such as $3 + 2i$ and $3 - 2i$ in Fig. 7.3, are reflections of each other in the real axis.

This representation is called an **Argand diagram**, named after Jean-Robert Argand (1786–1822), a Parisian bookkeeper and mathematician.

> An Argand diagram represents a complex number $z = x + yi$ by a point Z with coordinates (x,y).
>
> For any complex number z, the point representing the conjugate complex number $z^* = x - yi$ is the reflection of Z in the real axis.

The Argand diagram shows why you can't expect to use the inequality symbols $>$ and $<$ with complex numbers. On a real number line, the relation 'greater than' between two numbers is equivalent to the relation 'to the right of' between the corresponding points. But there is no comparable relation between pairs of points in a plane.

Example 7.6.1
Show in an Argand diagram the roots of
(a) $z^4 + 4 = 0$,   (b) $z^5 - 6z^3 - 2z^2 + 17z - 10 = 0$.

These are the equations in Examples 7.5.3 and 7.5.4, and the corresponding diagrams are Figs. 7.4 and 7.5, over the page. The symmetry of both diagrams about the real axis shows geometrically the property that the non-real roots occur in conjugate pairs.

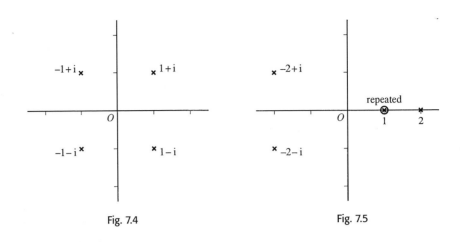

Fig. 7.4   Fig. 7.5

7.7   Arithmetic operations in the Argand diagram

On a real number line an operation such as 'add 3' can be represented by a translation of 3 units in the positive direction. In Fig. 7.6, if you take any point U on the line representing the real number u, the number $x = u + 3$ is represented by a point X which is 3 units to the right of U.

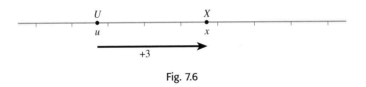

Fig. 7.6

> Notice the use of the 'alphabet convention' in which the same letter is used for the number (in lower case) as for the point which represents it (in capitals).

You can use a similar method to show addition of complex numbers in an Argand diagram. For example, the operation 'add $3 + 2\mathrm{i}$' translates any point W, representing the complex number $w = u + v\mathrm{i}$, to a point Z representing $z = x + y\mathrm{i}$ such that

$$x + y\mathrm{i} = (u + v\mathrm{i}) + (3 + 2\mathrm{i}).$$

That is,

$$x = u + 3 \quad \text{and} \quad y = v + 2.$$

This is shown in Fig. 7.7. The point Z is 3 units to the right of W and 2 units above it. So the operation 'add $3 + 2\mathrm{i}$' is represented by a translation of 3 units horizontally and 2 units vertically.

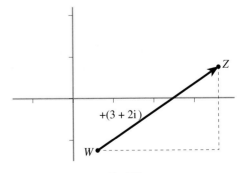

Fig. 7.7

In general, if s is any complex number $a + b\mathrm{i}$, the operation 'add s' is represented by a translation of a units horizontally and b units vertically. If this translation takes a point W in the Argand diagram to a point Z, then the relation between the corresponding complex numbers, $z = w + s$, is represented by Fig. 7.8.

This figure is especially important in the 'subtraction form' of the relation, $z - w = s$.

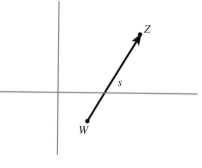

Fig. 7.8

> If the complex numbers z and w are represented in an Argand diagram by points Z and W, then the translation which takes W to Z represents the complex number $z - w$.

You may have noticed in this statement that the word 'represents' is used in two different senses. The complex numbers z and w are represented by points in an Argand diagram, but s is represented by a translation (shown by an arrow). Both ideas are useful, and in practice you will often find yourself switching from one to the other.

For example, Fig. 7.2 shows that the number s can also be represented by a point S in an Argand diagram. You can see from this figure that S is the point to which the origin (which of course represents the number 0) is translated by s. If you put Figs. 7.2 and 7.8 together you get Fig. 7.9.

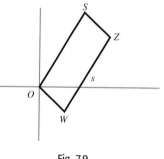

Fig. 7.9

In this figure, the translation which takes O to S also takes W to Z. It follows that $OSZW$ is a parallelogram. This gives another way of using the Argand diagram to show the addition of complex numbers.

> If complex numbers s, w and z are represented by points S, W and Z in an Argand diagram, and if $z = w + s$, then $OSZW$ is a parallelogram.

Example 7.7.1

Four complex numbers p, q, r, s are represented in an Argand diagram by points P, Q, R, S. Prove that, if $PQRS$ is a parallelogram, then $p + r = q + s$.

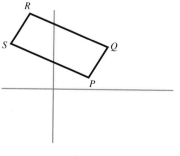

In Fig. 7.10, the translation which takes P to Q also takes S to R. Since these translations represent the complex numbers $q - p$ and $r - s$ respectively, $r - s = q - p$ Therefore $p + r = q + s$.

Fig. 7.10

Another operation which can be illustrated geometrically is multiplication by a real number. On a real number line, if c is a positive real number, the relation between the points U and X, where $x = cu$, is that X is c times as far from O as U, in the same direction (Fig. 7.11).

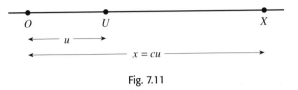

Fig. 7.11

Similarly, in an Argand diagram, the relation between the points W and Z, where $z = cw$, is that Z is c times as far from O as W, in the same direction (Fig. 7.12).

For example, in Fig. 7.3, the point representing $3 + 2i$ is twice as far from the origin in the same direction as $\frac{3}{2} + i$.

If the multiplying factor c is negative, Z is $|c|$ times as far from O as W, in the opposite direction.

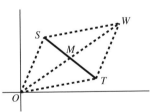

Fig. 7.12

Example 7.7.2

In Fig. 7.13, points S and T in the Argand diagram represent complex numbers s and t. Find the complex number corresponding to the mid-point M of ST.

Method 1   The translation which takes S to M is the same as the translation which takes M to T. So $m - s = t - m$, which gives $m = \frac{1}{2}(s + t)$.

Fig. 7.13

Method 2   Complete the parallelogram $OTWS$, where W represents the complex number w. Then $w = s + t$. The point M is half as far from O as W, in the same direction, so that $m = \frac{1}{2}w = \frac{1}{2}(s + t)$.

Exercise 7D

1   Draw (i) translation diagrams (like Fig. 7.7), (ii) Argand parallelograms (like Fig. 7.9) to represent the following relationships.

(a) $(3 + i) + (-1 + 2i) = (2 + 3i)$ (b) $(1 + 4i) - (3i) = (1 + i)$

2   Draw Argand diagrams to illustrate the following properties of complex numbers.

(a) $z + z^* = 2\,\mathrm{Re}\,z$ (b) $z - z^* = 2i\,\mathrm{Im}\,z$ (c) $(s + t)^* = s^* + t^*$
(d) $(kz)^* = kz^*$ where k is a real number

3 Draw Argand diagrams showing the roots of the following equations.

(a) $z^4 - 1 = 0$ (b) $z^3 + 1 = 0$ (c) $z^3 + 6z + 20 = 0$

(d) $z^4 + 4z^3 + 4z^2 - 9 = 0$ (e) $z^4 + z^3 + 5z^2 + 4z + 4 = 0$

4 Identify in an Argand diagram the points corresponding to the equation $z - z^* = 2i$.

7.8 Equations with complex coefficients

Complex numbers were introduced so that all real numbers should have square roots. But do complex numbers themselves have square roots?

Example 7.8.1

Find the square roots of   (a) $8i$,   (b) $3 - 4i$.

The problem is to find real numbers a and b such that $(a + bi)^2$ is equal to (a) $8i$ and (b) $3 - 4i$. To do this, note that $(a + bi)^2 = (a^2 - b^2) + 2abi$ and remember that, for two complex numbers to be equal, their real and imaginary parts must be equal.

(a) If $(a + bi)^2 = 8i$, then $a^2 - b^2 = 0$ and $2ab = 8$. Therefore $b = \dfrac{4}{a}$, and so

$$a^2 - \left(\frac{4}{a}\right)^2 = 0, \text{ or } a^4 = 16.$$ Since a is real, a^2 can't be negative: so $a^2 = 4$, $a = \pm 2$.

If $a = 2$, $b = \dfrac{4}{a} = 2$; if $a = -2$, $b = -2$. So $8i$ has two square roots, $2 + 2i$ and $-2 - 2i$.

(b) If $(a + bi)^2 = 3 - 4i$, then $a^2 - b^2 = 3$ and $2ab = -4$. Therefore $b = -\dfrac{2}{a}$, and so

$$a^2 - \left(-\frac{2}{a}\right)^2 = 3, \text{ or } a^4 - 3a^2 - 4 = 0.$$

This is a quadratic equation in a^2, which can be solved by factorising the left side, $(a^2 - 4)(a^2 + 1) = 0$. Since a is real, a^2 cannot equal -1; so $a^2 = 4$, $a = \pm 2$.

If $a = 2$, $b = -\dfrac{2}{a} = -1$; if $a = -2$, $b = 1$. So $3 - 4i$ has two square roots, $2 - i$ and $-2 + i$.

You can use this method to find the square root of any complex number. The equation for a^2 will always have two roots, one of which is positive, leading to two values of a, and hence two square roots.

You will see also that, if one root is $a + bi$ the other is $-a - bi$, so that the roots can be written as $\pm (a + bi)$. But of course you cannot say that one of the roots is 'positive' and the other 'negative', because these words have no meaning for complex numbers.

In Section 7.3 you saw that complex numbers make it possible to solve any quadratic equation with real coefficients. Now that you can find square roots of complex numbers, you can solve any quadratic equation even if the coefficients are complex numbers.

Example 7.8.2*

Solve the quadratic equation $(2 - i)z^2 + (4 + 3i)z + (-1 + 3i) = 0$.

Method 1   Using the standard formula with $a = 2 - i$, $b = 4 + 3i$ and $c = -1 + 3i$ gives

$$z = \frac{-(4 + 3i) \pm \sqrt{(4 + 3i)^2 - 4 \times (2 - i) \times (-1 + 3i)}}{2(2 - i)}$$

$$= \frac{-(4 + 3i) \pm \sqrt{7 + 24i - 4 \times (1 + 7i)}}{2(2 - i)}$$

$$= \frac{-(4 + 3i) \pm \sqrt{3 - 4i}}{2(2 - i)}$$

$$= \frac{-(4 + 3i) \pm (2 - i)}{2(2 - i)} \qquad \text{(using Example 7.8.1(b))}$$

$$= \frac{-2 - 4i}{2(2 - i)} \quad \text{or} \quad \frac{-6 - 2i}{2(2 - i)}$$

$$= \frac{-1 - 2i}{2 - i} \quad \text{or} \quad \frac{-3 - i}{2 - i}$$

$$= \frac{(-1 - 2i)(2 + i)}{(2 - i)(2 + i)} \quad \text{or} \quad \frac{(-3 - i)(2 + i)}{(2 - i)(2 + i)}$$

$$= \frac{-5i}{5} \quad \text{or} \quad \frac{-5 - 5i}{5}$$

$$= -i \quad \text{or} \quad -1 - i.$$

Method 2   You can often reduce the work by first making the coefficient of z^2 real. Multiplying through by $(2 - i)^* = 2 + i$, the equation becomes

$$(2 + i)(2 - i)z^2 + (2 + i)(4 + 3i)z + (2 + i)(-1 + 3i) = 0,$$
$$5z^2 + (5 + 10i)z + (-5 + 5i) = 0,$$
$$z^2 + (1 + 2i)z + (-1 + i) = 0.$$

The standard formula with $a = 1$, $b = 1 + 2i$ and $c = -1 + i$ then gives

$$z = \frac{-(1 + 2i) \pm \sqrt{(1 + 2i)^2 - 4 \times 1 \times (-1 + i)}}{2}$$

$$= \frac{-(1 + 2i) \pm \sqrt{-3 + 4i - 4(-1 + i)}}{2}$$

$$= \frac{-(1 + 2i) \pm \sqrt{1}}{2} = \frac{-(1 + 2i) \pm 1}{2}$$

$$= \frac{-2i}{2} \quad \text{or} \quad \frac{-2 - 2i}{2}$$

$$= -i \quad \text{or} \quad -1 - i.$$

It is important to notice that although the quadratic equation has two roots, these are not now conjugate complex numbers. The property in Section 7.4 that the roots occur in conjugate pairs holds only for equations whose coefficients are real.

The fact that, with complex numbers, every quadratic equation has two roots is a particular case of a more general result:

> Every polynomial equation of degree n has n roots.

You need to understand that for this to be true, repeated roots have to count more than once. If the polynomial p(z) has a factor $(z - s)^k$ with $k > 1$, then in the equation p(z) = 0 the root $z = s$ has to count as k roots. For example, the equation of degree 5 in Example 7.5.4 has only 4 different roots (1, 2, $-2 + i$ and $-2 - i$) but the repeated root 1 counts twice because $(z - 1)^2$ is a factor of p(z).

This remarkable result is one of the main reasons that complex numbers are important. Unfortunately the proof is too difficult to give here.

Exercise 7E

1 Find the square roots of

  (a) $-2i$,   (b) $-3 + 4i$,   (c) $5 + 12i$,   (d) $8 - 6i$.

2* Solve the following equations.

  (a) $z^2 + z + (1 - i) = 0$ (b) $z^2 + (1 - i)z + (-6 + 2i) = 0$
  (c) $z^2 + 4z + (4 + 2i) = 0$ (d) $(1 + i)z^2 + 2iz + 4i = 0$
  (e) $(2 - i)z^2 + (3 + i)z - 5 = 0$ (f) $z^4 - 6z^2 + (64 - 48i) = 0$

3 Find the fourth roots of

  (a) -64,   (b) $7 + 24i$.

  Show your answers on an Argand diagram.

4 If $(x + yi)^3 = 8i$, where x and y are real numbers, prove that either $x = 0$ or $x = \pm\sqrt{3}\, y$. Hence find all the cube roots of $8i$. Show your answers on an Argand diagram.

5* If $(x + yi)^3 = 2 - 2i$, where x and y are real numbers, prove that

$$x(x^2 - 3y^2) = y(y^2 - 3x^2) = 2.$$

  Show that these equations have one solution in which $x = y$, and hence find one cube root of $2 - 2i$.

  Find the quadratic equation satisfied by the other cube roots of $2 - 2i$, and solve it.

  Show all the roots on an Argand diagram.

Miscellaneous exercise 7

1 Given that z is a complex number such that $z + 3z^* = 12 + 8\,\mathrm{i}$, find z.   (OCR)

2 Given that $3\,\mathrm{i}$ is a root of the equation $3z^3 - 5z^2 + 27z - 45 = 0$, find the other two roots. Show all the roots in an Argand diagram.   (OCR, adapted)

3 Two of the roots of a cubic equation, in which all the coefficients are real, are 2 and $1 + 3\,\mathrm{i}$. State the third root and find the cubic equation.   (OCR)

4 It is given that $3 - \mathrm{i}$ is a root of the quadratic equation $z^2 - (a + b\,\mathrm{i})\,z + 4\,(1 + 3\,\mathrm{i}) = 0$, where a and b are real. In either order,

   (a) find the values of a and b,

   (b) find the other root of the quadratic equation, given that it is of the form $k\,\mathrm{i}$, where k is real.

   Explain why the roots do not form a conjugate complex pair.   (OCR, adapted)

5 Find the roots of the equation $z^2 = 21 - 20\,\mathrm{i}$. How are they related in an Argand diagram?   (OCR, adapted)

6 Verify that $(3 - 2\,\mathrm{i})^2 = 5 - 12\,\mathrm{i}$. Find the two roots of the equation $(z - \mathrm{i})^2 = 5 - 12\,\mathrm{i}$.   (OCR)

7 You are given the complex number $w = 1 - \mathrm{i}$. Express w^2, w^3 and w^4 in the form $a + b\,\mathrm{i}$.

   (a) Given that $w^4 + 3w^3 + pw^2 + qw + 8 = 0$, where p and q are real numbers, find the values of p and q.

   (b) Write down two roots of the equation $z^4 + 3z^3 + pz^2 + qz + 8 = 0$, where p and q are the real numbers found in part (a), and hence solve the equation completely.   (MEI, adapted)

8 Solve the simultaneous equations in Example 7.3.1,

$$\left. \begin{array}{l} \mathrm{i}z + (1 + 2\,\mathrm{i})\,w = 2 + 3\,\mathrm{i} \\ (1 + \mathrm{i})\,z + \qquad \mathrm{i}w = 2 + 4\,\mathrm{i} \end{array} \right\},$$

   by writing them in the form

$$\begin{pmatrix} \mathrm{i} & 1 + 2\,\mathrm{i} \\ 1 + \mathrm{i} & \mathrm{i} \end{pmatrix} \begin{pmatrix} z \\ w \end{pmatrix} = \begin{pmatrix} 2 + 3\,\mathrm{i} \\ 2 + 4\,\mathrm{i} \end{pmatrix}$$

   and using the inverse matrix method described in Section 4.5.

9 If $s = 0.8 + 0.6\mathrm{i}$, draw an accurate Argand diagram to show the points which represent $s^{-2}, s^{-1}, s^0, s^1, s^2, s^3$.

   What do you notice about these points?

8 Roots of polynomial equations

This chapter is about the connection between the roots and the coefficients of polynomial equations. When you have completed it, you should

- be able to construct a polynomial equation given its roots
- know how to find simple symmetric functions of the roots from the coefficients of an equation
- be able to find an equation whose roots are related in a simple way to the roots of a given equation.

8.1 Quadratic polynomials and quadratic equations

Suppose that you have a quadratic polynomial whose factors you know to be $x - 1$ and $x - 2$. You might be tempted to write it immediately as $(x - 1)(x - 2)$ or $x^2 - 3x + 2$.

The quadratic polynomial $x^2 - 3x + 2$ certainly does have factors $x - 1$ and $x - 2$, and it is the simplest quadratic polynomial with these factors. But other quadratic polynomials, such as $2x^2 - 6x + 4$, have the same factors. So also does the quadratic polynomial $a(x^2 - 3x + 2)$ where a is any number except 0.

More generally, if the quadratic $ax^2 + bx + c$ has factors $x - \alpha$ and $x - \beta$, then

$$ax^2 + bx + c \equiv k(x - \alpha)(x - \beta).$$

You can see at once, by equating coefficients of x^2, that $k = a$.

Then, putting $k = a$ and expanding the polynomial on the right,

$$ax^2 + bx + c \equiv a(x^2 - (\alpha + \beta)x + \alpha\beta).$$

By equating coefficients of x and the constant terms, you find that

$$b = -a(\alpha + \beta) \quad \text{and} \quad c = a\alpha\beta.$$

Summarising:

> If the quadratic $ax^2 + bx + c$ has factors $x - \alpha$ and $x - \beta$, then
> $$\alpha + \beta = -\frac{b}{a} \quad \text{and} \quad \alpha\beta = \frac{c}{a}.$$

Some quadratic polynomials, such as $3x^2 - 6x + 3 = 0$, factorise as $k(x - \alpha)^2$, rather than as $k(x - \alpha)(x - \beta)$ with $\alpha \neq \beta$. Such a polynomial is said to have a **repeated factor** $x - \alpha$ with **multiplicity** 2.

If you equate coefficients in

$$ax^2 + bx + c \equiv a(x - \alpha)^2 \equiv a(x^2 - 2\alpha x + \alpha^2),$$

you get $b = -2a\alpha$ and $c = a\alpha^2$, so

$$2\alpha = -\frac{b}{a} \quad \text{and} \quad \alpha^2 = \frac{c}{a}.$$

These are just the equations in the box above, with $\beta = \alpha$. So the statement in the box remains true for repeated factors, provided that you interpret a repeated factor $x - \alpha$ as two factors $x - \alpha$ and $x - \beta$ with $\beta = \alpha$.

You can also express these results in terms of the roots of quadratic equations. If the quadratic polynomial $ax^2 + bx + c$ has factors $x - \alpha$ and $x - \beta$, then the equation $ax^2 + bx + c = 0$ has roots α and β. The converse of this statement is also true: if the equation $ax^2 + bx + c = 0$ has roots α and β, then the quadratic polynomial $ax^2 + bx + c$ has factors $x - \alpha$ and $x - \beta$.

The repeated factor case corresponds to quadratic equations which have only one root (for which the discriminant $b^2 - 4ac = 0$). Again, the converse is also true: if the quadratic equation has only one root α, then the quadratic polynomial factorises as $a(x - \alpha)^2$.

It follows that:

> If the quadratic equation $ax^2 + bx + c = 0$ has distinct roots α and β, then
>
> $$\alpha + \beta = -\frac{b}{a} \quad \text{and} \quad \alpha\beta = \frac{c}{a}.$$
>
> If the equation has only one root α, these relations are modified by replacing β by α.

Because the equation with one root can be included in the general case by writing $\beta = \alpha$, it is sometimes said that to have 'two equal roots', or 'coincident roots'. You can regard this as a convenient fiction; there is in fact only one root, but you will come to no harm by treating it as a pair of roots which happen to have the same value.

Notice that the expressions for $\alpha + \beta$ and $\alpha\beta$ in the box are true whether the roots are real or complex. For example, the equation $x^2 + 2x + 5 = 0$ has roots $\alpha = -1 + 2\,\mathrm{i}$ and $\beta = -1 - 2\,\mathrm{i}$. You can easily check that

$$\alpha + \beta = (-1 + 2\,\mathrm{i}) + (-1 - 2\,\mathrm{i}) = -2, \text{ which is } -\frac{2}{1}, \text{ and that}$$
$$\alpha\beta = (-1 + 2\,\mathrm{i})(-1 - 2\,\mathrm{i}) = (-1)^2 + (-2)^2 = 1 + 4 = 5, \text{ which is } \frac{5}{1}.$$

Example 8.1.1

The quadratic equation $x^2 - 6x + 20 = 0$ has roots α and β. Find $\alpha + \beta$ and $\alpha\beta$, and the value of $\alpha^2 + \beta^2$. What can you deduce from the value of $\alpha^2 + \beta^2$?

From the relations $\alpha + \beta = -\dfrac{b}{a}$ and $\alpha\beta = \dfrac{c}{a}$, you get $\alpha + \beta = 6$ and $\alpha\beta = 20$.
Since $\alpha^2 + \beta^2 = (\alpha + \beta)^2 - 2\alpha\beta$, this gives $\alpha^2 + \beta^2 = 6^2 - 2 \times 20 = -4$.

If α and β were real, $\alpha^2 + \beta^2$ could not be negative. So α and β must be (conjugate) complex. You can check this for yourself by solving the quadratic equation directly.

Expressions such as $\alpha + \beta$, $\alpha\beta$, $\alpha^2 + \beta^2$ and $\dfrac{1}{\alpha} + \dfrac{1}{\beta}$ are called **symmetric functions** of α and β. The characteristic of a symmetric function is that if you interchange α and β, the expression is unchanged, apart from the order of the terms and factors. Thus $\alpha^2 - \alpha\beta + \beta^2$ is a symmetric function since changing α and β gives $\beta^2 - \beta\alpha + \alpha^2$, which is the same as $\alpha^2 - \alpha\beta + \beta^2$. However, $\alpha + 2\beta$ is not symmetric, as changing α and β gives $2\alpha + \beta$ which is not the same as $\alpha + 2\beta$.

Exercise 8A

1 Use the sum and product of the roots to find the simplest quadratic equation with the following roots.

(a) 2, 3   (b) −3, 1   (c) 2, −2   (d) 1, $-\frac{1}{2}$

2 Write down the sum and product of the roots for each of the following equations.

(a) $x^2 - 2x - 1 = 0$ (b) $2x^2 + 4x - 3 = 0$ (c) $3x^2 - x + 1 = 0$

3 Let the roots of the equation $x^2 - 4x + 2 = 0$ be α and β. Without finding α and β, find the values of each of the following symmetric functions.

(a) $3\alpha + 3\beta$ (b) $\alpha^2 + 2\alpha\beta + \beta^2$ (c) $\alpha^2 - \alpha\beta + \beta^2$

(d) $(\alpha - \beta)^2$ (e) $\dfrac{1}{\alpha} + \dfrac{1}{\beta}$ (f) $\dfrac{1}{\alpha^2} + \dfrac{1}{\beta^2}$

4 Write down a quadratic equation with integer coefficients such that the sum of the roots is the first number given, and the product is the second number given.

(a) 3, −2   (b) 2, 0   (c) $\frac{1}{2}$, 3   (d) $\frac{1}{3}$, $\frac{1}{2}$

8.2 Equations with given roots

Sometimes you may have a quadratic equation whose roots are α and β, and you want to find an equation whose roots are some functions of α and β. This is best illustrated by an example.

Example 8.2.1

The quadratic equation $x^2 + 5x + 7 = 0$ has roots α and β. Find an equation with roots 2α and 2β.

Two methods are given. The first uses 'brute force'; the second is more subtle and usually quicker.

Method 1   From the equation, $\alpha + \beta = -5$ and $\alpha\beta = 7$.

So the sum and the product of the roots of the new equation are

$$2\alpha + 2\beta = 2\,(\alpha + \beta) = -10 \quad \text{and} \quad (2\alpha)(2\beta) = 4\alpha\beta = 28.$$

An equation which has -10 as the sum of its roots and 28 as the product is

$$x^2 - (-10)\,x + 28 = 0 \quad \text{or} \quad x^2 + 10x + 28 = 0.$$

Method 2   If $u = 2\alpha$ or $u = 2\beta$, then $\alpha = \tfrac{1}{2}u$ or $\beta = \tfrac{1}{2}u$. Either way, $\tfrac{1}{2}u$ satisfies the equation $x^2 + 5x + 7 = 0$. Therefore $\left(\tfrac{1}{2}u\right)^2 + 5\left(\tfrac{1}{2}u\right) + 7 = 0$, or $\tfrac{1}{4}u^2 + \tfrac{5}{2}u + 7 = 0$. Multiplying through by 4 gives $u^2 + 10u + 28 = 0$.

Note that the equations $x^2 + 10x + 28 = 0$ and $u^2 + 10u + 28 = 0$ have the same roots. It does not matter what letter is given to the 'variable' in the polynomial. Either answer, $x^2 + 10x + 28 = 0$ or $u^2 + 10u + 28 = 0$, is acceptable.

In more complicated situations, Method 2 of Example 8.2.1 is usually more effective than Method 1, and you should use it in preference to Method 1 whenever you can.

Sometimes you may know a property of the roots of an equation, and you can deduce something about the coefficients.

Example 8.2.2

For the quadratic equation $ax^2 + bx + c = 0$, one root is twice the other. Prove that $2b^2 = 9ac$.

Suppose that the roots of $ax^2 + bx + c = 0$ are α and 2α. Then $\alpha + 2\alpha = -\dfrac{b}{a}$ and $\alpha \times 2\alpha = \dfrac{c}{a}$, so $3\alpha = -\dfrac{b}{a}$ and $2\alpha^2 = \dfrac{c}{a}$.

Therefore $\alpha = -\dfrac{b}{3a}$ and $\alpha^2 = \dfrac{c}{2a}$, so $\left(-\dfrac{b}{3a}\right)^2 = \dfrac{c}{2a}$.

Thus $\dfrac{b^2}{9a^2} = \dfrac{c}{2a}$, so $2b^2 = 9ac$.

Exercise 8B

1 The equation $x^2 + 2x + 5 = 0$ has roots α and β. Use Method 1 of Example 8.2.1 to find the equations which have the following roots.

(a) 3α, 3β (b) $1 + \alpha$, $1 + \beta$ (c) $\alpha + 2\beta$, $2\alpha + \beta$

(d) α^2, β^2 (e) $\dfrac{1}{\alpha}$, $\dfrac{1}{\beta}$ (f) $\dfrac{1}{\alpha^2}$, $\dfrac{1}{\beta^2}$

2 The equation $x^2 + 4x + 7 = 0$ has roots α and β. Use Method 2 of Example 8.2.1 to find the equations which have the following roots.

(a) 3α, 3β (b) $1 + \alpha$, $1 + \beta$ (c) $\alpha + 2\beta$, $2\alpha + \beta$

(d) α^2, β^2 (e) $\dfrac{1}{\alpha}$, $\dfrac{1}{\beta}$ (f) $\dfrac{1}{\alpha^2}$, $\dfrac{1}{\beta^2}$

3 One root of the equation $ax^2 + bx + c = 0$ is the reciprocal of the other. Prove that $c = a$.

4 One root of the equation $ax^2 + bx + c = 0$ is three times the other. Prove that $3b^2 = 16ac$.

5 The roots of the equation $ax^2 + bx + c = 0$ differ by 1. Prove that $b^2 - a^2 - 4ac = 0$.

8.3 Roots of cubic equations

The ideas of Section 8.1 can be extended to cubic equations.

A general cubic polynomial can be written as $ax^3 + bx^2 + cx + d$, where $a \neq 0$. If this has factors $x - \alpha$, $x - \beta$ and $x - \gamma$, then

$$ax^3 + bx^2 + cx + d \equiv k(x - \alpha)(x - \beta)(x - \gamma).$$

Equating coefficients of x^3 shows that $k = a$.

Expanding the product of the factors on the right gives

$$\begin{aligned}
(x - \alpha)(x - \beta)(x - \gamma) &= (x^2 - (\alpha + \beta)x + \alpha\beta)(x - \gamma) \\
&= (x^2 - (\alpha + \beta)x + \alpha\beta)x - (x^2 - (\alpha + \beta)x + \alpha\beta)\gamma \\
&= x^3 - (\alpha + \beta)x^2 + \alpha\beta x - \gamma x^2 + (\alpha + \beta)\gamma x - \alpha\beta\gamma \\
&= x^3 - (\alpha + \beta + \gamma)x^2 + (\beta\gamma + \gamma\alpha + \alpha\beta)x - \alpha\beta\gamma.
\end{aligned}$$

This gives the identity

$$ax^3 + bx^2 + cx + d \equiv a(x^3 - (\alpha + \beta + \gamma)x^2 + (\beta\gamma + \gamma\alpha + \alpha\beta)x - \alpha\beta\gamma).$$

Equating coefficients of x^2, x and the constant terms shows that

$$b = -a(\alpha + \beta + \gamma), \quad c = a(\beta\gamma + \gamma\alpha + \alpha\beta) \quad \text{and} \quad d = -a\alpha\beta\gamma.$$

These results can also be stated in terms of the roots of a cubic equation.

> If the cubic polynomial $ax^3 + bx^2 + cx + d$ has factors $x - \alpha$, $x - \beta$ and $x - \gamma$, or the cubic equation $ax^3 + bx^2 + cx + d = 0$ has roots α, β and γ, then
>
> $$\alpha + \beta + \gamma = -\frac{b}{a}, \quad \beta\gamma + \gamma\alpha + \alpha\beta = \frac{c}{a} \quad \text{and} \quad \alpha\beta\gamma = -\frac{d}{a}.$$

These relations are often written in the form $\sum \alpha = -\frac{b}{a}, \sum \beta\gamma = \frac{c}{a}, \alpha\beta\gamma = -\frac{d}{a}$, where $\sum \alpha$ denotes $\alpha + \beta + \gamma$ and $\sum \beta\gamma$ denotes $\beta\gamma + \gamma\alpha + \alpha\beta$. The reason why the terms of $\beta\gamma + \gamma\alpha + \alpha\beta$ are written in that order is that the first term, $\beta\gamma$, leaves out α; the second term, $\gamma\alpha$, leaves out β; and the third term, $\alpha\beta$, leaves out γ.

This notation is easily used for similar relations in quadratic and higher degree equations.

When the idea of a symmetric function is extended to roots of a cubic equation, the expression has to be unchanged if *any* of the pairs β and γ, γ and α, or α and β are swapped. You can check that $\alpha + \beta + \gamma$, $\beta\gamma + \gamma\alpha + \alpha\beta$ and $\alpha\beta\gamma$ all have this property. For example, swapping α and γ in $\beta\gamma + \gamma\alpha + \alpha\beta$ changes the expression to $\beta\alpha + \alpha\gamma + \gamma\beta$, which is just another way of writing $\beta\gamma + \gamma\alpha + \alpha\beta$.

A cubic may have repeated factors in two ways:

- It may have a repeated factor of multiplicity 2 and a distinct linear factor, so that it factorises as $a(x - \alpha)^2(x - \gamma)$. The results in the box are then modified by replacing β by α.

- It may have a repeated factor of multiplicity 3, so that it factorises as $a(x - \alpha)^3$. The results are then modified by replacing both β and γ by α.

Example 8.3.1
Which of   (a) $\alpha\beta + \alpha\gamma$,   (b) $(\beta + \gamma)(\gamma + \alpha)(\alpha + \beta)$,   (c) $\beta^2\gamma + \gamma^2\alpha + \alpha^2\beta$ are symmetric functions of α, β and γ?

(a) If you swap α and β in $\alpha\beta + \alpha\gamma$ you get $\beta\alpha + \beta\gamma$, which is not the same expression as $\alpha\beta + \alpha\gamma$. So $\alpha\beta + \alpha\gamma$ is not a symmetric function.

(b) Swapping α and β in $(\beta + \gamma)(\gamma + \alpha)(\alpha + \beta)$ gives $(\alpha + \gamma)(\gamma + \beta)(\beta + \alpha)$, swapping α and γ gives $(\beta + \alpha)(\alpha + \gamma)(\gamma + \beta)$, and swapping β and γ gives $(\gamma + \beta)(\beta + \alpha)(\alpha + \gamma)$. All these are the same as $(\beta + \gamma)(\gamma + \alpha)(\alpha + \beta)$, so the function is symmetric.

(c) Swapping α and β in $\beta^2\gamma + \gamma^2\alpha + \alpha^2\beta$ gives $\alpha^2\gamma + \gamma^2\beta + \beta^2\alpha$, which is not the same as $\beta^2\gamma + \gamma^2\alpha + \alpha^2\beta$, so $\beta^2\gamma + \gamma^2\alpha + \alpha^2\beta$ is not a symmetric function.

In Example 8.1.1 you found the symmetric function $\alpha^2 + \beta^2$ from the known functions $\alpha + \beta$ and $\alpha\beta$ by using the identity

$$\alpha^2 + \beta^2 \equiv (\alpha + \beta)^2 - 2\alpha\beta.$$

Similar identities, which are useful with cubic equations, are:

$$\alpha^2 + \beta^2 + \gamma^2 = (\alpha + \beta + \gamma)^2 - 2(\beta\gamma + \gamma\alpha + \alpha\beta)$$
$$\alpha^3 + \beta^3 + \gamma^3 - 3\alpha\beta\gamma \equiv (\alpha + \beta + \gamma)(\alpha^2 + \beta^2 + \gamma^2 - \beta\gamma - \gamma\alpha - \alpha\beta)$$
$$\equiv (\alpha + \beta + \gamma)((\alpha + \beta + \gamma)^2 - 3(\beta\gamma + \gamma\alpha + \alpha\beta))$$

You can check these identities for yourself.

Example 8.3.2
The cubic equation $2x^3 + 3x^2 + 4x + 5 = 0$ has roots α, β and γ. Find the values of
(a) $\alpha^2 + \beta^2 + \gamma^2$, (b) $\dfrac{1}{\alpha} + \dfrac{1}{\beta} + \dfrac{1}{\gamma}$.

Using the result in the first box, $\alpha + \beta + \gamma = -\frac{3}{2}$, $\beta\gamma + \gamma\alpha + \alpha\beta = \frac{4}{2} = 2$ and $\alpha\beta\gamma = -\frac{5}{2}$.

(a) Using the result in the second blue-tinted box,

$$\alpha^2 + \beta^2 + \gamma^2 = (\alpha + \beta + \gamma)^2 - 2(\beta\gamma + \gamma\alpha + \alpha\beta) = \left(-\tfrac{3}{2}\right)^2 - 2 \times 2 = -\tfrac{7}{4}.$$

(b) $\dfrac{1}{\alpha} + \dfrac{1}{\beta} + \dfrac{1}{\gamma} = \dfrac{\beta\gamma + \gamma\alpha + \alpha\beta}{\alpha\beta\gamma} = \dfrac{2}{-\frac{5}{2}} = -\tfrac{4}{5}.$

8.4 Finding equations with given roots

Suppose that a given equation $2x^3 + 3x^2 + 4x + 5 = 0$ has roots α, β and γ. How can you find the equation with roots α^{-1}, β^{-1} and γ^{-1}?

The best way is to use a substitution method, such as that in Method 2 of Example 8.2.1.

Let u be any one of the new roots, say $u = \alpha^{-1}$. Then $\alpha = u^{-1}$. But since α satisfies the original equation, $2\alpha^3 + 3\alpha^2 + 4\alpha + 5 = 0$, so

$$2(u^{-1})^3 + 3(u^{-1})^2 + 4(u^{-1}) + 5 = 0.$$

Multiplying by u^3 gives

$$2 + 3u + 4u^2 + 5u^3 = 0, \quad \text{or} \quad 5u^3 + 4u^2 + 3u + 2 = 0.$$

Since this is true if u is any one of α^{-1}, β^{-1} and γ^{-1}, it is the equation required.

Example 8.4.1

The cubic equation $x^3 - 2x^2 + 3x - 4 = 0$ has roots α, β and γ. Find the equation which has roots α^2, β^2 and γ^2.

Let $u = \alpha^2$.

Then $\alpha = \pm\sqrt{u}$, so $\pm\sqrt{u}$ satisfies $x^3 - 2x^2 + 3x - 4 = 0$.

Therefore

$$\left(\pm\sqrt{u}\right)^3 - 2\left(\pm\sqrt{u}\right)^2 + 3\left(\pm\sqrt{u}\right) - 4 = 0,$$
$$\pm u\sqrt{u} - 2u \pm 3\sqrt{u} - 4 = 0.$$

So $\pm\sqrt{u}(u + 3) = 2u + 4$.

Then, squaring both sides,

$$u(u + 3)^2 = (2u + 4)^2,$$

that is

$$u^3 + 6u^2 + 9u = 4u^2 + 16u + 16, \quad \text{or} \quad u^3 + 2u^2 - 7u - 16 = 0.$$

If you let $u = \beta^2$ or $u = \gamma^2$ you get the same result, so

$$u^3 + 2u^2 - 7u - 16 = 0$$

is the required equation.

Example 8.4.2

The cubic equation $x^3 + 3x^2 + 4x + 5 = 0$ has roots α, β and γ. Find an equation which has roots $\beta + \gamma$, $\gamma + \alpha$ and $\alpha + \beta$.

Let $u = \beta + \gamma$.

Then $u + \alpha = \alpha + \beta + \gamma = -3$, so $\alpha = -u - 3$.

But α satisfies the equation $x^3 + 3x^2 + 4x + 5 = 0$, so

$$(-u - 3)^3 + 3(-u - 3)^2 + 4(-u - 3) + 5 = 0,$$

which simplifies to

$$u^3 + 6u^2 + 13u + 7 = 0.$$

If you let $u = \gamma + \alpha$ or $u = \alpha + \beta$ you get the same result, so

$$u^3 + 6u^2 + 13u + 7 = 0 \text{ is the required equation.}$$

Example 8.4.3

The equation $x^3 - 9x^2 + 31x - 39 = 0$ has roots α, β and γ which are in arithmetic progression. Solve the equation.

In this type of problem it almost always results in easier algebra to let the roots be $\beta - d$, β and $\beta + d$, rather than α, $\alpha + d$ and $\alpha + 2d$.

Let the roots be $\beta - d$, β and $\beta + d$.

Then the sum of the roots is

$$(\beta - d) + \beta + (\beta + d) = 3\beta.$$

But the sum of the roots is $-(-9) = 9$, so $\beta = 3$.

So, factorising the cubic gives $x^3 - 9x^2 + 31x - 39 = (x - 3)(x^2 - 6x + 13)$.

The other roots of the equation $x^3 - 9x^2 + 31x - 39 = 0$ come from solving $x^2 - 6x + 13 = 0$, giving $x = 3 \pm 2i$.

So the roots are 3 and $3 \pm 2i$.

The numbers $3 - 2i$, 3 and $3 + 2i$ form an arithmetic progression with first term $3 - 2i$ and common difference $2i$. Or if you put the three terms in reverse order the common difference is $-2i$.

Example 8.4.4

The roots of the equation $x^3 + ax^2 + bx + c = 0$, where $c \neq 0$, are in geometric progression. Prove that $b^3 = a^3c$.

Let the roots be $\dfrac{\beta}{r}$, β and $r\beta$.

Then the product of the roots is β^3 which is $-c$.

If $\beta^3 = -c$, then $\sqrt[3]{-c}$ is a root of the equation $x^3 + ax^2 + bx + c = 0$, and so satisfies the equation.

Therefore $\left(\sqrt[3]{-c}\right)^3 + a\left(\sqrt[3]{-c}\right)^2 + b\left(\sqrt[3]{-c}\right) + c = 0$.

So $-c + ac^{\frac{2}{3}} - bc^{\frac{1}{3}} + c = 0$,   which reduces to $ac^{\frac{2}{3}} - bc^{\frac{1}{3}} = 0$.

Dividing through by $c^{\frac{1}{3}}$, and then cubing, gives $b^3 = a^3c$.

Exercise 8C

1 Find the simplest cubic equations with the following roots.

(a) 2, 3, 4   (b) −1, 0, 2   (c) 0, 2, −2

2 Which of the following are symmetric functions of α, β and γ?

(a) $\alpha + \beta + \gamma$ (b) $(\alpha - \beta)^2 + (\alpha - \gamma)^2$ (c) $(\alpha - \beta + \gamma)^2$

3 Let the roots of the equation $x^3 - 6x + 2 = 0$ be α, β and γ. Find the values of each of the following symmetric functions.

(a) $4\alpha + 4\beta + 4\gamma$

(b) $\alpha^2 + \beta^2 + \gamma^2$

(c) $(\beta - \gamma)^2 + (\gamma - \alpha)^2 + (\alpha - \beta)^2$

(d) $\dfrac{1}{\alpha} + \dfrac{1}{\beta} + \dfrac{1}{\gamma}$

4 The equation $x^3 + 2x^2 + 3x + 4 = 0$ has roots α, β and γ. Use Method 2 of Example 8.2.1 to find the equations which have the following roots.

(a) 2α, 2β, 2γ (b) $2 + \alpha$, $2 + \beta$, $2 + \gamma$

(c) α^2, β^2, γ^2 (d) $\dfrac{1}{\alpha}$, $\dfrac{1}{\beta}$, $\dfrac{1}{\gamma}$

5 The equation $2x^3 - 5x^2 + 3x + 4 = 0$ has roots α, β and γ. Find the equations which have the following roots.

(a) $\alpha - 1$, $\beta - 1$, $\gamma - 1$ (b) 3α, 3β, 3γ

6 The roots of the equation $x^3 - 3bx^2 + 3cx - d = 0$ are in arithmetic progression. Prove that one of the roots is b, and find a condition for the roots to be in arithmetic progression. Find the possible values of the common difference in terms of b and d.

7 Find a condition for the roots of the equation $x^3 - bx^2 + cx - d = 0$ to be in geometric progression. Find in terms of b and d a quadratic equation satisfied by the possible common ratios of the progression.

8 Write down the equation whose roots are p, q and r, where $p + q + r = 6$, $qr + rp + pq = 11$ and $pqr = 6$. Hence solve the equations.

9 Solve the simultaneous equations $p + q + r = 6$, $p^2 + q^2 + r^2 = 26$ and $pqr = -12$.

Miscellaneous exercise 8

1 The roots of $x^2 - 10x + 3 = 0$ are α and β. Find the values of $\alpha^2 + \beta^2$ and $\alpha^4 + \beta^4$.

2 You are given that the roots of the equation $x^3 + 3x^2 + 7x + 5 = 0$ are in arithmetic progression. Solve the equation.

3 The quadratic equation $x^2 + ax + b = 0$ has roots α and β. Find the equation which has roots $\dfrac{2}{\alpha}$ and $\dfrac{2}{\beta}$.

4 Solve the simultaneous equations $\alpha + \beta = 2$, $\alpha\beta = 2$.

5 (a) Show that $(p + q + r)(p^2 + q^2 + r^2 - qr - rp - pq) = p^3 + q^3 + r^3 - 3pqr$.

   (b) Hence solve the simultaneous equations $p + q + r = 2$, $p^2 + q^2 + r^2 = 6$ and $p^3 + q^3 + r^3 = 8$.

6 Find the equation whose roots are the fourth powers of the roots of the equation $x^3 + x + 1 = 0$. Hence find the sum of the fourth powers of the roots of the equation $x^3 + x + 1 = 0$.

7 The quadratic equation $x^2 + 5x + 13 = 0$ has roots α and β.

   (a) Show that $\alpha^2 + \beta^2 = -1$, and hence describe the nature of the roots α and β.

   (b) Find an equation with integer coefficients whose roots are $\dfrac{\alpha}{\beta} - 1$ and $\dfrac{\beta}{\alpha} - 1$.

8 The equation $x^2 + 6x + 10 = 0$ has roots α and β. Find the values of $\alpha^2 + \beta^2$ and $\alpha^3 + \beta^3$. Find a quadratic equation with integer coefficients having roots $\alpha^3\beta$ and $\alpha\beta^3$.

9 The equation $x^2 + 3x + 1 = 0$ has roots α and β. Find the values of $\alpha^2 + \beta^2$ and $\dfrac{\alpha}{\beta} + \dfrac{\beta}{\alpha}$.

   Find an equation with integer coefficients having roots $\dfrac{\alpha + 2\beta}{\beta}$ and $\dfrac{\beta + 2\alpha}{\alpha}$.

10 The equation $x^3 - 5x^2 + 8x - 6 = 0$ has roots α, β and γ. Find the equation whose roots are $\alpha - 3$, $\beta - 3$ and $\gamma - 3$, and solve the original equation.

11 The roots of the equation $x^3 - ax^2 + bx - c = 0$ are α, β and γ. Prove that if $\alpha\beta = \alpha + \beta$ then $\gamma = a + c - b$.

12 Without attempting to solve the equation $3x^3 - 2x^2 + x - 1 = 0$ find the sum of the squares of its roots. Hence show that the equation has one real and two complex roots.

13 The cubic equation $ax^3 + bx^2 + cx + d = 0$ has the property that two of its roots are the reciprocals of each other. Prove that $a^2 - d^2 = ac - bd$.

   Verify that this condition holds for the equation $9x^3 + 24x^2 - 11x - 6 = 0$, and solve it.

14* The roots of the equation $x^3 + ax + b = 0$ are α, β and γ. Find the equation with roots $\dfrac{\beta}{\gamma} + \dfrac{\gamma}{\beta}$, $\dfrac{\gamma}{\alpha} + \dfrac{\alpha}{\gamma}$ and $\dfrac{\alpha}{\beta} + \dfrac{\beta}{\alpha}$.

9 Modulus and argument

A complex number can be described by its real and imaginary parts. It can also be described by giving two other measurements, its modulus and argument. When you have completed this chapter, you should

- know the meaning of modulus, and be able to use it algebraically
- know what is meant by the argument of a complex number
- be able to use complex numbers in geometric contexts.

For Section 9.3 you will need to be familiar with the measurement of angles in radians, as explained in C2 Section 9.1.

9.1 The modulus of a complex number

You saw in Section 7.6 that a complex number can be represented by a translation in an Argand diagram. In Fig. 7.8, reproduced here as Fig. 9.1, the distance covered by the translation $s = a + b\text{i}$ is $\sqrt{a^2 + b^2}$. If s is represented by a point S in an Argand diagram (Fig. 9.2) this is the distance of the point S from O. It is called the **modulus** of s, and is denoted by $|s|$.

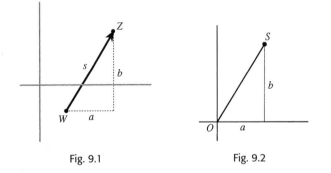

Fig. 9.1   Fig. 9.2

You have already seen this notation used for the modulus of a real number (see Section 0.2). But there is no danger of confusion; if s is the real number $a + 0\text{i}$, then $|s|$ is $\sqrt{a^2 + 0^2} = \sqrt{a^2}$, which is $|a|$ as defined for the real number a (see C3 Section 7.7). So the modulus of a complex number is just an extension of the modulus of a real number.

But beware! If s is complex, then $|s|$ does not equal $\sqrt{s^2}$.

In fact, you have met the expression $a^2 + b^2$ already (in Sections 7.2 and 7.3), as $(a + b\text{i})(a - b\text{i})$, or ss^*. So the correct generalisation of $|a| = \sqrt{a^2}$ is $|s| = \sqrt{ss^*}$. (Notice that, if a is real, then $a^* = a$, so that $a^2 = aa^*$. Thus the rule $|s| = \sqrt{ss^*}$ holds whether s is real or complex.)

If s is a complex number, then

$$|s| = \sqrt{ss^*}.$$

If $s = a + b\,\mathrm{i}$, where a and b are real, then

$$|s| = \sqrt{(a + b\,\mathrm{i})(a - b\,\mathrm{i})} = \sqrt{a^2 + b^2}.$$

You can use the modulus and an Argand diagram to link complex numbers with coordinate geometry. If S and T represent complex numbers s and t, where $s = a + b\mathrm{i}$ and $t = c + d\mathrm{i}$, then

$$\begin{aligned} \text{distance } ST = |t - s| &= \sqrt{(t - s)(t - s)^*} \\ &= \sqrt{((c - a) + (d - b)\,\mathrm{i})((c - a) - (d - b)\,\mathrm{i})} \\ &= \sqrt{(c - a)^2 + (d - b)^2}, \end{aligned}$$

which is the familiar expression for the distance between the points (a, b) and (c, d).

In problems which require the interpretation of the modulus of a complex number in terms of coordinates, you have a choice between writing $|s| = \sqrt{ss^*}$ and using complex number algebra as long as you can, or of going directly to $|s| = \sqrt{a^2 + b^2}$ and using real number algebra. In Examples 9.1.1 and 9.1.2 these are Method 1 and Method 2 respectively.

Example 9.1.1

In an Argand diagram, what can you say about a point Z representing a complex number z if $|z - 2\mathrm{i}| = 3$? Verify the answer by expressing this equation in cartesian coordinates.

In Fig. 9.3, the expression $z - 2\mathrm{i}$ corresponds to the translation which takes the point C representing the number $2\mathrm{i}$ to the point Z. So the equation $|z - 2\mathrm{i}| = 3$ states that the distance CZ is equal to 3. That is, Z lies on a circle with centre C and radius 3.

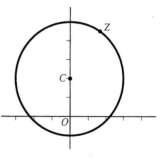

Method 1 To express this in cartesian form, begin by noting that $|z - 2\mathrm{i}|^2$ is equal to $(z - 2\mathrm{i})(z - 2\mathrm{i})^*$, and recall from Section 7.4 that $(z - 2\mathrm{i})^* = z^* - (2\mathrm{i})^* = z^* - (-2\mathrm{i}) = z^* + 2\mathrm{i}$. So $(z - 2\mathrm{i})(z^* + 2\mathrm{i}) = 9$.

Fig. 9.3

Multiplying out the left side gives

$$(z - 2\mathrm{i})(z^* + 2\mathrm{i}) = zz^* + 2\mathrm{i}(z - z^*) + 4.$$

Recalling that, if $z = x + y\mathrm{i}$, $zz^* = x^2 + y^2$ and $z - z^* = 2y\mathrm{i}$, the equation becomes

$$x^2 + y^2 + 4y\,\mathrm{i}^2 + 4 = 9, \quad \text{which is} \quad x^2 + y^2 - 4y + 4 = 9.$$

This equation can be written as

$$x^2 + (y - 2)^2 = 9,$$

which you will recognise as the equation of a circle with centre $(0, 2)$ and radius 3 (see C1 Section 13.1).

Method 2   Write $z = x + y\,\mathrm{i}$, so that $z - 2\mathrm{i} = x + y\,\mathrm{i} - 2\mathrm{i} = x + (y - 2)\,\mathrm{i}$.

Then $|z - 2\,\mathrm{i}| = \sqrt{x^2 + (y - 2)^2}$.

So the equation $|z - 2\,\mathrm{i}| = 3$ in cartesian form is

$$\sqrt{x^2 + (y - 2)^2} = 3,$$

which is

$$x^2 + (y - 2)^2 = 9.$$

Example 9.1.2
In an Argand diagram, points S and T represent 4 and $2\,\mathrm{i}$ respectively (see Fig. 9.4). Identify the points P such that $PS < PT$.

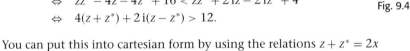

Fig. 9.4

Method 1
$$
\begin{aligned}
PS < PT \quad &\Leftrightarrow \quad |z - 4| < |z - 2\,\mathrm{i}| \\
&\Leftrightarrow \quad |z - 4|^2 < |z - 2\,\mathrm{i}|^2 \\
&\Leftrightarrow \quad (z - 4)(z^* - 4^*) < (z - 2\,\mathrm{i})(z^* - (2\,\mathrm{i})^*) \\
&\Leftrightarrow \quad (z - 4)(z^* - 4) < (z - 2\,\mathrm{i})(z^* + 2\,\mathrm{i}) \\
&\Leftrightarrow \quad zz^* - 4z - 4z^* + 16 < zz^* + 2\,\mathrm{i}z - 2\,\mathrm{i}z^* + 4 \\
&\Leftrightarrow \quad 4(z + z^*) + 2\,\mathrm{i}(z - z^*) > 12.
\end{aligned}
$$

You can put this into cartesian form by using the relations $z + z^* = 2x$ and $z - z^* = 2y\,\mathrm{i}$ from Section 7.3. Then

$$
\begin{aligned}
PS < PT \quad &\Leftrightarrow \quad 8x + 2\,\mathrm{i}(2y\,\mathrm{i}) > 12 \\
&\Leftrightarrow \quad 8x - 4y > 12 \quad \Leftrightarrow \quad 2x - y > 3.
\end{aligned}
$$

Method 2   In cartesian coordinates, S is the point $(4, 0)$, T is $(0, 2)$ and P is (x, y).

So $PS = \sqrt{(x - 4)^2 + (y - 0)^2}$ and $PT = \sqrt{(x - 0)^2 + (y - 2)^2}$.

Then $
\begin{aligned}
PS < PT \quad &\Leftrightarrow \quad \sqrt{(x - 4)^2 + y^2} < \sqrt{x^2 + (y - 2)^2} \\
&\Leftrightarrow \quad (x - 4)^2 + y^2 < x^2 + (y - 2)^2 \\
&\Leftrightarrow \quad x^2 - 8x + 16 + y^2 < x^2 + y^2 - 4y + 4 \\
&\Leftrightarrow \quad 12 < 8x - 4y \\
&\Leftrightarrow \quad 2x - y > 3.
\end{aligned}
$

The line $2x - y = 3$ is the perpendicular bisector of ST, shown as a dotted line in Fig. 9.4. This cuts the axes at $(\frac{3}{2}, 0)$ and $(0, -3)$; as complex numbers, these are the points $\frac{3}{2}$ and $-3\,\mathrm{i}$. You can check that these points are equidistant from the points 4 and $2\,\mathrm{i}$; that is, $|\frac{3}{2} - 4| = |\frac{3}{2} - 2\,\mathrm{i}|$ and $|-3\,\mathrm{i} - 4| = |-3\,\mathrm{i} - 2\,\mathrm{i}|$.

Example 9.1.3
In an Argand diagram the points S and T represent the numbers 4 and 1 respectively (see Fig. 9.5). Show that the points such that $SP = 2TP$ lie on a circle.

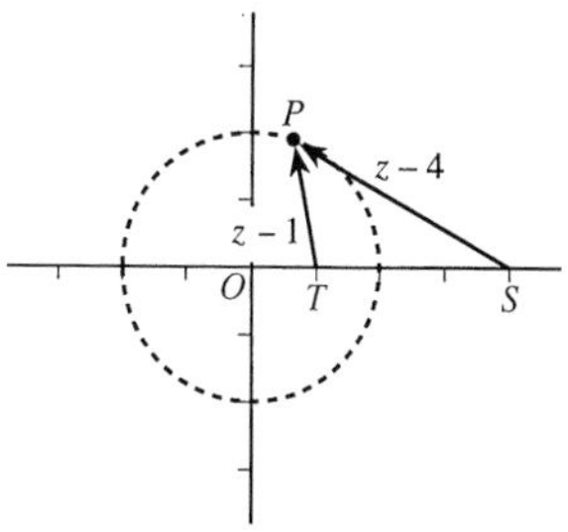

If P represents z,

$$SP = 2TP \quad \Leftrightarrow \quad |z - 4| = 2|z - 1|$$
$$\Leftrightarrow \quad |z - 4|^2 = 4|z - 1|^2$$
$$\Leftrightarrow \quad (z - 4)(z^* - 4^*) = 4(z - 1)(z^* - 1^*)$$
$$\Leftrightarrow \quad (z - 4)(z^* - 4) = 4(z - 1)(z^* - 1)$$
$$\Leftrightarrow \quad zz^* - 4z - 4z^* + 16 = 4(zz^* - z - z^* + 1)$$
$$\Leftrightarrow \quad zz^* - 4z - 4z^* + 16 = 4zz^* - 4z - 4z^* + 4$$
$$\Leftrightarrow \quad 12 = 3zz^*$$
$$\Leftrightarrow \quad zz^* = 4.$$

Fig. 9.5

Since $zz^* = |z|^2$, this can be written as

$$|z|^2 = 4, \quad \text{so} \quad |z| = 2.$$

That is, the distance of P from the origin is 2. So P lies on a circle with centre O and radius 2.

9.2* Algebraic properties of the modulus

Two important properties of the modulus are:

$$|st| = |s||t|, \quad \left|\frac{s}{t}\right| = \frac{|s|}{|t|}.$$

These are easy to prove by using $|z| = \sqrt{zz^*}$:

$$|st|^2 = (st)(st)^* = (st)(s^*t^*) \quad \text{and} \quad \left|\frac{s}{t}\right|^2 = \left(\frac{s}{t}\right)\left(\frac{s}{t}\right)^* = \left(\frac{s}{t}\right)\left(\frac{s^*}{t^*}\right).$$

So

$$|st|^2 = (ss^*)(tt^*) = |s|^2|t|^2 \quad \text{and} \quad \left|\frac{s}{t}\right|^2 = \frac{ss^*}{tt^*} = \frac{|s|^2}{|t|^2}.$$

The results follow by taking the square roots.

There are no similar equations for $|s + t|$ and $|s - t|$, but there are inequalities connecting them with $|s|$ and $|t|$. Fig. 9.6 shows the parallelogram construction for getting the point in the Argand diagram representing $s + t$ from the points representing s and t (see Section 7.7). This parallelogram has sides of length $|s|$ and $|t|$, and the diagonal has length $|s + t|$. Using the geometrical theorem that the sum of two sides of a triangle is greater than the third side (or equal, if the triangle collapses so that the vertices are all in one line),

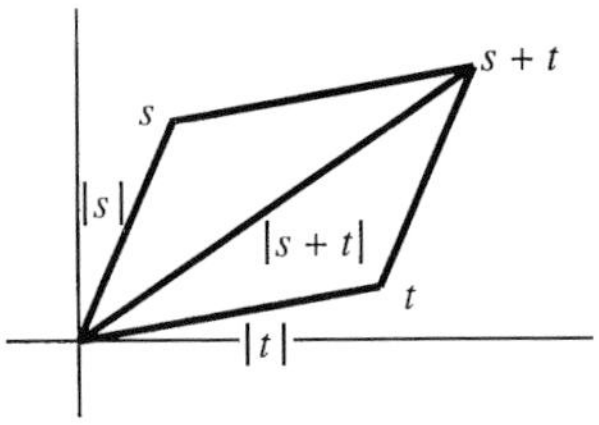

Fig. 9.6

$$|s| + |t| \geqslant |s + t|.$$

That is,

$$|s + t| \leqslant |s| + |t|.$$

Fig. 9.7 shows a similar situation for $s - t$, based on the equation

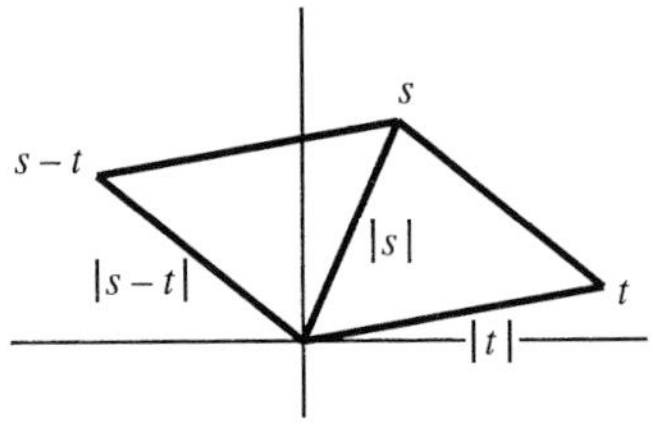

$$(s - t) + t = s.$$

This time the sides of the parallelogram are $|s - t|$ and $|t|$, and the diagonal has length $|s|$. So

$$|s - t| + |t| \geqslant |s|.$$

Fig. 9.7

That is,

$$|s - t| \geqslant |s| - |t|.$$

Example 9.2.1

S and T are the points representing -4 and 4 in an Argand diagram. A point P moves so that $SP + TP = 10$ (see Fig. 9.8). Prove that $3 \leqslant OP \leqslant 5$.

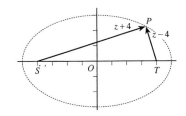

Fig. 9.8

If P represents z, then $SP + TP = |z + 4| + |z - 4|$, so that z satisfies $|z + 4| + |z - 4| = 10$.

Then

$$
\begin{aligned}
OP &= |z| = \left|\tfrac{1}{2}((z + 4) + (z - 4))\right| \\
&\leqslant \tfrac{1}{2}(|z + 4| + |z - 4|) \quad \text{(using } |s + t| \leqslant |s| + |t|) \\
&\leqslant \tfrac{1}{2} \times 10 = 5.
\end{aligned}
$$

Also, $(|z + 4| + |z - 4|)^2 = 100$, and $(|z + 4| - |z - 4|)^2 \geqslant 0$; adding,

$$(|z + 4| + |z - 4|)^2 + (|z + 4| - |z - 4|)^2 \geqslant 100,$$
$$2|z + 4|^2 + 2|z - 4|^2 \geqslant 100,$$
$$(z + 4)(z^* + 4^*) + (z - 4)(z^* - 4^*) \geqslant 50,$$
$$2zz^* + 32 \geqslant 50, \quad \text{which is} \quad |z|^2 \geqslant 9; \quad \text{that is,} \quad OP \geqslant 3.$$

You probably know that the property $SP + TP = 10$ defines an ellipse. OP takes its greatest value of 5 when S, T and P are in a straight line, at the ends of the major axis; and it takes its smallest value of 3 when $|z + 4| = |z - 4|$, that is when $SP = TP$, at the ends of the minor axis.

Exercise 9A

1 Draw an Argand diagram to illustrate the property $\operatorname{Re} z \leqslant |z| \leqslant |\operatorname{Re} z| + |\operatorname{Im} z|$.

2 Represent the roots of the equation $z^4 - z^3 + z - 1 = 0$ in an Argand diagram, and show that they all have the same modulus.

3 Identify in an Argand diagram the points corresponding to the following equations.

    (a) $|z| = 5$ (b) $\operatorname{Re} z = 3$ (c) $z + z^* = 6$

    (d) $|z - 2| = 2$ (e) $|z - 4| = |z|$ (f) $|z + 2\mathrm{i}| = |z + 4|$

    (g) $|z + 4| = 3|z|$ (h) $1 + \operatorname{Re} z = |z - 1|$

4 Identify in an Argand diagram the points corresponding to the following inequalities.

    (a) $|z| > 2$ (b) $|z - 3\mathrm{i}| \leqslant 1$ (c) $|z + 1| \leqslant |z - \mathrm{i}|$ (d) $|z - 3| > 2|z|$

5* P is a point in an Argand diagram corresponding to a complex number z, and $|z - 5| + |z + 5| = 26$. Prove that $12 \leqslant OP \leqslant 13$, and draw a diagram to illustrate this result.

6* P is a point in an Argand diagram corresponding to a complex number z which satisfies the equation $|4 + z| - |4 - z| = 6$. Prove that $|4 + z|^2 - |4 - z|^2 \geqslant 48$, and deduce that $\operatorname{Re} z \geqslant 3$. Draw a diagram to illustrate this result.

7* Use mathematical induction to prove that, if z is a complex number and n is a positive integer, $|z^n| = |z|^n$.

Show that all the roots of the equation $z^n + a^n = 0$, where a is a positive real number, have modulus a.

8* Assuming that the inequality $|s + t| \leqslant |s| + |t|$ holds for any two complex numbers s and t, prove that $|z - w| \geqslant ||z| - |w||$ holds for any two complex numbers z and w.

9* If s and t are two complex numbers, prove the following.

(a) $|s + t|^2 = |s|^2 + |t|^2 + (st^* + s^*t)$

(b) $|s - t|^2 = |s|^2 + |t|^2 - (st^* + s^*t)$

(c) $|s + t|^2 + |s - t|^2 = 2|s|^2 + 2|t|^2$

Interpret the result of part (c) as a geometrical theorem.

10* If s and t are two complex numbers, prove the following.

(a) $(s^*t)^* = st^*$

(b) $st^* + s^*t$ is a real number, and $st^* - s^*t$ is an imaginary number.

(c) $(st^* + s^*t)^2 - (st^* - s^*t)^2 = (2|st|)^2$

(d) $(|s| + |t|)^2 - |s + t|^2 = 2|st| - (st^* + s^*t)$

Use these results to deduce that $|s + t| \leqslant |s| + |t|$.

9.3   The argument of a complex number

Knowing the modulus of a complex number gives you some idea of its position on an Argand diagram, but does not of course fix it completely. If you know that $|z| = 2$, the point Z may be anywhere on a circle with its centre at the origin O with radius 2.

A second piece of information which will determine the precise position of Z is its direction when viewed from the origin. This can be described by giving the angle of rotation from the positive real axis to the line OZ, as shown in Fig. 9.9. The usual convention is adopted, that anticlockwise rotation is positive and clockwise negative. This angle is called the **argument** of the number z; it is denoted by $\arg z$. To make the definition completely precise, the argument is measured in radians and is always chosen so that $-\pi < \arg z \leqslant \pi$.

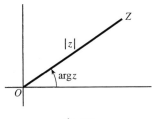

Fig. 9.9

Example 9.3.1
Give the argument of the complex numbers (a) $2 + 2i$,   (b) -3,   (c) $-i$.

These angles are the angles of rotation α, β and γ in Fig. 9.10.

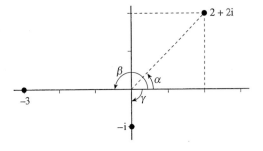

Fig. 9.10

(a) The line joining O to $2 + 2\,\mathrm{i}$ is the diagonal of a square with sides parallel to the axes, so $\arg(2 + 2\,\mathrm{i}) = \frac{1}{4}\pi$.

(b) The rotation is described anticlockwise because π is an acceptable value for $\arg z$, but $-\pi$ is not. So $\arg(-3) = \pi$.

(c) The angle γ is described clockwise, so $\arg(-\mathrm{i}) = -\frac{1}{2}\pi$.

The trigonometric definitions in C2 Sections 1.1 and 1.2 can be used to give equations for calculating $\arg z$ for a general complex number $z = x + y\,\mathrm{i}$. Denoting $\arg z$ by θ, Fig. 9.11 shows that

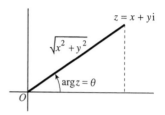

$$\cos\theta = \frac{x}{\sqrt{x^2 + y^2}} \quad \text{and} \quad \sin\theta = \frac{y}{\sqrt{x^2 + y^2}}.$$

Fig. 9.11

From the definition of $\arg z$, θ must be chosen so that $-\pi < \theta \le \pi$.

Thus in Example 9.3.1 the arguments can be calculated as follows.

(a) $x = 2$ and $y = 2$; $\cos\theta = \dfrac{2}{\sqrt{8}} = \dfrac{1}{\sqrt{2}}$ and $\sin\theta = \dfrac{2}{\sqrt{8}} = \dfrac{1}{\sqrt{2}}$, so $\arg z = \frac{1}{4}\pi$.

(b) $x = -3$ and $y = 0$; $\cos\theta = \dfrac{-3}{\sqrt{9}} = -1$ and $\sin\theta = \dfrac{0}{\sqrt{9}} = 0$, so $\arg z = \pi$.

(c) $x = 0$ and $y = -1$; $\cos\theta = \dfrac{0}{\sqrt{1}} = 0$ and $\sin\theta = \dfrac{-1}{\sqrt{1}} = -1$, so $\arg z = -\frac{1}{2}\pi$.

Notice that both equations are usually needed to determine θ uniquely. For example, in (a) there are two angles in the interval $-\pi < \theta \le \pi$ such that $\cos\theta = \dfrac{1}{\sqrt{2}}$ (that is, $\frac{1}{4}\pi$ and $-\frac{1}{4}\pi$), but only $\frac{1}{4}\pi$ also has $\sin\theta = \dfrac{1}{\sqrt{2}}$.

There is one number z for which the equations for θ cannot be used, when both x and y are 0. It is obvious from Fig. 9.9 that the description of the argument is meaningless when $z = 0$.

Example 9.3.2

What can you say about the point Z in an Argand diagram, representing a complex number z, if (a) $\arg z = \frac{1}{6}\pi$, (b) $\arg(z - 1 + \mathrm{i}) = -\frac{1}{6}\pi$, (c) $\arg z = \arg(z - 1 + \mathrm{i})$?

(a) The line OZ makes an angle $\frac{1}{6}\pi$ with the positive real axis, so Z lies on the half-line labelled a in Fig. 9.12.

Notice that only points on this part of the line have argument $\frac{1}{6}\pi$; points on the part of the line which extends into the third quadrant have argument $-\frac{5}{6}\pi$.

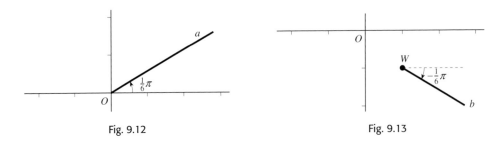

Fig. 9.12   Fig. 9.13

(b) The expression $z - 1 + i$ can be written as $z - (1 - i)$. So, if W is the point representing $1 - i$, $z - 1 + i$ is represented by the translation which takes W to Z. This translation has argument $-\frac{1}{6}\pi$, so Z lies on the half-line labelled b in Fig. 9.13.

(c) This equation states that the arguments of the translations OZ and WZ are the same. For this to happen, the points O, W and Z must be collinear: Z can be either on the half-line labelled c (where both translations have argument $\frac{3}{4}\pi$) or on the half-line labelled c' (where both translations have argument $-\frac{1}{4}\pi$). See Fig. 9.14. But Z cannot be between O and W, where the translation OZ has argument $-\frac{1}{4}\pi$, but the translation WZ has argument $\frac{3}{4}\pi$.

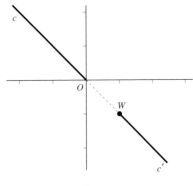

Fig. 9.14

Example 9.3.3
If $\arg z = \frac{1}{4}\pi$ and $\arg(z - 3) = \frac{1}{2}\pi$, find $\arg(z - 6i)$.

This is best done with an Argand diagram (Fig. 9.15).

Since $\arg z = \frac{1}{4}\pi$, the point z lies on the half-line u starting at O at an angle $\frac{1}{4}\pi$ to the real axis. (Points on the other half of the line, in the third quadrant, have $\arg z = -\frac{3}{4}\pi$.)

As $\arg(z - 3) = \frac{1}{2}\pi$, the translation from 3 to z makes an angle $\frac{1}{2}\pi$ with the real axis, so the point z lies on the half-line v in the direction of the imaginary axis.

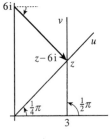

Fig. 9.15

These two half-lines meet at $z = 3 + 3i$, so $\arg(z - 6i) = \arg(3 - 3i)$. The translation $3 - 3i$ is at an angle $\frac{1}{4}\pi$ with the real axis in the clockwise sense, so that $\arg(z - 6i) = -\frac{1}{4}\pi$.

Example 9.3.4

Given that $|z - 2| = 2$ and that $\arg z = \frac{1}{3}\pi$, find $|z|$ and z.

Fig. 9.16 shows an Argand diagram in which Z represents z and C represents 2.

Since $|z - 2| = 2$, Z lies on a circle with centre C and radius 2. Also, since $\arg z = \frac{1}{3}\pi$, the line OZ makes an angle $\frac{1}{3}\pi$ (that is, 60°) with the real axis.

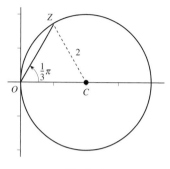

Both CO and CZ are radii of this circle, so triangle COZ is isosceles. Therefore angle OZC is also $\frac{1}{3}\pi$, and angle OCZ is $\pi - \left(\frac{1}{3}\pi + \frac{1}{3}\pi\right) = \frac{1}{3}\pi$. It follows that the triangle COZ is equilateral, so $OZ = 2$. That is, $|z| = 2$.

Fig. 9.16

Therefore, if $z = a + b\,\mathrm{i}$, then

$$a = 2\cos\tfrac{1}{3}\pi = 2 \times \tfrac{1}{2} = 1 \quad \text{and} \quad b = 2\sin\tfrac{1}{3}\pi = 2 \times \tfrac{1}{2}\sqrt{3} = \sqrt{3}.$$

So $z = 1 + \sqrt{3}\,\mathrm{i}$.

Example 9.3.5

If $|z - 2\,\mathrm{i}| = 1$, find the least and greatest possible values of $\arg(z - 1)$.

If Z represents the complex number z, $|z - 2\,\mathrm{i}|$ is the distance of Z from the point C representing $2\,\mathrm{i}$. So Z lies on the circle with centre C and radius 1, shown in Fig. 9.17.

As a translation, the number $z - 1$ takes you to a point Z on the circle from the point U which represents 1. The least and greatest values of $\arg(z - 1)$ are therefore the angles marked α and β in the figure, when Z is at A and B respectively.

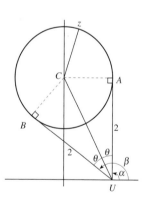

When Z is at the point A, it represents the number $1 + 2\,\mathrm{i}$. So UA is parallel to the imaginary axis, and $\alpha = \frac{1}{2}\pi$.

Also, UA is a tangent to the circle, and its length is 2. The other tangent UB also has length 2. Therefore, if θ is the size of the angles CUA and CUB, $\tan\theta = \frac{1}{2}$.

Fig. 9.17

The least and greatest possible values of $\arg(z - 1)$ are therefore

$$\alpha = \tfrac{1}{2}\pi \quad \text{and} \quad \beta = \alpha + 2\theta = \tfrac{1}{2}\pi + 2\tan^{-1}\tfrac{1}{2} = 2.50,$$

correct to 2 decimal places.

Exercise 9B

1 Find the arguments of the following complex numbers. Give the answer where appropriate as a rational multiple of π, otherwise give the argument correct to 2 decimal places.

(a) $1 + 2i$ (b) $3 - 4i$ (c) $-5 + 6i$ (d) $-7 - 8i$

(e) 1 (f) $2i$ (g) -3 (h) $-4i$

(i) $\sqrt{2} - \sqrt{2}i$ (j) $-1 + \sqrt{3}i$

2 Show in an Argand diagram the sets of points satisfying the following equations.

(a) $\arg z = \frac{1}{5}\pi$ (b) $\arg z = -\frac{2}{3}\pi$ (c) $\arg z = \pi$

(d) $\arg(z - 2) = \frac{1}{2}\pi$ (e) $\arg(2z - 1) = 0$ (f) $\arg(z + i) = \pi$

(g) $\arg(z - 1 - 2i) = \frac{3}{4}\pi$ (h) $\arg(z + 1 - i) = -\frac{2}{5}\pi$

3 Show in an Argand diagram the sets of points satisfying the following inequalities. Use a solid line to show boundary points which are included, and a dotted line for boundary points which are not included.

(a) $0 < \arg z < \frac{1}{6}\pi$ (b) $\frac{1}{2}\pi \leqslant \arg z \leqslant \pi$

(c) $\frac{1}{3}\pi < \arg(z - 1) \leqslant \frac{2}{3}\pi$ (d) $-\frac{1}{4}\pi < \arg(z + 1 - i) < \frac{1}{4}\pi$

4 Use an Argand diagram to find, in the form $a + bi$, the complex number which satisfies the following pairs of equations.

(a) $\arg(z + 2) = \frac{1}{2}\pi$, $\arg z = \frac{2}{3}\pi$ (b) $\arg(z + 1) = \frac{1}{4}\pi$, $\arg(z - 3) = \frac{3}{4}\pi$

(c) $\arg(z - 3) = -\frac{3}{4}\pi$, $\arg(z + 3) = -\frac{1}{2}\pi$ (d) $\arg(z + 2i) = \frac{1}{6}\pi$, $\arg(z - 2i) = -\frac{1}{3}\pi$

(e) $\arg(z - 2 - 3i) = -\frac{5}{6}\pi$, $\arg(z - 2 + i) = \frac{5}{6}\pi$ (f) $\arg z = \frac{7}{12}\pi$, $\arg(z - 2 - 2i) = \frac{11}{12}\pi$

5 Use an Argand diagram to find, in the form $a + bi$, the complex number(s) satisfying the following pairs of equations.

(a) $\arg z = \frac{1}{6}\pi$, $|z| = 2$ (b) $\arg(z - 3) = \frac{1}{2}\pi$, $|z| = 5$

(c) $\arg(z - 4i) = \pi$, $|z + 6| = 5$ (d) $\arg(z - 2) = \frac{3}{4}\pi$, $|z + 2| = 3$

6 If $\arg(z - \frac{1}{2}) = \frac{1}{5}\pi$, what is $\arg(2z - 1)$?

7 If $\arg(\frac{1}{3} - z) = \frac{1}{6}\pi$, what is $\arg(3z - 1)$?

8 If $\arg(z - 1) = \frac{1}{3}\pi$ and $\arg(z - i) = \frac{1}{6}\pi$, what is $\arg z$?

9 If $\arg(z + 1) = \frac{1}{6}\pi$ and $\arg(z - 1) = \frac{2}{3}\pi$, what is $\arg z$?

10 If $\arg(z + i) = 0$ and $\arg(z - i) = -\frac{1}{4}\pi$, what is $|z|$?

11 If $\arg(z - 2) = \frac{2}{3}\pi$ and $|z| = 2$, what is $\arg z$?

Miscellaneous exercise 9

1 Two complex numbers, z and w, satisfy the inequalities $|z - 3 - 2\,\mathrm{i}| \leqslant 2$ and $|w - 7 - 5\,\mathrm{i}| < 1$. By drawing an Argand diagram, find the least possible value of $|z - w|$. (OCR)

2 In an Argand diagram, the point P represents the complex number z. On a single diagram, illustrate the set of possible positions of P for each of the cases

  (a) $|z - 3\,\mathrm{i}| \leqslant 3$,   (b) $\arg(z + 3 - 3\,\mathrm{i}) = \frac{1}{4}\pi$.

  Given that z satisfies both (a) and (b), find the greatest possible value of $|z|$. (OCR)

3 A complex number z satisfies $|z - 3 - 4\,\mathrm{i}| = 2$. Describe in geometrical terms, with the aid of a sketch, the locus of the point which represents z in an Argand diagram. Find

  (a) the greatest value of $|z|$,

  (b) the difference between the greatest and least values of $\arg z$. (OCR)

4 Given that $|z - 5| = |z - 2 - 3\,\mathrm{i}|$, show on an Argand diagram the locus of the point which represents z. Using your diagram, show that there is no value of z satisfying both $|z - 5| = |z - 2 - 3\,\mathrm{i}|$ and $\arg z = \frac{1}{4}\pi$. (OCR)

5 A complex number z satisfies the inequality $|z + 2 - 2\sqrt{3}\,\mathrm{i}| \leqslant 2$. Describe, in geometrical terms, with the aid of a sketch, the corresponding region in an Argand diagram. Find

  (a) the least possible value of $|z|$,   (b) the greatest possible value of $\arg z$. (OCR)

6 The quadratic equation $z^2 + 6z + 34 = 0$ has complex roots α and β.

  (a) Find the roots, in the form $a + b\,\mathrm{i}$.

  (b) Find the modulus and argument of each root, and illustrate the two roots on an Argand diagram.

  (c) Find $|\alpha - \beta|$. (MEI)

7 (a) Given that $\alpha = -1 + 2\,\mathrm{i}$, express α^2 and α^3 in the form $a + b\,\mathrm{i}$. Hence show that α is a root of the cubic equation $z^3 + 7z^2 + 15z + 25 = 0$. Find the other two roots.

  (b) Illustrate the three roots of the cubic equation on an Argand diagram, and find the modulus and argument of each root.

  (c) L is the locus of points in the Argand diagram representing complex numbers z for which $\left|z + \frac{5}{2}\right| = \frac{5}{2}$. Show that all three roots of the cubic equation lie on L and draw the locus L on your diagram. (MEI)

10 Determinants and inverses of 3 × 3 matrices

This chapter develops the ideas of linear equations and matrices in Chapter 4 to sets of three linear equations in three unknowns. When you have completed it, you should know

- that the equations have a unique solution if and only if the determinant of the associated matrix is non-zero
- how to evaluate determinants of 3 × 3 matrices
- how to find the inverses, if they exist, of 3 × 3 matrices.

10.1 Three equations and three unknowns

The purpose of this section is to find when the equations

$$\left. \begin{array}{l} ax + by + cz = p \\ dx + ey + fz = q \\ gx + hy + jz = r \end{array} \right\}$$

have a unique solution for x, y and z.

In principle the argument is similar to that for two equations with two unknowns which is given in Section 4.2.

Start by finding an equivalent set of equations in triangular form,

$$\left. \begin{array}{l} Ax + By + Cz = P \\ Dy + Ez = Q \\ Fz = R \end{array} \right\}.$$

If $F \neq 0$, the third of these equations has a solution $z = \dfrac{R}{F}$. Then, substituting this value of z in the second equation gives $Dy = Q - E\dfrac{R}{F}$ which has a unique solution for y provided that $D \neq 0$. If you solve this equation for y you can then substitute this value in the first equation which has a unique solution for x provided that $A \neq 0$.

So the simultaneous equations have a unique solution for x, y and z if, and only if, $A \neq 0$, $D \neq 0$ and $F \neq 0$.

Returning to the problem at the beginning of this section, you have to express these conditions in terms of a, b, c, d, e, f, g, h and j.

Case 1   Suppose first that $a \neq 0$.

Then, if you multiply the second and third equations by a and then subtract d times the first equation from the second, and g times the first equation from the third you get

$$\left.\begin{matrix} ax + by + cz = p \\ dx + ey + fz = q \\ gx + hy + jz = r \end{matrix}\right\} \quad \Leftrightarrow \quad \left.\begin{matrix} ax + \qquad by + \qquad cz = p \\ (ae - db)y + (af - dc)z = aq - dp \\ (ah - gb)y + (aj - gc)z = ar - gp \end{matrix}\right\}.$$

Now look at the last two equations, containing only y and z.

From Section 4.2, you know that these two equations have a unique solution if, and only if,

$$(ae - db)(aj - gc) - (af - dc)(ah - gb) \neq 0.$$

Calling this expression T, for the moment, the value of T is given by

$$\begin{aligned} T &= (ae - db)(aj - gc) - (af - dc)(ah - gb) \\ &= a^2ej - dbaj - aegc + dbgc - (a^2fh - dcah - afgb + dcgb) \\ &= a^2ej - abdj - aceg + bcdg - a^2fh + acdh + abfg - bcdg \\ &= a^2ej - abdj - aceg - a^2fh + acdh + abfg \\ &= a(aej - bdj - ceg - afh + cdh + bfg) \end{aligned}$$

Since $a \neq 0$, the equations have a unique solution if $T \neq 0$. And since $a \neq 0$, this leaves

$$aej - bdj - ceg - afh + cdh + bfg \neq 0.$$

Case 2   If $a = 0$, find a coefficient which isn't 0 and put it in the top left corner. For example, if $f \neq 0$, write the equations as

$$\left.\begin{matrix} fz + dx + ey = q \\ cz + ax + by = p \\ jz + gx + hy = r \end{matrix}\right\}.$$

Using the same argument as in Case 1, these equations have a solution if, and only if,

$$fah - dch - eaj - fbg + ecg + dbj \neq 0$$

which, after rearranging, is the same condition as before, but with the signs reversed.

In fact, you get the same condition whichever non-zero coefficient is placed in the top left corner.

Case 3   If all the coefficients are 0, it is obvious that the equations do not have a unique solution, and $aej - bdj - ceg - afh + cdh + bfg = 0$.

So the linear equations $\left.\begin{array}{l} ax + by + cz = p \\ dx + ey + fz = q \\ gx + hy + jz = r \end{array}\right\}$ have a unique solution if, and only if,

$aej - bdj - ceg - afh + cdh + bfg \neq 0$.

10.2   Matrix notation

As in Section 4.3, the equations $\left.\begin{array}{l} ax + by + cz = p \\ dx + ey + fz = q \\ gx + hy + jz = r \end{array}\right\}$ can be written in matrix notation as

$$\begin{pmatrix} a & b & c \\ d & e & f \\ g & h & j \end{pmatrix} \begin{pmatrix} x \\ y \\ z \end{pmatrix} = \begin{pmatrix} p \\ q \\ r \end{pmatrix}.$$

Section 10.1 shows that this set of equations has a unique solution if, and only if,

$aej - bdj - ceg - afh + cdh + bfg \neq 0$

This expression, $aej - bdj - ceg - afh + cdh + bfg$, is called the **determinant** of the

matrix $\begin{pmatrix} a & b & c \\ d & e & f \\ g & h & j \end{pmatrix}$, and is denoted by $\det \begin{pmatrix} a & b & c \\ d & e & f \\ g & h & j \end{pmatrix}$.

In some books you will find the notation $\begin{vmatrix} a & b & c \\ d & e & f \\ g & h & j \end{vmatrix}$ for the determinant.

The linear equations $\left.\begin{array}{l} ax + by + cz = p \\ dx + ey + fz = q \\ gx + hy + jz = r \end{array}\right\}$ can be written as the matrix

equation $\begin{pmatrix} a & b & c \\ d & e & f \\ g & h & j \end{pmatrix} \begin{pmatrix} x \\ y \\ z \end{pmatrix} = \begin{pmatrix} p \\ q \\ r \end{pmatrix}.$

$\begin{pmatrix} a & b & c \\ d & e & f \\ g & h & j \end{pmatrix} \begin{pmatrix} x \\ y \\ z \end{pmatrix} = \begin{pmatrix} p \\ q \\ r \end{pmatrix}$ has a unique solution for $\begin{pmatrix} x \\ y \\ z \end{pmatrix} \Leftrightarrow \det \begin{pmatrix} a & b & c \\ d & e & f \\ g & h & j \end{pmatrix} \neq 0.$

The Greek capital delta, Δ, is often used as a shorthand for the value of a determinant.

Unfortunately the expression $aej - bdj - ceg - afh + cdh + bfg$ for the determinant is almost impossible to remember. The next section shows you how to work with it.

10.3   Organising 3×3 determinants

When dealing with three equations it is helpful to use a different notation because the

notation $\left.\begin{array}{l} ax + by + cz = p \\ dx + ey + fz = q \\ gx + hy + jz = r \end{array}\right\}$ simply uses too many letters to be clear about what is

happening. For example, if you see the letter h there is nothing about h which tells you which coefficient it is. You have to look back at the original equations.

It is better to use the notation $\left.\begin{array}{l} a_1x + b_1y + c_1z = p \\ a_2x + b_2y + c_2z = q \\ a_3x + b_3y + c_3z = r \end{array}\right\}$ where the letters a, b and c are attached

to the unknowns x, y and z respectively and the suffix attached to a, b and c tells you which equation it comes from.

The determinant $aej - bdj - ceg - afh + cdh + bfg$ then takes the form

$$a_1b_2c_3 - b_1a_2c_3 - c_1b_2a_3 - a_1c_2b_3 + c_1a_2b_3 + b_1c_2a_3,$$

so $\qquad \det \begin{pmatrix} a_1 & b_1 & c_1 \\ a_2 & b_2 & c_2 \\ a_3 & b_3 & c_3 \end{pmatrix} = a_1b_2c_3 - b_1a_2c_3 - c_1b_2a_3 - a_1c_2b_3 + c_1a_2b_3 + b_1c_2a_3.$

> Already there is more organisation. Every term in the determinant has one of the letters a, b and c, and one of the numbers 1, 2 and 3.

If you look at the determinant $a_1b_2c_3 - b_1a_2c_3 - c_1b_2a_3 - a_1c_2b_3 + c_1a_2b_3 + b_1c_2a_3$ and rewrite it in the form

$$a_1 (b_2c_3 - c_2b_3) + b_1 (c_2a_3 - a_2c_3) + c_1 (a_2b_3 - b_2a_3),$$

you can then think of it in a different way.

If you start with the matrix $\begin{pmatrix} a_1 & b_1 & c_1 \\ a_2 & b_2 & c_2 \\ a_3 & b_3 & c_3 \end{pmatrix}$ and cross out the row and column containing a_1

you get

$$\begin{pmatrix} \cancel{a_1} & \cancel{b_1} & \cancel{c_1} \\ \cancel{a_2} & b_2 & c_2 \\ \cancel{a_3} & b_3 & c_3 \end{pmatrix},$$

where what remains is $\begin{pmatrix} b_2 & c_2 \\ b_3 & c_3 \end{pmatrix}$. The determinant $\det \begin{pmatrix} b_2 & c_2 \\ b_3 & c_3 \end{pmatrix} = b_2c_3 - c_2b_3.$

If you now cross out the row and column containing b_1 you get $\begin{pmatrix} \cancel{a_1} & \cancel{b_1} & \cancel{c_1} \\ a_2 & \cancel{b_2} & c_2 \\ a_3 & \cancel{b_3} & c_3 \end{pmatrix}$, where the

determinant of what remains is $\det \begin{pmatrix} a_2 & c_2 \\ a_3 & c_3 \end{pmatrix} = a_2 c_3 - c_2 a_3.$

(Notice the sign of this expression compared with the middle bracket of the original 3×3 determinant.)

Finally if you cross out the row and column containing c_1 you get $\begin{pmatrix} \cancel{a_1} & \cancel{b_1} & \cancel{c_1} \\ a_2 & b_2 & \cancel{c_2} \\ a_3 & b_3 & \cancel{c_3} \end{pmatrix}$, where the

determinant of what remains is $\det \begin{pmatrix} a_2 & b_2 \\ a_3 & b_3 \end{pmatrix} = a_2 b_3 - b_2 a_3.$

Thus,

$$\det \begin{pmatrix} a_1 & b_1 & c_1 \\ a_2 & b_2 & c_2 \\ a_3 & b_3 & c_3 \end{pmatrix} = a_1 \det \begin{pmatrix} b_2 & c_2 \\ b_3 & c_3 \end{pmatrix} + b_1 \left(-\det \begin{pmatrix} a_2 & c_2 \\ a_3 & c_3 \end{pmatrix} \right) + c_1 \det \begin{pmatrix} a_2 & b_2 \\ a_3 & b_3 \end{pmatrix}.$$

This is called the **expansion of the determinant** $\det \begin{pmatrix} a_1 & b_1 & c_1 \\ a_2 & b_2 & c_2 \\ a_3 & b_3 & c_3 \end{pmatrix}$ **by the first row.**

Example 10.3.1

Find the value of $\det \begin{pmatrix} 0 & 3 & 0 \\ 1 & 4 & 2 \\ 3 & 1 & 5 \end{pmatrix}.$

Expanding by the first row,

$$\det \begin{pmatrix} 0 & 3 & 0 \\ 1 & 4 & 2 \\ 3 & 1 & 5 \end{pmatrix} = 0 \times \det \begin{pmatrix} 4 & 2 \\ 1 & 5 \end{pmatrix} + 3 \times \left(-\det \begin{pmatrix} 1 & 2 \\ 3 & 5 \end{pmatrix} \right) + 0 \times \det \begin{pmatrix} 1 & 4 \\ 3 & 1 \end{pmatrix}$$

$$= 3 \times \left(-\det \begin{pmatrix} 1 & 2 \\ 3 & 5 \end{pmatrix} \right) = 3(-(1 \times 5 - 2 \times 3)) = 3(-5 + 6) = 3.$$

Example 10.3.2

(a) Find the value of k such that the equations $\left. \begin{array}{r} x + 2y + 4z = 11 \\ 3x + y + 2z = 13 \\ 8x + y + kz = c \end{array} \right\}$ do not have a unique

solution.

(b) For this value of k, solve the equations in the cases $c = 28$ and $c = 29$.

(a) The equations $\left. \begin{array}{l} x + 2y + 4z = 11 \\ 3x + y + 2z = 13 \\ 8x + y + kz = c \end{array} \right\}$ do not have a unique solution if, and only if,

$\det \begin{pmatrix} 1 & 2 & 4 \\ 3 & 1 & 2 \\ 8 & 1 & k \end{pmatrix} = 0$. Expanding the determinant by the first row,

$$\det \begin{pmatrix} 1 & 2 & 4 \\ 3 & 1 & 2 \\ 8 & 1 & k \end{pmatrix} = 1 \times \det \begin{pmatrix} 1 & 2 \\ 1 & k \end{pmatrix} + 2 \times \left(-\det \begin{pmatrix} 3 & 2 \\ 8 & k \end{pmatrix} \right) + 4 \times \det \begin{pmatrix} 3 & 1 \\ 8 & 1 \end{pmatrix}$$
$$= 1 \times (k - 2) + 2 \times (-3k + 16) + 4 \times (3 - 8)$$
$$= k - 2 - 6k + 32 - 20$$
$$= -5k + 10.$$

So the equations do not have a unique solution when $-5k + 10 = 0$, that is, when $k = 2$.

(b) Using the method of Chapter 1,

$$\left. \begin{array}{l} x + 2y + 4z = 11 \\ 3x + y + 2z = 13 \\ 8x + y + 2z = c \end{array} \right\} \Leftrightarrow \left. \begin{array}{l} x + 2y + 4z = 11 \\ -5y - 10z = -20 \\ -15y - 30z = c - 88 \end{array} \right\} \quad \begin{array}{l} r_2' = r_2 - 3r_1 \\ r_3' = r_3 - 8r_1 \end{array}$$

$$\Leftrightarrow \left. \begin{array}{l} x + 2y + 4z = 11 \\ -5y - 10z = -20 \\ 0z = c - 28 \end{array} \right\} . \quad r_3' = r_3 - 3r_2$$

If $c = 28$, the equations become $\left. \begin{array}{l} x + 2y + 4z = 11 \\ -5y - 10z = -20 \end{array} \right\}$ or $\left. \begin{array}{l} x + 2y + 4z = 11 \\ y + 2z = 4 \end{array} \right\}$.

Putting $z = t \in \mathbb{R}$ gives $y = 4 - 2t$ and $x = 11 - 2(4 - 2t) - 4t = 3$.

So the solution when $c = 28$ is $x = 3$, $y = 4 - 2t$, $z = t$, $t \in \mathbb{R}$.

If $c = 29$, the last equation becomes $0z = 1$, so the equations are inconsistent, and there is no solution.

Example 10.3.3

Find the values of k such that $\det \begin{pmatrix} 1 & k & 0 \\ 3 & 0 & k \\ k & 1 & 1 \end{pmatrix} = 0$. Interpret your solution in terms of simultaneous equations.

Denoting $\det \begin{pmatrix} 1 & k & 0 \\ 3 & 0 & k \\ k & 1 & 1 \end{pmatrix}$ by Δ and expanding it by the first row gives

$$\Delta = 1 \times \left(\det \begin{pmatrix} 0 & k \\ 1 & 1 \end{pmatrix} \right) + k \times \left(-\det \begin{pmatrix} 3 & k \\ k & 1 \end{pmatrix} \right) + 0 \times \det \begin{pmatrix} 3 & 0 \\ k & 1 \end{pmatrix}$$
$$= 1 \times (-k) + k \times (-3 + k^2) + 0$$
$$= k^3 - 4k.$$

Thus the determinant is zero when $k^3 - 4k = 0$, that is when $k = 0$ or ± 2.

This shows that the equations $\left. \begin{array}{r} x + ky \qquad = p \\ 3x + \qquad kz = q \\ kx + y + z = r \end{array} \right\}$ do not have a unique solution

when $k = 0$ or ± 2.

You can check this for yourself by putting these values of k in the equations and solving them by the methods in Section 1.6.

Exercise 10A

1 Find the values of the following determinants.

(a) $\det \begin{pmatrix} 1 & 2 & 3 \\ 4 & 5 & 6 \\ 7 & 8 & 9 \end{pmatrix}$
(b) $\det \begin{pmatrix} 1 & 2 & 3 \\ 4 & 5 & 6 \\ 7 & 8 & 10 \end{pmatrix}$
(c) $\det \begin{pmatrix} 4 & 5 & 7 \\ 4 & 5 & 3 \\ 4 & 6 & 2 \end{pmatrix}$

2 Find the value or values of k for which each of the following determinants is zero.

(a) $\det \begin{pmatrix} 4 & 3 & 4 \\ -3 & -2 & -1 \\ 2 & 1 & k \end{pmatrix}$
(b) $\det \begin{pmatrix} 5 & k & 8 \\ 2 & 6 & 3 \\ -1 & 4 & -2 \end{pmatrix}$
(c) $\det \begin{pmatrix} k & 1 & 1 \\ 1 & k & 1 \\ 1 & 1 & k \end{pmatrix}$

3 Find the value of k for which each of the following sets of equations does not have a unique solution. Do not solve the equations.

(a) $\left. \begin{array}{r} 3x + 4y + 2z = 0 \\ 2x + 3y + 5z = 0 \\ 3x + 5y + kz = 0 \end{array} \right\}$
(b) $\left. \begin{array}{r} 4x - 2y + 6z = 0 \\ x + ky - 3z = 0 \\ 3x - 5y + 9z = 0 \end{array} \right\}$
(c) $\left. \begin{array}{r} kx + y - z = 0 \\ x + 3y - 2z = 0 \\ 5x + \qquad z = 0 \end{array} \right\}$

4 Find the value of k such that the equations $\left. \begin{array}{r} x + 2y + 3z = 0 \\ x + 3y - 2z = 0 \\ x + 4y + kz = 0 \end{array} \right\}$ do not have a unique solution.

(a) Solve them for this value of k.

(b) Solve the equations when k does not take the value you used in part (a).

5 (a) Find the value of k such that the equations $\left. \begin{array}{r} 3x - y + 6z = 4 \\ 2x + 4y + 5z = -2 \\ 4x - 6y + kz = r \end{array} \right\}$ do not have a unique solution.

(b) For this value of k solve the equations for $r = 10$.

(c) For this value of k solve the equations for $r = 9$.

10.4 Expansions by other rows and columns

In Section 10.3 you saw how to expand a determinant by the first row. There is nothing special about choosing the first row to expand the determinant. For example, you could write the expression for the determinant in Section 10.3 as

$$a_1 b_2 c_3 - b_1 a_2 c_3 - c_1 b_2 a_3 - a_1 c_2 b_3 + c_1 a_2 b_3 + b_1 c_2 a_3$$
$$= (b_1 c_2 a_3 - c_1 b_2 a_3) + (c_1 a_2 b_3 - a_1 c_2 b_3) + (a_1 b_2 c_3 - b_1 a_2 c_3)$$
$$= a_3 (b_1 c_2 - c_1 b_2) + b_3 (c_1 a_2 - a_1 c_2) + c_3 (a_1 b_2 - b_1 a_2)$$
$$= a_3 \det \begin{pmatrix} b_1 & c_1 \\ b_2 & c_2 \end{pmatrix} + b_3 \left(-\det \begin{pmatrix} a_1 & c_1 \\ a_2 & c_2 \end{pmatrix} \right) + c_3 \det \begin{pmatrix} a_1 & b_1 \\ a_2 & b_2 \end{pmatrix}.$$

This is called the **expansion of the determinant by the third row**.

You can also expand by columns. To get the expansion by the second column, go back to the expression for the determinant and group the terms which include the second column, namely b_1, b_2 and b_3.

$$a_1 b_2 c_3 - b_1 a_2 c_3 - c_1 b_2 a_3 - a_1 c_2 b_3 + c_1 a_2 b_3 + b_1 c_2 a_3$$
$$= (b_1 c_2 a_3 - b_1 a_2 c_3) + (a_1 b_2 c_3 - c_1 b_2 a_3) + (c_1 a_2 b_3 - a_1 c_2 b_3)$$
$$= b_1 (c_2 a_3 - a_2 c_3) + b_2 (a_1 c_3 - c_1 a_3) + b_3 (c_1 a_2 - a_1 c_2)$$
$$= b_1 \left(-\det \begin{pmatrix} a_2 & c_2 \\ a_3 & c_3 \end{pmatrix} \right) + b_2 \det \begin{pmatrix} a_1 & c_1 \\ a_3 & c_3 \end{pmatrix} + b_3 \left(-\det \begin{pmatrix} a_1 & c_1 \\ a_2 & c_2 \end{pmatrix} \right).$$

So $\det \begin{pmatrix} a_1 & b_1 & c_1 \\ a_2 & b_2 & c_2 \\ a_3 & b_3 & c_3 \end{pmatrix} = b_1 \left(-\det \begin{pmatrix} a_2 & c_2 \\ a_3 & c_3 \end{pmatrix} \right) + b_2 \det \begin{pmatrix} a_1 & c_1 \\ a_3 & c_3 \end{pmatrix} + b_3 \left(-\det \begin{pmatrix} a_1 & c_1 \\ a_2 & c_2 \end{pmatrix} \right).$

This is called the **expansion of the determinant by the second column.**

Exercise 10B

1 Find expansions for $\det \begin{pmatrix} a_1 & b_1 & c_1 \\ a_2 & b_2 & c_2 \\ a_3 & b_3 & c_3 \end{pmatrix}$ by the other columns and rows similar to those for

the first row and second column. Note carefully the pattern of signs in front of the 2 × 2 determinants obtained in the course of these expansions.

10.5 Cofactors

In Exercise 10B you were asked to find various expansions by rows and columns for the determinant. You should have found that there are 6 possibilities, one for each row and one for each column, where the small determinants have signs according to the pattern

$$\begin{pmatrix} + & - & + \\ - & + & - \\ + & - & + \end{pmatrix}.$$

It is useful to define the small determinants, together with the signs taken from the pattern above.

The **cofactor** A_1 of a_1 in det $\begin{pmatrix} a_1 & b_1 & c_1 \\ a_2 & b_2 & c_2 \\ a_3 & b_3 & c_3 \end{pmatrix}$ is found by crossing out the row and column

containing a_1 in the matrix $\begin{pmatrix} a_1 & b_1 & c_1 \\ a_2 & b_2 & c_2 \\ a_3 & b_3 & c_3 \end{pmatrix}$, calculating the determinant of the 2×2 matrix

which remains and attaching the sign from the pattern of signs above.

Similar definitions apply to the cofactors of other elements in det $\begin{pmatrix} a_1 & b_1 & c_1 \\ a_2 & b_2 & c_2 \\ a_3 & b_3 & c_3 \end{pmatrix}$.

Thus the 9 cofactors in det $\begin{pmatrix} a_1 & b_1 & c_1 \\ a_2 & b_2 & c_2 \\ a_3 & b_3 & c_3 \end{pmatrix}$ are

$$A_1 = + \det\begin{pmatrix} b_2 & c_2 \\ b_3 & c_3 \end{pmatrix}, \quad B_1 = - \det\begin{pmatrix} a_2 & c_2 \\ a_3 & c_3 \end{pmatrix}, \quad C_1 = + \det\begin{pmatrix} a_2 & b_2 \\ a_3 & b_3 \end{pmatrix},$$

$$A_2 = - \det\begin{pmatrix} b_1 & c_1 \\ b_3 & c_3 \end{pmatrix}, \quad B_2 = + \det\begin{pmatrix} a_1 & c_1 \\ a_3 & c_3 \end{pmatrix}, \quad C_2 = - \det\begin{pmatrix} a_1 & b_1 \\ a_3 & b_3 \end{pmatrix},$$

$$A_3 = + \det\begin{pmatrix} b_1 & c_1 \\ b_2 & c_2 \end{pmatrix}, \quad B_3 = - \det\begin{pmatrix} a_1 & c_1 \\ a_2 & c_2 \end{pmatrix}, \quad C_3 = + \det\begin{pmatrix} a_1 & b_1 \\ a_2 & b_2 \end{pmatrix}.$$

The row expansions of the determinant then take one of the forms in Table 10.1.

Row expansions	Column expansions
$a_1 A_1 + b_1 B_1 + c_1 C_1$	$a_1 A_1 + a_2 A_2 + a_3 A_3$
$a_2 A_2 + b_2 B_2 + c_2 C_2$	$b_1 B_1 + b_2 B_2 + b_3 B_3$
$a_3 A_3 + b_3 B_3 + c_3 C_3$	$c_1 C_1 + c_2 C_2 + c_3 C_3$

Table 10.1

Example 10.5.1

Find all the cofactors of the determinant det $\begin{pmatrix} 2 & 4 & 5 \\ 3 & 1 & 2 \\ 4 & 5 & 6 \end{pmatrix}$, and use them to expand the

determinant by

(a) the first column,   (b) the second row,   (c) the third column.

The cofactors are

$$+ \det\begin{pmatrix} 1 & 2 \\ 5 & 6 \end{pmatrix} = -4, \quad - \det\begin{pmatrix} 3 & 2 \\ 4 & 6 \end{pmatrix} = -10, \quad + \det\begin{pmatrix} 3 & 1 \\ 4 & 5 \end{pmatrix} = 11,$$

$$- \det\begin{pmatrix} 4 & 5 \\ 5 & 6 \end{pmatrix} = 1, \quad + \det\begin{pmatrix} 2 & 5 \\ 4 & 6 \end{pmatrix} = -8, \quad - \det\begin{pmatrix} 2 & 4 \\ 4 & 5 \end{pmatrix} = 6,$$

$$+ \det\begin{pmatrix} 4 & 5 \\ 1 & 2 \end{pmatrix} = 3, \quad - \det\begin{pmatrix} 2 & 5 \\ 3 & 2 \end{pmatrix} = 11, \quad + \det\begin{pmatrix} 2 & 4 \\ 3 & 1 \end{pmatrix} = -10.$$

(a) The expansion by the first column is

$$2 \times (-4) + 3 \times 1 + 4 \times 3 = -8 + 3 + 12 = 7.$$

(b) The expansion by the second row is

$$3 \times 1 + 1 \times (-8) + 2 \times 6 = 3 - 8 + 12 = 7.$$

(c) The expansion by the third column is

$$5 \times 11 + 2 \times 6 + 6 \times (-10) = 55 + 12 - 60 = 7.$$

Sometimes you can save quite a lot of work by expanding a determinant by the most appropriate row or column.

Example 10.5.2

Find the value of $\det \begin{pmatrix} 4 & 0 & 3 \\ 0 & 1 & 0 \\ 6 & 2 & 5 \end{pmatrix}$.

If you expand by the middle row you can see that the expansion takes the form

$$0 \times \text{something} + 1 \times \left(+\det \begin{pmatrix} 4 & 3 \\ 6 & 5 \end{pmatrix} \right) + 0 \times \text{something} = 1 \times (20 - 18) = 2.$$

The determinant $\det \begin{pmatrix} a_1 & b_1 & c_1 \\ a_2 & b_2 & c_2 \\ a_3 & b_3 & c_3 \end{pmatrix}$ has cofactors $\begin{matrix} A_1 & B_1 & C_1 \\ A_2 & B_2 & C_2 \\ A_3 & B_3 & C_3 \end{matrix}$ where

$$A_1 = +\det \begin{pmatrix} b_2 & c_2 \\ b_3 & c_3 \end{pmatrix}, \quad B_1 = -\det \begin{pmatrix} a_2 & c_2 \\ a_3 & c_3 \end{pmatrix}, \quad C_1 = +\det \begin{pmatrix} a_2 & b_2 \\ a_3 & b_3 \end{pmatrix},$$

$$A_2 = -\det \begin{pmatrix} b_1 & c_1 \\ b_3 & c_3 \end{pmatrix}, \quad B_2 = +\det \begin{pmatrix} a_1 & c_1 \\ a_3 & c_3 \end{pmatrix}, \quad C_2 = -\det \begin{pmatrix} a_1 & b_1 \\ a_3 & b_3 \end{pmatrix},$$

$$A_3 = +\det \begin{pmatrix} b_1 & c_1 \\ b_2 & c_2 \end{pmatrix}, \quad B_3 = -\det \begin{pmatrix} a_1 & c_1 \\ a_2 & c_2 \end{pmatrix}, \quad C_3 = +\det \begin{pmatrix} a_1 & b_1 \\ a_2 & b_2 \end{pmatrix}.$$

The value of the determinant is found by combining the elements of any row (or column) and the cofactors of the corresponding row (or column); for example,

for the first row, $\Delta = \det \begin{pmatrix} a_1 & b_1 & c_1 \\ a_2 & b_2 & c_2 \\ a_3 & b_3 & c_3 \end{pmatrix} = a_1 A_1 + b_1 B_1 + c_1 C_1,$

and for the second column, $\Delta = \det \begin{pmatrix} a_1 & b_1 & c_1 \\ a_2 & b_2 & c_2 \\ a_3 & b_3 & c_3 \end{pmatrix} = b_1 B_1 + b_2 B_2 + b_3 B_3.$

In Exercise 10c which follows, Question 4 contains some useful theoretical results.

Exercise 10C

1 Find all the cofactors of the determinant $\det \begin{pmatrix} 3 & -2 & 6 \\ 5 & 4 & 2 \\ 1 & 3 & -7 \end{pmatrix}$, and use them to expand the

determinant by

(a) the first column,   (b) the third row.

2 Find the values of the following determinants using whichever row or column you think easiest.

(a) $\det \begin{pmatrix} 4 & 3 & -1 \\ -2 & 0 & 4 \\ 1 & 0 & 16 \end{pmatrix}$ (b) $\det \begin{pmatrix} -1 & 3 & 11 \\ 14 & 2 & 0 \\ 13 & 0 & 4 \end{pmatrix}$ (c) $\det \begin{pmatrix} 5 & 4 & 0 \\ 1 & 0 & 0 \\ -3 & 0 & 1 \end{pmatrix}$

3 Calculate the values of the following determinants in terms of k.

(a) $\det \begin{pmatrix} 1 & 4 & 2 \\ 3 & 0 & 5 \\ 1 & 0 & k \end{pmatrix}$ (b) $\det \begin{pmatrix} 2 & 7 & -1 \\ 4 & 3 & 5 \\ 0 & 2 & k \end{pmatrix}$ (c) $\det \begin{pmatrix} k & 0 & 1 \\ 0 & 1 & k \\ 1 & k & 0 \end{pmatrix}$

4 (a) Show that the expansion of $\det \begin{pmatrix} a_1 & b_1 & c_1 \\ a_2 & b_2 & c_2 \\ a_3 & b_3 & c_3 \end{pmatrix}$ by the first row is equal to the expansion

of $\det \begin{pmatrix} a_1 & a_2 & a_3 \\ b_1 & b_2 & b_3 \\ c_1 & c_2 & c_3 \end{pmatrix}$ by the first column.

(b) Explain why the equations $\left. \begin{array}{l} a_1 x + b_1 y + c_1 z = p \\ a_1 x + b_1 y + c_1 z = q \\ a_3 x + b_3 y + c_3 z = r \end{array} \right\}$ do not have a unique solution.

(c) Deduce from part (b), that if a determinant has two rows which are the same, then the determinant is zero.

(d) Deduce from parts (a) and (c), that if a determinant has two columns which are the same, then the determinant is zero.

(e) Verify parts (c) and (d) directly by calculating $\det \begin{pmatrix} a_1 & b_1 & c_1 \\ a_1 & b_1 & c_1 \\ a_3 & b_3 & c_3 \end{pmatrix}$ and $\det \begin{pmatrix} a_1 & a_1 & c_1 \\ a_2 & a_2 & c_2 \\ a_3 & a_3 & c_3 \end{pmatrix}$.

10.6   Alien cofactors

In Section 10.5 you saw that elements of one row (or column) combined with the cofactors of their own row (or column) give you the value of the determinant.

But what happens if you take the elements of one row (or column) and combine them with the cofactors of another row (or column)?

Return to Example 10.5.1 in which the cofactors of the determinant $\det \begin{pmatrix} 2 & 4 & 5 \\ 3 & 1 & 2 \\ 4 & 5 & 6 \end{pmatrix}$ were found to be

$$-4, \quad -10, \quad 11,$$
$$1, \quad -8, \quad 6,$$
$$3, \quad 11, \quad -10.$$

Combining the elements of the first row with the cofactors of the second row and then the third row gives

$$2 \times 1 + 4 \times (-8) + 5 \times 6 = 2 - 32 + 30 = 0,$$
$$2 \times 3 + 4 \times 11 + 5 \times (-10) = 6 + 44 - 50 = 0.$$

A similar property holds for columns. Combining the elements of the second column with the cofactors of the first and third columns gives

$$4 \times (-4) + 1 \times 1 + 5 \times 3 = -16 + 1 + 15 = 0,$$
$$4 \times 11 + 1 \times 6 + 5 \times (-10) = 44 + 6 - 50 = 0.$$

This is quite a surprise!

In general, if you take the elements of the determinant $\det \begin{pmatrix} a_1 & b_1 & c_1 \\ a_2 & b_2 & c_2 \\ a_3 & b_3 & c_3 \end{pmatrix}$ and the corresponding cofactors

$$A_1, \quad B_1, \quad C_1,$$
$$A_2, \quad B_2, \quad C_2,$$
$$A_3, \quad B_3, \quad C_3,$$

and combine the elements of one row with the cofactors of another row, you will get 0.

You could show this by brute force. For example, combining the elements of the third row with the cofactors of the second row gives

$$a_3 A_2 + b_3 B_2 + c_3 C_2 = a_3 \times \left(-\det \begin{pmatrix} b_1 & c_1 \\ b_3 & c_3 \end{pmatrix}\right) + b_3 \times \left(+\det \begin{pmatrix} a_1 & c_1 \\ a_3 & c_3 \end{pmatrix}\right)$$
$$+ c_3 \times \left(-\det \begin{pmatrix} a_1 & b_1 \\ a_3 & b_3 \end{pmatrix}\right)$$
$$= a_3(-b_1 c_3 + c_1 b_3) + b_3(a_1 c_3 - c_1 a_3) + c_3(-a_1 b_3 + b_1 a_3)$$
$$= -a_3 b_1 c_3 + a_3 c_1 b_3 + b_3 a_1 c_3 - b_3 c_1 a_3 - c_3 a_1 b_3 + c_3 b_1 a_3$$
$$= -a_3 b_1 c_3 + a_3 b_3 c_1 + a_1 b_3 c_3 - a_3 b_3 c_1 - a_1 b_3 c_3 + a_3 b_1 c_3$$
$$= 0.$$

Here is a more subtle method. Start with $\det \begin{pmatrix} a_1 & b_1 & c_1 \\ a_2 & b_2 & c_2 \\ a_3 & b_3 & c_3 \end{pmatrix}$, and now consider

$\det \begin{pmatrix} a_1 & b_1 & c_1 \\ a_3 & b_3 & c_3 \\ a_3 & b_3 & c_3 \end{pmatrix}$. From Exercise 10C Question 4 you know that as two rows are identical, the value of the determinant is 0.

If you expand $\det \begin{pmatrix} a_1 & b_1 & c_1 \\ a_3 & b_3 & c_3 \\ a_3 & b_3 & c_3 \end{pmatrix}$ by the middle row, you get

$$\det \begin{pmatrix} a_1 & b_1 & c_1 \\ a_3 & b_3 & c_3 \\ a_3 & b_3 & c_3 \end{pmatrix} = a_3 A_2 + b_3 B_2 + c_3 C_2,$$

as the values of the cofactors A_2, B_2 and C_2 are unaffected by the entries in the second row. It follows that

$$a_3 A_2 + b_3 B_2 + c_3 C_2 = 0.$$

The proofs for the other rows and columns are similar.

> If you combine the elements of one row (or column) of a determinant with the cofactors of another row (or column) you get 0; for example
>
> $$b_1 A_1 + b_2 A_2 + b_3 A_3 = 0.$$
>
> This property is called the property of **alien cofactors**.

10.7   The inverse of a 3×3 matrix

The expansion of a determinant and the properties of cofactors enable you to find the inverse of a 3×3 matrix. Here is the method.

> To find the inverse of the matrix $\mathbf{A} = \begin{pmatrix} a_1 & b_1 & c_1 \\ a_2 & b_2 & c_2 \\ a_3 & b_3 & c_3 \end{pmatrix}$:
>
> **Step 1** Find the matrix of cofactors $\begin{pmatrix} A_1 & B_1 & C_1 \\ A_2 & B_2 & C_2 \\ A_3 & B_3 & C_3 \end{pmatrix}$.
>
> **Step 2** Swap the rows and columns of the cofactor matrix to get
>
> $\begin{pmatrix} A_1 & A_2 & A_3 \\ B_1 & B_2 & B_3 \\ C_1 & C_2 & C_3 \end{pmatrix}$. This is called **transposing** the matrix.
>
> **Step 3** Calculate $\begin{pmatrix} a_1 & b_1 & c_1 \\ a_2 & b_2 & c_2 \\ a_3 & b_3 & c_3 \end{pmatrix} \begin{pmatrix} A_1 & A_2 & A_3 \\ B_1 & B_2 & B_3 \\ C_1 & C_2 & C_3 \end{pmatrix}$. You should get $\begin{pmatrix} \Delta & 0 & 0 \\ 0 & \Delta & 0 \\ 0 & 0 & \Delta \end{pmatrix}$.
>
> **Step 4** Divide the transposed matrix by Δ to get: $\mathbf{A}^{-1} = \dfrac{1}{\Delta} \times \begin{pmatrix} A_1 & A_2 & A_3 \\ B_1 & B_2 & B_3 \\ C_1 & C_2 & C_3 \end{pmatrix}$.

To show that this is true,

$$\begin{pmatrix} a_1 & b_1 & c_1 \\ a_2 & b_2 & c_2 \\ a_3 & b_3 & c_3 \end{pmatrix} \begin{pmatrix} A_1 & A_2 & A_3 \\ B_1 & B_2 & B_3 \\ C_1 & C_2 & C_3 \end{pmatrix}$$

$$= \begin{pmatrix} a_1 A_1 + b_1 B_1 + c_1 C_1 & a_1 A_2 + b_1 B_2 + c_1 C_2 & a_1 A_3 + b_1 B_3 + c_1 C_3 \\ a_2 A_1 + b_2 B_1 + c_2 C_1 & a_2 A_2 + b_2 B_2 + c_2 C_2 & a_2 A_3 + b_2 B_3 + c_2 C_3 \\ a_3 A_1 + b_3 B_1 + c_3 C_1 & a_3 A_2 + b_3 B_2 + c_3 C_2 & a_3 A_3 + b_3 B_3 + c_3 C_3 \end{pmatrix}$$

$$= \begin{pmatrix} \Delta & 0 & 0 \\ 0 & \Delta & 0 \\ 0 & 0 & \Delta \end{pmatrix} = \Delta \begin{pmatrix} 1 & 0 & 0 \\ 0 & 1 & 0 \\ 0 & 0 & 1 \end{pmatrix} = \Delta \mathbf{I}.$$

The elements of the product which are 0 come from the alien cofactor property; the elements which are Δ come from the expansions of the determinant.

Thus $\begin{pmatrix} a_1 & b_1 & c_1 \\ a_2 & b_2 & c_2 \\ a_3 & b_3 & c_3 \end{pmatrix} \begin{pmatrix} A_1 & A_2 & A_3 \\ B_1 & B_2 & B_3 \\ C_1 & C_2 & C_3 \end{pmatrix} = \Delta \mathbf{I}$, so $\dfrac{1}{\Delta} \begin{pmatrix} A_1 & A_2 & A_3 \\ B_1 & B_2 & B_3 \\ C_1 & C_2 & C_3 \end{pmatrix}$ is the inverse of $\begin{pmatrix} a_1 & b_1 & c_1 \\ a_2 & b_2 & c_2 \\ a_3 & b_3 & c_3 \end{pmatrix}$.

Example 10.7.1

Find the inverse of the matrix $\mathbf{A} = \begin{pmatrix} 4 & 1 & -1 \\ 3 & -1 & 2 \\ 4 & 0 & -3 \end{pmatrix}$.

Step 1   Using the method in the box, find the matrix of cofactors:

$$\begin{pmatrix} 3 & 17 & 4 \\ 3 & -8 & 4 \\ 1 & -11 & -7 \end{pmatrix}.$$

Step 2   Transpose it (by switching rows and columns) $\begin{pmatrix} 3 & 3 & 1 \\ 17 & -8 & -11 \\ 4 & 4 & -7 \end{pmatrix}$.

Step 3   Calculate $\begin{pmatrix} 4 & 1 & -1 \\ 3 & -1 & 2 \\ 4 & 0 & -3 \end{pmatrix} \begin{pmatrix} 3 & 3 & 1 \\ 17 & -8 & -11 \\ 4 & 4 & -7 \end{pmatrix}$ to get $\begin{pmatrix} 25 & 0 & 0 \\ 0 & 25 & 0 \\ 0 & 0 & 25 \end{pmatrix}$.

Step 4   The inverse of $\mathbf{A}$ is $\mathbf{A}^{-1} = \dfrac{1}{25} \begin{pmatrix} 3 & 3 & 1 \\ 17 & -8 & -11 \\ 4 & 4 & -7 \end{pmatrix}$.

Finding the inverse of a matrix is very prone to errors. Step 3 is important for checking.

Inverse matrices can also be used for solving linear equations. See Example 4.5.2.

Example 10.7.2

$$\text{Solve the equations} \quad \left.\begin{array}{r} 4x + y - z = 12 \\ 3x - y + 2z = -1 \\ 4x \phantom{{}-y} - 3z = 17 \end{array}\right\}.$$

You can write these equations as $\mathbf{A}\begin{pmatrix} x \\ y \\ z \end{pmatrix} = \begin{pmatrix} 12 \\ -1 \\ 17 \end{pmatrix}$, with $\mathbf{A} = \begin{pmatrix} 4 & 1 & -1 \\ 3 & -1 & 2 \\ 4 & 0 & -3 \end{pmatrix}$.

Then multiplying on the left by $\mathbf{A}^{-1}$ (which exists, since $\mathbf{A}$ is the matrix of Example 10.7.1) you find

$$\mathbf{A}^{-1}\mathbf{A}\begin{pmatrix} x \\ y \\ z \end{pmatrix} = \mathbf{A}^{-1}\begin{pmatrix} 12 \\ -1 \\ 17 \end{pmatrix} \Leftrightarrow \mathbf{I}\begin{pmatrix} x \\ y \\ z \end{pmatrix} = \mathbf{A}^{-1}\begin{pmatrix} 12 \\ -1 \\ 17 \end{pmatrix} \Leftrightarrow \begin{pmatrix} x \\ y \\ z \end{pmatrix} = \mathbf{A}^{-1}\begin{pmatrix} 12 \\ -1 \\ 17 \end{pmatrix}.$$

Thus

$$\begin{pmatrix} x \\ y \\ z \end{pmatrix} = \tfrac{1}{25}\begin{pmatrix} 3 & 3 & 1 \\ 17 & -8 & -11 \\ 4 & 4 & -7 \end{pmatrix}\begin{pmatrix} 12 \\ -1 \\ 17 \end{pmatrix} = \tfrac{1}{25}\begin{pmatrix} 36 - 3 + 17 \\ 204 + 8 - 187 \\ 48 - 4 - 119 \end{pmatrix} = \tfrac{1}{25}\begin{pmatrix} 50 \\ 25 \\ -75 \end{pmatrix} = \begin{pmatrix} 2 \\ 1 \\ -3 \end{pmatrix}.$$

So $x = 2$, $y = 1$, $z = -3$.

Example 10.7.3

Find the matrix $\mathbf{M}$ which transforms $\begin{pmatrix} 1 \\ 2 \\ 3 \end{pmatrix}$ to $\begin{pmatrix} 4 \\ 8 \\ 5 \end{pmatrix}$, $\begin{pmatrix} 4 \\ 1 \\ 2 \end{pmatrix}$ to $\begin{pmatrix} 6 \\ 1 \\ 3 \end{pmatrix}$ and $\begin{pmatrix} 3 \\ 4 \\ -1 \end{pmatrix}$ to $\begin{pmatrix} 2 \\ 8 \\ 3 \end{pmatrix}$.

Since $\mathbf{M}\begin{pmatrix} 1 \\ 2 \\ 3 \end{pmatrix} = \begin{pmatrix} 4 \\ 8 \\ 5 \end{pmatrix}$, $\mathbf{M}\begin{pmatrix} 4 \\ 1 \\ 2 \end{pmatrix} = \begin{pmatrix} 6 \\ 1 \\ 3 \end{pmatrix}$ and $\mathbf{M}\begin{pmatrix} 3 \\ 4 \\ -1 \end{pmatrix} = \begin{pmatrix} 2 \\ 8 \\ 3 \end{pmatrix}$,

$$\mathbf{M}\begin{pmatrix} 1 & 4 & 3 \\ 2 & 1 & 4 \\ 3 & 2 & -1 \end{pmatrix} = \begin{pmatrix} 4 & 6 & 2 \\ 8 & 1 & 8 \\ 5 & 3 & 3 \end{pmatrix}, \text{ so } \mathbf{M} = \begin{pmatrix} 4 & 6 & 2 \\ 8 & 1 & 8 \\ 5 & 3 & 3 \end{pmatrix}\begin{pmatrix} 1 & 4 & 3 \\ 2 & 1 & 4 \\ 3 & 2 & -1 \end{pmatrix}^{-1}.$$

Using the procedure for calculating the inverse gives

$$\begin{pmatrix} 1 & 4 & 3 \\ 2 & 1 & 4 \\ 3 & 2 & -1 \end{pmatrix}^{-1} = \tfrac{1}{50}\begin{pmatrix} -9 & 10 & 13 \\ 14 & -10 & 2 \\ 1 & 10 & -7 \end{pmatrix},$$

so $\mathbf{M} = \begin{pmatrix} 4 & 6 & 2 \\ 8 & 1 & 8 \\ 5 & 3 & 3 \end{pmatrix} \times \tfrac{1}{50}\begin{pmatrix} -9 & 10 & 13 \\ 14 & -10 & 2 \\ 1 & 10 & -7 \end{pmatrix} = \begin{pmatrix} 1 & 0 & 1 \\ -1 & 3 & 1 \\ 0 & 1 & 1 \end{pmatrix}.$

What happens when you use the procedure for finding the inverse of a matrix on a matrix which is singular?

Example 10.7.4

Use the procedure for finding an inverse matrix on the singular matrix $\mathbf{A} = \begin{pmatrix} 1 & 2 & 3 \\ 4 & 5 & 6 \\ 7 & 8 & 9 \end{pmatrix}$.

Step 1 Using the method in the box, find the matrix of cofactors:

$$\begin{pmatrix} -3 & 6 & -3 \\ 6 & -12 & 6 \\ -3 & 6 & -3 \end{pmatrix}.$$

Step 2 Transpose it (by switching rows and columns) $\begin{pmatrix} -3 & 6 & -3 \\ 6 & -12 & 6 \\ -3 & 6 & -3 \end{pmatrix}.$

Step 3 Calculate $\begin{pmatrix} 1 & 2 & 3 \\ 4 & 5 & 6 \\ 7 & 8 & 9 \end{pmatrix} \begin{pmatrix} -3 & 6 & -3 \\ 6 & -12 & 6 \\ -3 & 6 & -3 \end{pmatrix}$ to get $\begin{pmatrix} 0 & 0 & 0 \\ 0 & 0 & 0 \\ 0 & 0 & 0 \end{pmatrix}.$

At this stage you cannot carry out Step 4 of the procedure, because you cannot divide by $\det \mathbf{A}$, which is 0.

So the procedure breaks down.

10.8 Tying things together

A considerable part of this book has been about sets of linear equations. Chapter 1 was about solving them. Chapter 4 was about the matrix interpretation of two linear equations with two unknowns, using the ideas introduced in Chapter 3: it also introduced the determinant of a 2×2 matrix. This chapter took those ideas further still using three linear equations with three unknowns, and introduced the determinant of a 3×3 matrix.

In this section, for completeness, all these ideas are gathered together in one set of results. The results are given in terms of three equations with three unknowns, together with the associated 3×3 matrix, but they apply in an obvious way to a set of n equations with n unknowns, and its associated $n \times n$ matrix. The only problem is that you do not know how to calculate the determinant of a square matrix which is larger than 3×3.

The set of equations $\left. \begin{array}{l} a_1 x + b_1 y + c_1 z = p \\ a_1 x + b_1 y + c_1 z = q \\ a_3 x + b_3 y + c_3 z = r \end{array} \right\}$ has a unique solution

$\Leftrightarrow \quad \det \mathbf{A} \neq 0$, where $\mathbf{A} = \begin{pmatrix} a_1 & b_1 & c_1 \\ a_2 & b_2 & c_2 \\ a_3 & b_3 & c_3 \end{pmatrix}$

$\Leftrightarrow \quad$ the inverse of $\mathbf{A}$, written $\mathbf{A}^{-1}$, exists.

If the equations, written as $\mathbf{A}\mathbf{x} = \mathbf{p}$ where $\mathbf{x} = \begin{pmatrix} x \\ y \\ z \end{pmatrix}$ and $\mathbf{p} = \begin{pmatrix} p \\ q \\ r \end{pmatrix}$, have a

unique solution, the solution is $\mathbf{x} = \mathbf{A}^{-1}\mathbf{p}$.

Exercise 10D

1 Find the inverse, if it exists, of each of the following matrices.

(a) $\begin{pmatrix} 1 & -2 & 3 \\ 1 & -1 & 2 \\ -2 & 4 & -5 \end{pmatrix}$
(b) $\begin{pmatrix} 1 & 1 & 1 \\ -1 & 0 & 1 \\ -2 & -2 & 0 \end{pmatrix}$
(c) $\begin{pmatrix} 1 & -2 & -1 \\ 2 & -1 & -1 \\ 1 & -2 & 1 \end{pmatrix}$

(d) $\begin{pmatrix} 1 & -2 & -3 \\ 2 & -1 & -4 \\ 3 & -3 & -5 \end{pmatrix}$
(e) $\begin{pmatrix} 1 & -2 & -1 \\ 2 & 1 & 5 \\ 3 & -2 & 3 \end{pmatrix}$
(f) $\begin{pmatrix} 2 & -1 & 3 \\ 1 & 2 & 1 \\ 3 & -4 & 5 \end{pmatrix}$

2 By finding the appropriate inverse matrices, find the solutions of the following equations.

(a) $\left.\begin{array}{l} 2x - y - z = 4 \\ x + 2y \quad\;\; = 10 \\ y - z = 2 \end{array}\right\}$
(b) $\left.\begin{array}{l} x + y - z = 3 \\ 3x - 2y - z = 1 \\ 2x + 3y - z = 9 \end{array}\right\}$
(c) $\left.\begin{array}{l} 2x - 3y + 4z = 7 \\ x - 2y + 3z = 5 \\ 3x - 5y + 2z = 2 \end{array}\right\}$

3 Solve for **X** the following matrix equations.

(a) $\begin{pmatrix} 1 & 3 & 2 \\ 4 & 0 & -1 \\ 2 & 3 & -3 \end{pmatrix} \mathbf{X} = \begin{pmatrix} 0 & -6 & 3 \\ 21 & 6 & -9 \\ -9 & 5 & -4 \end{pmatrix}$
(b) $\mathbf{X} \begin{pmatrix} 3 & -1 & 5 \\ 2 & 4 & -2 \\ 1 & 2 & 0 \end{pmatrix} = \begin{pmatrix} 18 & 29 & -3 \\ 7 & 0 & 12 \\ 7 & 0 & 10 \end{pmatrix}$

4 $\mathbf{A} = \begin{pmatrix} 1 & 3 & 0 \\ 2 & 1 & 2 \\ 3 & 2 & 3 \end{pmatrix}$ and $\mathbf{B}^{-1} = \begin{pmatrix} 4 & 2 & 2 \\ 1 & 0 & 1 \\ 0 & 1 & 0 \end{pmatrix}$. Calculate $\mathbf{BA}^{-1}$.

5 Find the matrix which transforms $\begin{pmatrix} 0 \\ 1 \\ 1 \end{pmatrix}$ to $\begin{pmatrix} 2 \\ 1 \\ 1 \end{pmatrix}$, $\begin{pmatrix} 1 \\ 0 \\ 1 \end{pmatrix}$ to $\begin{pmatrix} 3 \\ 0 \\ 1 \end{pmatrix}$ and $\begin{pmatrix} 1 \\ 1 \\ 0 \end{pmatrix}$ to $\begin{pmatrix} 3 \\ -1 \\ 2 \end{pmatrix}$.

Miscellaneous exercise 10

Notice that, as in Question 1, some examination questions may use the $|\;|$ notation for determinants.

1 (a) Solve the equation $\begin{vmatrix} x & 10 \\ 2 & x-1 \end{vmatrix} = 0$.

(b) Show that, for each of these values of x, $\begin{vmatrix} 3 & 0 & y \\ 6 & x & 10 \\ 0 & 2 & x-1 \end{vmatrix} = 12y$.   (OCR)

2 Determine the value of the constant k for which the system of equations

$$\left.\begin{array}{l} 2x - y - z = 3 \\ -4x + 7y + 3z = -5 \\ kx + y - z = 5 \end{array}\right\}$$

does not have a unique solution.

For this value of k, determine the complete solution to this system.   (OCR, adapted)

3 Find a 3×3 matrix $\mathbf{M}$ such that $\mathbf{Mp} = \mathbf{q}$, $\mathbf{Mq} = -2\mathbf{r}$, and $\mathbf{Mr} = 2\mathbf{p} + 4\mathbf{r}$, where

$$\mathbf{p} = \begin{pmatrix} 2 \\ 0 \\ -1 \end{pmatrix}, \quad \mathbf{q} = \begin{pmatrix} -3 \\ -2 \\ 1 \end{pmatrix}, \quad \mathbf{r} = \begin{pmatrix} 1 \\ 3 \\ 0 \end{pmatrix}.$$

Find also the column matrix $\mathbf{M}^{-1}\mathbf{p}$. (OCR)

4 (a) Given that $\mathbf{M} = \begin{pmatrix} 1 & 5 & a \\ 2 & -4 & 1 \\ 4 & 6 & 7 \end{pmatrix}$, evaluate $\det \mathbf{M}$ in terms of a.

(b) Hence show that, whatever the values of p, q and r, the equations

$$\begin{aligned} x + 5y + az &= p, \\ 2x - 4y + z &= q, \\ 4x + 6y + 7z &= r, \end{aligned}$$

have a unique solution provided $a \neq 3$.

(c) For the case where $\mathbf{M}$ is non-singular, find $\mathbf{M}^{-1}$ and hence find, in terms of a, the solution of the equations when $p = 1$, $q = 0$, $r = -2$. (OCR, adapted)

5 It is given that the matrix $\mathbf{M} = \begin{pmatrix} 2 & 0 & -1 \\ 0 & 4 & a \\ 9 & -5 & -7 \end{pmatrix}$ is non-singular.

(a) Find the set of possible values of a.

(b) Find the inverse of $\mathbf{M}$.

(c) Solve the equations

$$\begin{aligned} 2x \quad\;\;\; - z &= 1, \\ 4y + az &= -3, \\ 9x - 5y - 7z &= 2, \end{aligned}$$

for x, y, z in terms of a. (OCR)

6 (a) The square matrices $\mathbf{P}$ and $\mathbf{Q}$, of the same size, have inverses $\mathbf{P}^{-1}$ and $\mathbf{Q}^{-1}$. Simplify $(\mathbf{PQ})(\mathbf{Q}^{-1}\mathbf{P}^{-1})$, and hence write down the inverse of $\mathbf{PQ}$.

(b) Evaluate the matrix product $\begin{pmatrix} a & a^2 & a^2 \\ -1 & a & a \\ 0 & 0 & -a \end{pmatrix} \begin{pmatrix} a & -a^2 & 0 \\ 1 & a & 2a \\ 0 & 0 & -2a \end{pmatrix}$ and hence write down

the inverse of the matrix $\begin{pmatrix} a & -a^2 & 0 \\ 1 & a & 2a \\ 0 & 0 & -2a \end{pmatrix}$ (when $a \neq 0$).

(c) Let $\mathbf{A} = \begin{pmatrix} 1 & -1 & 0 \\ 1 & 1 & 2 \\ 0 & 0 & -2 \end{pmatrix}$, $\mathbf{B} = \begin{pmatrix} 2 & 4 & 4 \\ -1 & 2 & 2 \\ 0 & 0 & -2 \end{pmatrix}$ and $\mathbf{C} = \mathbf{AB}$. Use your answers to

part (b) to find $\mathbf{A}^{-1}$ and $\mathbf{B}^{-1}$, and hence find $\mathbf{C}^{-1}$. (MEI)

7 The matrix $\mathbf{A}$ is given by $\mathbf{A} = \begin{pmatrix} 2 & -1 & 1 \\ 0 & 3 & 1 \\ 1 & 1 & a \end{pmatrix}$, where $a \neq 1$. Find the inverse of $\mathbf{A}$.

Hence, or otherwise, solve the equations

$$\begin{aligned} 2x - y + z &= 0, \\ 3y + z &= 1, \\ x + y + az &= 3. \end{aligned}$$

(OCR)

8 Find the values of k for which the simultaneous equations

$$\begin{aligned} kx + 2y + z &= 0, \\ 3x \quad\quad - 2z &= 4, \\ 3x - 6ky - 4z &= 14, \end{aligned}$$

do not have a unique solution for x, y and z.

Show that, when $k = -2$, the equations are inconsistent. (OCR, adapted)

9 The matrix $\mathbf{A} = \begin{pmatrix} 3 & 1 & -3 \\ 2 & 4 & 3 \\ -4 & 2 & -1 \end{pmatrix}$.

(a) (i) Show that $\mathbf{A}^2 = \mathbf{A} + 20\mathbf{I}$ where $\mathbf{I}$ is the 3×3 identity matrix.
(ii) Deduce the inverse matrix, $\mathbf{A}^{-1}$, of $\mathbf{A}$.

(b) Determine the unique solution of the system of equations

$$\left.\begin{aligned} 3x + y - 3z &= 9 \\ 2x + 4y + 3z &= 11 \\ -4x + 2y - z &= 23 \end{aligned}\right\}.$$

10 The matrices $\mathbf{A}$ and $\mathbf{B}$ are given by $\mathbf{A} = \begin{pmatrix} 2 & 3 & -1 \\ 3 & -1 & 2 \\ 5 & 3 & 0 \end{pmatrix}$ and $\mathbf{B} = \begin{pmatrix} -6 & -3 & 5 \\ 10 & 5 & -7 \\ 14 & 9 & -11 \end{pmatrix}$.

(a) Calculate the matrix $\mathbf{AB}$, and hence find $\mathbf{A}^{-1}$.

(b) Use the matrix $\mathbf{A}^{-1}$ to solve the equations $\left.\begin{aligned} 2x + 3y - z &= 11 \\ 3x - y + 2z &= 19 \\ 5x + 3y &= 23 \end{aligned}\right\}.$

Revision exercise 2

1 The matrices $\mathbf{A}$ and $\mathbf{B}$ are given by $\mathbf{A} = \begin{pmatrix} 3 & 1 & 1 \\ a & 1 & 1 \\ 3a+2 & 3 & 2 \end{pmatrix}$, $\mathbf{B} = \begin{pmatrix} -1 & 1 & 0 \\ a+2 & 4-3a & a-3 \\ -2 & 3a-7 & 3-a \end{pmatrix}$.

Evaluate $\mathbf{AB}$, and hence or otherwise find $\mathbf{A}^{-1}$, given that $a \neq 3$.
Show that, if $a \neq 3$, the equations

$$3x + y + z = 1,$$
$$ax + y + z = 0,$$
$$(3a+2)x + 3y + 2z = 2,$$

have a unique solution, and find this solution, simplifying your results for x, y, z as much as possible.

Determine whether there are any solutions when $a = 3$. (OCR, adapted)

2 The following set of simultaneous equations is given.

$$x + 2y + az = 1,$$
$$2x - y + 5z = 11,$$
$$3x + y + 8z = b.$$

(a) Show that if $a \neq 3$ then the equations have a unique solution.

(b) Show that if $a = 3$ and $b \neq 12$ then the equations have no solution.

(c) Solve the equations when $a = 3$ and $b = 12$. (OCR, adapted)

3 The matrix $\mathbf{A}$ is given by $\mathbf{A} = \begin{pmatrix} 1 & a & 0 \\ -1 & 1 & 0 \\ a & 5 & 1 \end{pmatrix}$, where $a \neq -1$.

(a) Find $\mathbf{A}^{-1}$.

(b) Given that $a = 2$, solve $\mathbf{A} \begin{pmatrix} x \\ y \\ z \end{pmatrix} = \begin{pmatrix} 1 \\ 2 \\ 3 \end{pmatrix}$. (OCR, adapted)

4 Matrices $\mathbf{A}$ and $\mathbf{B}$ are given by $\mathbf{A} = \begin{pmatrix} 1 & 0 & 0 \\ 1 & -1 & 0 \\ 1 & 0 & a \end{pmatrix}$ and $\mathbf{B} = \begin{pmatrix} 1 & 1 & 1 \\ 0 & 1 & -1 \\ 0 & 0 & 2 \end{pmatrix}$, where $a \neq 0$.

(a) Find the inverse of $\mathbf{A}$.

(b) Given that $\mathbf{B}^{-1} = \begin{pmatrix} 1 & -1 & -1 \\ 0 & 1 & \frac{1}{2} \\ 0 & 0 & \frac{1}{2} \end{pmatrix}$, find the matrix $\mathbf{C}$ such that $\mathbf{ABC} = \mathbf{I}$, where $\mathbf{I}$ is the identity matrix.

5 Find the value of c for which the system of equations

$$5x + 2y \qquad = 3,$$
$$2x + 3y - 5z = 1,$$
$$cx - 5y + 15z = c,$$

does not have a unique solution.

For this value of c, determine whether or not the equations are consistent. (OCR, adapted)

6 It is given that $S_n = 2 \times 2 + 3 \times 2^2 + 4 \times 2^3 + \cdots + (n+1)2^n$.

(a) Find S_1, S_2, S_3 and S_4.

(b) Hence make a conjecture about a formula for S_n in the form $nf(n)$, where $f(n)$ is to be determined.

(c) Use induction to test if your conjecture is correct. (OCR)

7 (a) Find, in the form $a + ib$, the roots of the equation $w^2 + 6w + 25 = 0$.

(b) Hence find, in the form $a + ib$, the roots of the equation $z^4 + 6z^2 + 25 = 0$.

(c) Represent the roots of the equation in part (b) on an Argand diagram.

(d) The root z_1 of the equation in part (b) is such that $0 < \arg(z_1) < \frac{1}{2}\pi$. Find the maximum value of $|z|$ such that $|z - z_1| \leqslant 2$. (OCR)

8 A sequence $u_1, u_2, u_3, \ldots$ is defined by $u_n = 3^{2n} - 1$.

(a) Show that $u_{n+1} - u_n = 8 \times 3^{2n}$.

(b) Hence prove by induction that each term of the sequence is a multiple of 8. (OCR)

9 A point Z on an Argand diagram represents a complex number z.
If $\arg(z - 1) - \arg(z + 1) = \frac{1}{2}\pi$, show that Z lies on a semicircle whose bounding diameter is the line segment joining the points representing -1 and 1.

What is the value of $\arg(z - 1) - \arg(z + 1)$ for points on the other semicircle with the same bounding diameter?

10 Calculate the values of

$$\left(1 - \frac{1}{2^2}\right), \quad \left(1 - \frac{1}{2^2}\right)\left(1 - \frac{1}{3^2}\right), \quad \left(1 - \frac{1}{2^2}\right)\left(1 - \frac{1}{3^2}\right)\left(1 - \frac{1}{4^2}\right), \quad \ldots,$$

until you see a pattern occurring and can make a conjecture about the product

$$\left(1 - \frac{1}{2^2}\right)\left(1 - \frac{1}{3^2}\right)\left(1 - \frac{1}{4^2}\right) \cdots \left(1 - \frac{1}{n^2}\right).$$

Then use the principle of mathematical induction to prove that your conjecture is correct.

11 (a) Given that $f(k) = 5^k - 4k + 15$, show that $f(k+1) - 5f(k) = 16k - 64$.

(b) Hence, or otherwise, prove by induction that $5^n - 4n + 15$ is divisible by 16 for all integers $n \geqslant 1$. (OCR)

12 (a) Use the substitution $x = 1 + y$ in the equation $x^4 - 4x^3 + x^2 + 6x + 2 = 0$ to show that $y^4 - 5y^2 + 6 = 0$.

(b) Hence find the exact roots of the equation in x.

13 (a) The roots of the equation $x^3 - 5x^2 + px - 8 = 0$ are consecutive terms in a geometric progression. Find the value of the constant p.

(b) Solve the equation for this value of p, and show the roots as points in an Argand diagram. Prove that all the roots have the same modulus. (OCR, adapted)

14 Find the complex number z such that $\arg(z - 1) = \frac{1}{6}\pi$ and $|z - 3| = 2$.

15 The equation $ax^3 + bx^2 + cx + d = 0$ has roots α, β and γ. One of the roots, α, is the sum of the other two.

(a) Prove that $\alpha = -\dfrac{b}{2a}$.

(b) Deduce that $b^3 - 4abc + 8a^2d = 0$.

You may assume that the condition in part (b) is true only for equations in which one of the roots is the sum of the other two.

(c) Verify that this condition is satisfied for the equation $9x^3 + 12x^2 - 2x - 4 = 0$ and hence or otherwise find its exact roots. (OCR)

16 The matrix $\mathbf{A}$ is given by $\mathbf{A} = \begin{pmatrix} 1 & 1 & -1 \\ 1 & 2 & -3 \\ 1 & -1 & p \end{pmatrix}$, where p is a constant and $p \neq 3$. Find

(a) the determinant of $\mathbf{A}$,

(b) the inverse of $\mathbf{A}$.

(c) Solve the equations $\begin{aligned} x + y - z &= 1, \\ x + 2y - 3z &= 2, \\ x - y + pz &= 4. \end{aligned}$ (OCR, adapted)

17 (a) Find the values of the constant k for which the matrix $\begin{pmatrix} 1 & 1 & k \\ 2 & -1 & 1 \\ k & 3 & -1 \end{pmatrix}$ is singular.

(b) Find the solution of the equations $\begin{aligned} x + y &= 9, \\ 2x - y + z &= 5, \\ 3y - z &= 18. \end{aligned}$ (OCR)

18 Use the method of mathematical induction to prove that

$$\frac{1^2}{1 \times 3} + \frac{2^2}{3 \times 5} + \cdots + \frac{n^2}{(2n-1)(2n+1)} = \frac{n(n+1)}{2(2n+1)}.$$

19 (a) Find the values of the constants A and B for which $x^3 + 1 \equiv (x + 1)(x^2 + Ax + B)$.

(b) Prove by induction that $\sum_{r=1}^{n} r(2r^2 - 3r + 2) = \frac{1}{2}n(n^3 + 1)$ for all positive integers n. (OCR)

20 If $\mathbf{M} = \begin{pmatrix} 1 - 2i & -2 & 2 + i \\ i & 1 & -1 \\ 2 & -1 & 1 + 2i \end{pmatrix}$, show that $\det \mathbf{M} = 1$. Hence find $\mathbf{M}^{-1}$.

21 Prove by mathematical induction that

$$\left(1 - \frac{1}{2}\right)\left(1 - \frac{1}{3}\right)\left(1 - \frac{1}{4}\right)\cdots\left(1 - \frac{1}{n}\right) = \frac{1}{n}.$$

22 Suppose that $a_0 = 1$, and that $a_1, a_2, \ldots, a_n, \ldots$ are positive numbers such that $a_{r+1}{}^2 > a_r a_{r+2}$ for $r = 0, 1, 2, \ldots$ Prove that

$$a_1 > a_2{}^{\frac{1}{2}} > a_3{}^{\frac{1}{3}} > a_4{}^{\frac{1}{4}} > \ldots > a_n{}^{\frac{1}{n}} > \ldots$$

23 Find the complex numbers which satisfy the following equations.

(a) $(1 + \mathrm{i})z = 1 + 3\mathrm{i}$

(b) $z^2 + 4z + 13 = 0$

(c) $(1 - \mathrm{i})z^2 - 4z + (1 + 3\mathrm{i}) = 0$

(d) $\left.\begin{array}{l} (1 - \mathrm{i})z + (1 + \mathrm{i})w = 2 \\ (1 + 3\mathrm{i})z - (4 + \mathrm{i})w = 3\mathrm{i} \end{array}\right\}$

24 Here is a 'spoof proof' of the obviously false proposition that all candidates who take the FP1 module examination get the same number of marks. Your task is to find the error in the proof.

Proposition Let $\mathrm{P}(n)$ be 'all sets of n candidates get the same mark'.

Basis case The theorem is clearly true for $n = 1$ as any candidate gets the same mark as him or herself.

Inductive step Suppose that $\mathrm{P}(k)$ is true. Then all sets of k candidates get the same mark as each other. Let $\{c_1, c_2, \ldots, c_k\}$ be one such set of k candidates. Now add candidate c_{k+1} and consider the set $\{c_2, \ldots, c_k, c_{k+1}\}$ where c_{k+1} replaces c_1. This is also a set of k candidates, so they all get the same mark, so c_{k+1} gets the same mark as $c_1, c_2, \ldots, c_k$. Therefore, if $\mathrm{P}(k)$ is true, then $\mathrm{P}(k + 1)$ is true.

Completion Using the principle of mathematical induction, $P(n)$ is true for all positive integers, so all sets of n candidates get the same mark.

25 The equation $16x^3 + kx^2 + 27 = 0$ (where k is a real constant) has roots α, β and γ.
   (a) Write down the values of $\beta\gamma + \gamma\alpha + \alpha\beta$ and $\alpha\beta\gamma$, and express k in terms of α, β and γ.
   (b) For the case where there is a repeated root, say $\beta = \gamma$, solve the equation, and find the value of k.
   (c) For the case $k = 9$, find a cubic equation with integer coefficients which has

   roots $\dfrac{1}{\alpha} + 1$, $\dfrac{1}{\beta} + 1$, $\dfrac{1}{\gamma} + 1$.   (MEI)

26 The cubic equation $2x^3 - 3x^2 - 12x - 4 = 0$ has roots α, β and γ.
   (a) Write down the values of $\alpha + \beta + \gamma$, $\beta\gamma + \gamma\alpha + \alpha\beta$ and $\alpha\beta\gamma$.
   (b) Find $\alpha^2 + \beta^2 + \gamma^2$ and $(\beta\gamma)^2 + (\gamma\alpha)^2 + (\alpha\beta)^2$.
   (c) By considering $(\alpha + \beta + \gamma)(\beta\gamma + \gamma\alpha + \alpha\beta)$, show that

   $$\alpha^2\beta + \alpha^2\gamma + \beta^2\gamma + \beta^2\alpha + \gamma^2\alpha + \gamma^2\beta = -15.$$

   (d) Find a cubic equation with integer coefficients which has roots $\alpha - \beta\gamma$, $\beta - \gamma\alpha$ and $\gamma - \alpha\beta$.   (MEI)

27 Let **A**, **B** and **C** be real 2×2 matrices and denote $\mathbf{AB} - \mathbf{BA}$ by $[\mathbf{A}, \mathbf{B}]$.
Prove that

(a) $[\mathbf{A}, \mathbf{A}] = \mathbf{O}$;

(b) $[[\mathbf{A}, \mathbf{B}], \mathbf{C}] + [[\mathbf{B}, \mathbf{C}], \mathbf{A}] + [[\mathbf{C}, \mathbf{A}], \mathbf{B}] = \mathbf{O}$;

(c) $[\mathbf{A}, \mathbf{B}] = \mathbf{I} \quad \Rightarrow \quad [\mathbf{A}, \mathbf{B}^m] = m\mathbf{B}^{m-1}$ for all positive integers m.

The trace $\mathrm{Tr}(\mathbf{A})$ of a matrix $\mathbf{A} = \begin{pmatrix} a_{11} & a_{12} \\ a_{21} & a_{22} \end{pmatrix}$ is defined by $\mathrm{Tr}(\mathbf{A}) = a_{11} + a_{22}$.

Prove that

(d) $\mathrm{Tr}(\mathbf{A} + \mathbf{B}) = \mathrm{Tr}(\mathbf{A}) + \mathrm{Tr}(\mathbf{B})$;

(e) $\mathrm{Tr}(\mathbf{AB}) = \mathrm{Tr}(\mathbf{BA})$;

(f) $\mathrm{Tr}(\mathbf{I}) = 2$.

Deduce that there are no matrices satisfying $[\mathbf{A}, \mathbf{B}] = \mathbf{I}$. Does this in any way invalidate the statement in part (c)?

(MEI)

Practice examination 1

Time 1 hour 30 minutes

Answer all the questions.

You are permitted to use a graphic calculator in this paper.

1 Use formulae for $\sum_{r=1}^{n} r^2$ and $\sum_{r=1}^{n} r^3$ to show that

$$\sum_{r=1}^{n} r^2(r-1) = \tfrac{1}{12}(n-1)n(n+1)(3n+2).$$ [5]

2 (i) Find the value of the constant a for which the matrix $\begin{pmatrix} a & 2 \\ 3 & 6 \end{pmatrix}$ is singular. [2]

(ii) With this value of a, the matrix represents a transformation in the x-y plane. Find the image of the point corresponding to $\begin{pmatrix} x \\ y \end{pmatrix}$, and hence show that the image of any point of the plane lies on a certain straight line, whose equation is to be stated. [4]

3 (i) Calculate the matrix product

$$\begin{pmatrix} 1 & 0 & 2 \\ 0 & 2 & -1 \\ 2 & 1 & 0 \end{pmatrix} \begin{pmatrix} -1 & -2 & 4 \\ 2 & 4 & -1 \\ 4 & 1 & -2 \end{pmatrix}.$$ [2]

(ii) Hence

(a) find the inverse of the matrix $\begin{pmatrix} -1 & -2 & 4 \\ 2 & 4 & -1 \\ 4 & 1 & -2 \end{pmatrix}$, [2]

(b) express x, y and z in terms of a, given the set of equations

$$\begin{aligned} -x - 2y + 4z &= a, \\ 2x + 4y - z &= a, \\ 4x + y - 2z &= 0. \end{aligned}$$ [3]

4 (i) Show that $(\sqrt{r+1} - \sqrt{r})(\sqrt{r+1} + \sqrt{r}) = 1$. [2]

(ii) Use the method of differences to find the sum of the series

$$\frac{1}{\sqrt{2} + \sqrt{1}} + \frac{1}{\sqrt{3} + \sqrt{2}} + \frac{1}{\sqrt{4} + \sqrt{3}} + \cdots + \frac{1}{\sqrt{n+1} + \sqrt{n}}.$$ [4]

(iii) Does the series in part (ii) converge as $n \to \infty$? Justify your answer. [2]

5 The matrix $\begin{pmatrix} 2 & 0 \\ 1 & 1 \end{pmatrix}$ represents a transformation in the x-y plane, and the point A_0 has

column matrix $\begin{pmatrix} 1 \\ 0 \end{pmatrix}$. Under this transformation, the image of A_0 is A_1, the image of A_1 is A_2, and so on.

 (i) Find the column matrices corrresponding to the points A_1, A_2, A_3 and A_4.   [3]

 (ii) Hence make a conjecture about the column matrix corrresponding to A_n.   [2]

 (iii) Use mathematical induction to determine whether your conjecture is correct.   [5]

6 The complex number $3 - 4\,\mathrm{i}$ is denoted by z, and the complex conjugate of z is denoted by z^*.

 (i) Express $\frac{z}{z^*}$ in the form $a + b\,\mathrm{i}$, where a and b are real.   [4]

 (ii) Let $z = (p + q\mathrm{i})^2$, where p and q are real. Show that $p^4 - 3p^2 - 4 = 0$, and hence find the two square roots of $3 - 4\,\mathrm{i}$.   [7]

7 The quadratic equation $x^2 - 5x + 7 = 0$ has roots α and β.

 (i) Write down the values of $\alpha + \beta$ and $\alpha\beta$, and hence show that $\alpha^2 + \beta^2 = 11$.   [4]

 (ii) Hence find a quadratic equation, with integer coefficients, whose roots are α^2 and β^2.   [3]

 (iii) Show how the equation whose roots are α^2 and β^2 may alternatively be obtained from the original quadratic equation by means of the substitution $y = x^2$.   [4]

8 (i) Show that $(1 + 2\,\mathrm{i})^3 = -11 - 2\,\mathrm{i}$.   [2]

   The complex number $1 + 2\,\mathrm{i}$ is a root of the cubic equation $z^3 + az + 10 = 0$.

 (ii) Find the value of the real constant a.   [2]

 (iii) State the other two roots of the equation.   [3]

 (iv) Show all three roots of the equation in an Argand diagram.   [2]

 (v) Show that all three roots satisfy the equation $|\,6z - 1\,| = 13$, and show the locus represented by this equation in your diagram.   [5]

Practice examination 2

Time 1 hour 30 minutes

Answer all the questions.

You are permitted to use a graphic calculator in this paper.

1 Find an expression in terms of n for the sum

$$1 \times 2 + 2 \times 3 + 3 \times 4 + \cdots + r(r+1) + \cdots + n(n+1),$$

factorising your answer fully. [5]

2 A sequence of numbers $u_1,\ u_2,\ u_3,\ \ldots$ is defined by

$$u_1 = 1 \quad \text{and} \quad u_{n+1} = 2u_n + 1 \ \text{ for } \ n \geqslant 1.$$

(i) Evaluate $u_2,\ u_3,\ u_4$ and u_5. [2]

(ii) Hence conjecture a formula for u_n in terms of n, and prove your conjecture by induction. [5]

3 The cubic equation $x^3 + ax + b = 0$, where a and b are constants, has roots $\alpha,\ \beta$ and γ.

(i) Write down expressions for a and b in terms of $\alpha,\ \beta$ and γ. [2]

It is given that the roots are such that $\alpha\beta = \gamma$.

(ii) Express each of a and b in terms of γ only. [4]

(iii) Hence show that $(a-b)^2 + b = 0$. [2]

4 The complex numbers $2 + 3\,\mathrm{i}$ and $1 - 2\,\mathrm{i}$ are denoted by z_1 and z_2 respectively.

(i) Draw an Argand diagram showing the points representing $z_1,\ z_2$ and $z_1 + z_2$. State what type of quadrilateral is formed by these three points and the origin. [4]

(ii) Find $\dfrac{z_1}{z_2}$, and calculate the modulus and argument of this complex number. [5]

5 (i) Show that $\dfrac{r+1}{2^r} - \dfrac{r+2}{2^{r+1}} = \dfrac{r}{2^{r+1}}$. [2]

(ii) Hence show that

$$\frac{1}{4} + \frac{2}{8} + \frac{3}{16} + \cdots + \frac{n}{2^{n+1}} = 1 - \frac{n+2}{2^{n+1}}.$$ [4]

(iii) You are given that $2^n > n^2$ for all $n > 4$. Explain carefully how you can deduce from this that the series in part (ii) is convergent, and state the sum to infinity. [3]

6 (i) By evaluating a suitable determinant, show that the simultaneous equations

$$-x + 2y + z = a,$$
$$x + y + z = b,$$
$$4x + y + 2z = c,$$

where a, b and c are constants, do not have a unique solution.   [3]

(ii) Find the relation between a, b and c for which the equations are consistent.   [4]

(iii) Given that the equations are consistent and also that $c = a + b$, express y and z in terms of x and a.   [4]

7 (i) Draw an Argand diagram showing the locus given by the equation

$$|z - 2 - 2i| = 2.$$ [3]

(ii) Mark the point on this locus at which $|z|$ is greatest, and state the values of $|z|$ and $\arg z$ for this point.   [4]

(iii) Show on the same diagram the locus given by the equation

$$\arg(z + 2) = \tfrac{1}{4}\pi,$$

and state the complex numbers represented by the two points of intersection of this locus and the locus in part (i).   [4]

8 The 2×2 matrices **R** and **S** represent the following transformations in the x-y plane.

   R : rotation through an angle θ anticlockwise about the origin

   S : stretch with scale factor 2 parallel to the x-axis (with the y-axis invariant)

(i) Write down the matrices **R** and **S**.   [3]

The matrix **RSR**$^{-1}$ is denoted by **M**.

(ii) Show that $\mathbf{M} = \begin{pmatrix} 1 + \cos^2\theta & \sin\theta\cos\theta \\ \sin\theta\cos\theta & 1 + \sin^2\theta \end{pmatrix}$.   [4]

(iii) The point P has column matrix $\begin{pmatrix} x \\ y \end{pmatrix}$ and the point Q is the image of P under the transformation represented by **M**. Find the column matrix of Q, and hence show that the line joining P to Q makes an angle θ with the x-axis.   [5]

Answers

1 Sets of linear equations

Your answers may differ in form from those given. The parameters s and t are real numbers. The solution $z = t, t \in \mathbb{R}$ means that z can take any real value. To save space, the answers are not given in column form.

Exercise 1A (page 12)

1. (a) $x = 13, y = -2$
   (b) $x = -2, y = -5$
   (c) $x = 1, y = 12$

2. (a) $x = 3, y = 1, z = -1$
   (b) $x = -2, y = -1, z = 3$
   (c) $x = 2, y = 1, z = 0$
   (d) $x = 3, y = -1, z = 5$
   (e) $x = 2, y = 3, z = 1$
   (f) $x = 2, y = 1, z = 1$

Exercise 1B (page 20)

1. (a) $x = 2 + t, y = t, \quad t \in \mathbb{R}$
   (b) No solution
   (c) $x = t, y = 3t, \quad t \in \mathbb{R}$
   (d) $x = 3 + 2t, y = t, \quad t \in \mathbb{R}$
   (e) No solution
   (f) $x = 2 + 3t, y = 5t, \quad t \in \mathbb{R}$

2. (a) $x = t, y = 4t - 11, z = 3t - 8, \quad t \in \mathbb{R}$
   (b) $x = 2t, y = t - 3, z = 3t - 2, \quad t \in \mathbb{R}$
   (c) No solution
   (d) $x = s, y = 2 - 2s + 3t, z = t, \quad s, t \in \mathbb{R}$
   (e) $x = s, y = t, z = s + t - 3, \quad s, t \in \mathbb{R}$
   (f) $x = 2 + t, y = 1 + t, z = t, \quad t \in \mathbb{R}$
   (g) $x = 4s - 5t, y = 3s, z = 3t, \quad s, t \in \mathbb{R}$
   (h) No solution
   (i) $x = t, y = 2s - 3t + 4, z = s, \quad s, t \in \mathbb{R}$

3. (a) $x = 1, y = 2, z = -1$
   (b) No solution
   (c) $x = 2 - t, y = 3 - t, z = t, \quad t \in \mathbb{R}$
   (d) $x = -1 - 2t, y = 2 + t, z = t, \quad t \in \mathbb{R}$
   (e) $x = 1 + t, y = 2 - t, z = t, \quad t \in \mathbb{R}$
   (f) $x = -2, y = -3, z = -4$

4. (a) $x = 3, y = \frac{1}{2}k - 1, z = \frac{1}{2}k - 2$
   (b) If $k \neq 3$, no solution;
      if $k = 3$,
      $x = 13 - t, y = 3t - 18, z = t, \quad t \in \mathbb{R}$

   (c) If $k \neq 16$, no solution;
      if $k = 16$, $x = 5 - t, y = 2 + t, z = t, \quad t \in \mathbb{R}$

5. (a) $x = 8 - 8z, y = 11z - 8$
   (b) $x = z - 6, y = 5 - 2z$
   (c) $x = 7 - z, y = 3 - z$

Miscellaneous exercise 1 (page 21)

1. $x = 2 - 3t, y = 2t, \quad t \in \mathbb{R}$

2. $x = -10s + 10t, y = 15s, z = 6t, \quad s, t \in \mathbb{R}$

3. $x = 2t, y = -9t, z = 5t, \quad t \in \mathbb{R}$

4. (a) $x = 3, y = -1, z = -2$
   (b) $x = 2t, y = t, z = 7t - 8, \quad t \in \mathbb{R}$
   (c) $x = 1, y = -t, z = t, \quad t \in \mathbb{R}$
   (d) $x = 9 - 3t, y = 2t, z = t, \quad t \in \mathbb{R}$
   (e) $x = 1, y = -1, z = 1$
   (f) $x = 2 - t, y = 1 + t, z = t, \quad t \in \mathbb{R}$

5. (a) If $k \neq -16$, no solution;
      if $k = -16$, $x = 4 + 3t, y = t, \quad t \in \mathbb{R}$
   (b) $x = \frac{1}{4}(k + 3), y = \frac{1}{4}(k - 9)$
   (c) $x = k - 3, y = 3$

6. (a) If $k \neq 3$, no solution;
      if $k = 3$, $x = 1 - t, y = t, z = 0, \quad t \in \mathbb{R}$
   (b) $x = k, y = k - 1, z = 1$
   (c) No solution for any value of k.

7. (a) $x = t - 1, y = t - 1, z = t, \quad t \in \mathbb{R}$
   (b) $x = 1 - s - t, y = s, z = t, \quad s, t \in \mathbb{R}$

8. (a) $x = -t, y = t, \quad t \in \mathbb{R}$
   (b) $x = 8t, y = 5t, \quad t \in \mathbb{R}$

2 Summing series

Exercise 2A (page 26)

1. (a) $338\,350$ (b) $333\,298$ (c) 3080

2. (a) $\frac{1}{2}(n + 1)(n + 2)$ (b) $n(n + 2)$
   (c) $\frac{1}{2}n(2n^2 + 3n + 3)$

3. $n, \frac{1}{2}n(n + 1); \quad \frac{1}{2}n(2a + (n - 1)d)$

4. (a) $71\,071$ (b) $7\,142\,142$

5. (a) $112\,761$ (b) $215\,589$

6. $np^2 - \frac{1}{6}n(n + 1)(2n + 1)$

7. $\frac{1}{6}n(n + 1)(n + 2)$

Exercise 2B (page 29)

1 (a) 24 497 550 (b) 25 497 444

2 (a) $\frac{1}{12}(n-1)n(n+1)(3n+2)$

 (b) $\frac{1}{6}n(n+1)(3n^2+n-1)$

 (c) $\frac{1}{3}n(2n+1)(2n-1)(3n+1)$

 (d) $\frac{1}{6}(n+1)(n+2)(3n^2+7n+3)$

3 (a) 13 005 000 (b) 12 005 000

4 1 999 000

5 $\frac{1}{12}n(n+1)(n+2)(3n+5)$

6 $\frac{1}{12}n(n+1)(3n^2+11n+4)$

7 $\frac{1}{12}n(n+1)^2(n+2)$

8 (a) 27 224 550

 (b) 25 497 450

 (c) 28 638 550

Exercise 2C (page 35)

1 (b) $\dfrac{2n}{2n+1}$

2 (b) $(n+1)!-1$

4 $r(r+1)(r+2)$, $\frac{1}{4}n(n+1)(n+2)(n+3)$

5 $2(80r^4+40r^2+1)$,

 $\frac{1}{30}n(n+1)(2n+1)(3n^2+3n-1)$

6 $\frac{1}{2}-\dfrac{1}{(n+1)(n+2)}$; $\frac{1}{2}$

7 $\dfrac{na^{n+1}-(n+1)a^n+1}{(a-1)^2}$

8 $\frac{3}{4}$

9 $\dfrac{2n+1+(-1)^{n-1}}{2(2n+1)}$, $\frac{1}{2}$

Miscellaneous exercise 2 (page 35)

1 (a) 1683   (b) 3367

2 (a) 2420   (b) 90 240

3 109 428

4 111 150

6 (a) $\frac{1}{3}$ (b) 1166 650

7 25 512 600

8 $4r+1$, $(n+1)(6n+1)$

11 $64r^3+16r$

13 $\frac{1}{3}n(n+1)(n+2)$; $\frac{1}{2}n(6n^2+15n+11)$

14 (b) $\dfrac{(N-1)(N+2)}{4N(N+1)}$ (c) $\frac{1}{4}$

3 Matrices

Exercise 3A (page 44)

1 (a) $\begin{pmatrix} 3 & 5 \\ 7 & 3 \end{pmatrix}$ (b) $\begin{pmatrix} -1 & -1 \\ -1 & 5 \end{pmatrix}$

 (c) $\begin{pmatrix} 7 & 12 \\ 17 & 10 \end{pmatrix}$ (d) $\begin{pmatrix} -2 & -1 \\ 0 & 19 \end{pmatrix}$

2 $\mathbf{X}=\frac{3}{2}(\mathbf{A}+\mathbf{B})$; they are all the same size.

4 $\begin{pmatrix} 10 & 1 \\ 22 & 5 \end{pmatrix}$, $\begin{pmatrix} 11 & 16 \\ 1 & 4 \end{pmatrix}$

5 $\begin{pmatrix} 21 & 3 & -1 \\ 29 & -19 & 8 \\ -18 & -4 & 7 \end{pmatrix}$, $\begin{pmatrix} 15 & 12 & -20 \\ 5 & 14 & 4 \\ -3 & -8 & -20 \end{pmatrix}$

6 $\begin{pmatrix} 0 & -8 \\ 13 & 0 \end{pmatrix}$, $\begin{pmatrix} -14 & 10 & 40 \\ -5 & 4 & 22 \\ -8 & 5 & 10 \end{pmatrix}$

7 For example, $\begin{pmatrix} 1 & -2 \\ -2 & 1 \end{pmatrix}$ and $\begin{pmatrix} 2 & -3 \\ -3 & 2 \end{pmatrix}$.

8 (a) Does not exist.   (b) $\begin{pmatrix} -3 \\ -8 \end{pmatrix}$

 (c) $\begin{pmatrix} 2 & 3 & 1 \\ -2 & -3 & -1 \\ 2 & 3 & 1 \end{pmatrix}$ (d) (0)

 (e) Does not exist.   (f) Does not exist.

 (g) Does not exist.   (h) Does not exist.

9 $\begin{pmatrix} 7 & -2 \\ -3 & 1 \end{pmatrix}$, $\begin{pmatrix} 1 & 0 \\ 0 & 1 \end{pmatrix}$; no such matrix.

11 $\begin{pmatrix} 19 & -2 & -8 \\ -7 & 1 & 3 \\ -2 & 0 & 1 \end{pmatrix}$, $\begin{pmatrix} 1 & 0 & 0 \\ 0 & 1 & 0 \\ 0 & 0 & 1 \end{pmatrix}$

14 $\mathbf{OA}=\mathbf{AO}=\mathbf{O}$

Exercise 3B (page 50)

1 $\begin{pmatrix} 2 & -3 \\ -3 & 5 \end{pmatrix}$

2 $\begin{pmatrix} 3 & -2 \\ -7 & 5 \end{pmatrix}$

3 (a) $\begin{pmatrix} 2 & -1 \\ -\frac{3}{2} & 1 \end{pmatrix}$ (b) $\begin{pmatrix} 7 & 5 \\ -3 & -2 \end{pmatrix}$

 (c) $\dfrac{1}{ad-bc}\begin{pmatrix} d & -b \\ -c & a \end{pmatrix}$, provided $ad-bc \neq 0$

4 $\begin{pmatrix} -\frac{9}{2} & -\frac{5}{2} \\ \frac{5}{2} & \frac{3}{2} \end{pmatrix}$

 (a) $\begin{pmatrix} -38 \\ 22 \end{pmatrix}$ (b) $\begin{pmatrix} -38 & -12 \\ 22 & 8 \end{pmatrix}$

6 $\begin{pmatrix} -\frac{5}{2} & \frac{3}{2} \\ 2 & -1 \end{pmatrix}$, $x = 2, y = -1$

7 $\begin{pmatrix} 1 & 0 & 0 \\ -4 - 2k & 3 + k & 2 + k \\ 0 & 0 & 1 \end{pmatrix}$, $\begin{pmatrix} 1 & 4 & -5 \\ 1 & 5 & -2 \\ 1 & 3 & -7 \end{pmatrix}$

Miscellaneous exercise 3 (page 51)

2 It is the 3×3 identity matrix.

4 $\mathbf{P} = \begin{pmatrix} -1 & 2 \\ 0 & 1 \end{pmatrix}$, $a = -1, b = 2, d = 1$;

$\mathbf{Q} = \begin{pmatrix} 1 & 0 \\ -3 & 1 \end{pmatrix}$

5 (a) -1 (b) $\begin{pmatrix} -1 & 1 \\ 1 & 3 \end{pmatrix}$

7 (a) $\begin{pmatrix} 20 + 3p & 0 & 0 \\ -28 + 2p & 62 & 0 \\ 28 - 2p & 0 & 62 \end{pmatrix}$

(b) (i) $p = 14, k = 62$

(ii) $\dfrac{1}{62} \begin{pmatrix} -4 & 13 & 7 \\ 12 & -8 & 10 \\ 14 & 1 & -9 \end{pmatrix}$

4 Determinants and inverses of 2×2 matrices

Exercise 4A (page 53)

1 (a) If $a \neq 0$, $x = 2a^{-1}$;
if $a = 0$, no solution
(b) If $a \neq 0$, $x = 1 + a^{-1}$;
if $a = 0$, no solution
(c) If $b \neq 0$, $x = b$;
if $b = 0$, $x = t$, $t \in \mathbb{R}$

Exercise 4B (page 58)

1 (a) 1 (b) 17 (c) 0 (d) 1
2 (a) $k \neq 6$ (b) $k \neq 2\frac{1}{4}$ (c) $k \neq -\frac{3}{4}$
(d) $k \neq \pm 4$ (e) $k \neq 1, 2$ (f) $k \neq -3, 6$
3 (a) $x = 4, y = -1$
(b) $x = 3, y = -1$
(c) No unique solution
4 (a) -1; $x = 2 - t, y = t$, $t \in \mathbb{R}$
(b) -9; no unique solution
(c) -8; $x = \frac{1}{2} - 3t, y = 4t$, $t \in \mathbb{R}$
5 (a) If $a \neq 1$, $x = (5 - a^2)(1 - a)^{-1}$;
$y = (a^2 - 2a - 3)(1 - a)^{-1}$;
if $a = 1$, no unique solution

(b) If $a \neq 1$, $x = 1 + a, y = 1 - a$;
if $a = 1$, $x = 2 - t, y = t$, $t \in \mathbb{R}$
(c) If $a \neq 1$, $x = 2 + 2a, y = -2a$;
if $a = 1$, $x = 2 - t, y = t$, $t \in \mathbb{R}$

Exercise 4C (page 64)

1 (a) $\begin{pmatrix} \frac{1}{2} & \frac{1}{2} \\ -\frac{1}{2} & \frac{1}{2} \end{pmatrix}$ (b) $\begin{pmatrix} 7 & -9 \\ -3 & 4 \end{pmatrix}$

(c) $\begin{pmatrix} 7 & 5 \\ 4 & 3 \end{pmatrix}$ (d) $\begin{pmatrix} \frac{4}{3} & \frac{1}{3} \\ \frac{5}{3} & \frac{2}{3} \end{pmatrix}$

(e) No inverse (f) $\begin{pmatrix} -1 & \frac{3}{5} \\ -2 & 1 \end{pmatrix}$

2 (a) $x = 4, y = -3$ (b) $x = -3, y = 2$
(c) $x = 2, y = 1$

3 (a) $\begin{pmatrix} 1 & 3 \\ -1 & 2 \end{pmatrix}$ (b) $\begin{pmatrix} 13 & -\frac{15}{2} \\ 18 & -10 \end{pmatrix}$

(c) $\begin{pmatrix} \frac{2}{5} & -\frac{3}{5} \\ \frac{1}{5} & \frac{1}{5} \end{pmatrix}$

4 $\begin{pmatrix} -2 & 0 \\ 1 & 5 \end{pmatrix}$

5 $\frac{1}{3}\begin{pmatrix} -3 & 4 \\ 6 & -7 \end{pmatrix}$

6 $\frac{1}{2}\begin{pmatrix} -3 & 7 \\ 2 & -4 \end{pmatrix}$, $\frac{1}{2}\begin{pmatrix} -6 & 4 \\ 5 & -3 \end{pmatrix}$, $\frac{1}{4}\begin{pmatrix} 53 & -33 \\ -32 & 20 \end{pmatrix}$

Miscellaneous exercise 4 (page 65)

1 (a) 2 and -2
(b) For $k = 2$, $x = 1 - t, y = t$, $t \in \mathbb{R}$
For $k = -2$, no solution

2 (a) 3 and -2
(b) For $a = 3$, no solution
For $a = -2$, $x = -1 + 3t, y = -2 + t$,
$t \in \mathbb{R}$

3 (a) 9 and -2
(b) For $\lambda = 9$, $x = t, y = 3t$, $t \in \mathbb{R}$
For $\lambda = -2$, $x = -2t, y = 5t$, $t \in \mathbb{R}$

4 (b) $x = 0, y = 0$

6 $\frac{1}{2}\begin{pmatrix} 5 & 2 \\ -1 & 0 \end{pmatrix}$

7 (b) $x = -7, y = -15$

8 (a) $41\begin{pmatrix} 1 & 0 \\ 0 & 1 \end{pmatrix}$, $\frac{1}{41}\begin{pmatrix} 7 & 5 \\ -4 & 3 \end{pmatrix}$
(b) $x = 17, y = -4$

9 -1

10 (a) $(ax^2 + 2bx + c)$

5   Matrices and transformations

Exercise 5A (page 68)

1 (a) $\begin{pmatrix} 3 \\ 2 \end{pmatrix}$ (b) (6, 4)

   (c) O, P, Q lie in a straight line with Q twice as far from O as P.

2 Replace twice by half.

3 OPQ would still be a straight line, but Q and P are on opposite sides of O, and equidistant from it.

4 (9, 8); find the point which is twice as far from the origin in the same straight line as P, and the point which is three times as far from the origin in the same straight line as Q, and then complete the parallelogram to find R.

5 $(2a + 3c, 2b + 3d)$; find the point which is twice as far from the origin in the same straight line as P, and the point which is three times as far from the origin in the same straight line as Q, and then complete the parallelogram to find R.

6 (a) These points, $(1, -1)$, $(2, 0)$, $(3, 1)$ and $(4, 2)$, all lie on a line through $(1, -1)$ parallel to the line joining the origin to $(1, 1)$.

   (b) These points are all the points with integer coordinates; all lie on a line through $(1, -1)$ parallel to the line joining the origin to $(1, 1)$.

   (c) These points form a lattice of parallelograms covering the whole plane based on $(0, 0)$, $(1, -1)$, $(2, 0)$ and $(1, 1)$.

Exercise 5B (page 72)

1 (a) Reflection in the x-axis.
   (b) Reflection in the line $y = x$.
   (c) Rotation $\frac{1}{2}\pi$ clockwise about the origin.
   (d) Shear parallel to x-axis of angle $\frac{1}{4}\pi$.
   (e) Half-turn about the origin.
   (f) Stretch in x-direction, scale factor 2.
   (g) Enlargement about the origin, scale factor 2, and half-turn about the origin.
   (h) Projection onto the line $y = x$, followed by enlargement about the origin with scale factor 2.

2 Rotation anticlockwise about the origin through angle of $\cos^{-1} 0.8$.

3 Enlargement factor 5 about the origin with a rotation about the origin of angle $\cos^{-1} 0.6$.

4 All points are transformed to $(0, 0)$.

5 The original points, which lie in a square grid with six squares, are transformed to the vertices of another grid of six parallelograms.

6 The original points, which lie in a parallelogram grid with six parallelograms, are transformed to the vertices of another grid of six parallelograms.

7 $3y = 4x$; they are perpendicular.

Exercise 5C (page 76)

1 The images are $(0, 0)$, $(1, 1)$, $(0, 2)$ and $(-1, 1)$ in that order, and $(0, 0)$, $(-1, 1)$, $(0, 2)$ and $(1, 1)$ in that order. The first matrix rotates the unit square through 45° and enlarges it by a factor of $\sqrt{2}$; the second reflects the unit square in the line at $67\frac{1}{2}°$ to the x-axis and enlarges it by a factor of $\sqrt{2}$.

2 The image of the unit square is the parallelogram with vertices at $(0, 0)$, $(1, 0)$, $(3, 1)$, $(2, 1)$; its area is 1.

3 (a) $\begin{pmatrix} 4 \\ 2 \end{pmatrix}$ (b) $\begin{pmatrix} 1 \\ 4 \end{pmatrix}$ (c) $\begin{pmatrix} 5 \\ 6 \end{pmatrix}$

4 $\begin{pmatrix} 4 & 2 \\ 4 & 1 \end{pmatrix}$

5 (a) $\begin{pmatrix} 2 & -3 \\ -3 & 5 \end{pmatrix}$

   (b) The image of the unit square is $(0, 0)$, $(5, 3)$, $(8, 5)$ and $(3, 2)$.

   (c) $\mathbf{M}^{-1}$ transforms $OA'B'C'$ to $OABC$.

Exercise 5D (page 82)

1 (a) $\begin{pmatrix} -1 & 0 \\ 0 & 1 \end{pmatrix}$ (b) $\begin{pmatrix} 0 & -1 \\ -1 & 0 \end{pmatrix}$

   (c) $\begin{pmatrix} c & 0 \\ 0 & c \end{pmatrix}$ (d) $\begin{pmatrix} 1 & 1 \\ 0 & 1 \end{pmatrix}$

2 (a) Reflection in the y-axis; $\begin{pmatrix} -1 & 0 \\ 0 & 1 \end{pmatrix}$

   (b) Reflection in $y = -x$; $\begin{pmatrix} 0 & -1 \\ -1 & 0 \end{pmatrix}$

   (c) Enlargement with factor $\frac{1}{c}$; $\begin{pmatrix} 1/c & 0 \\ 0 & 1/c \end{pmatrix}$

   (d) A shear in which the point $(7, 3)$ is transformed to $(4, 3)$ and the x-axis remains fixed; $\begin{pmatrix} 1 & -1 \\ 0 & 1 \end{pmatrix}$

3 (a) $\begin{pmatrix} \frac{1}{2} & -\frac{1}{2}\sqrt{3} \\ \frac{1}{2}\sqrt{3} & \frac{1}{2} \end{pmatrix}$ (b) $\begin{pmatrix} \frac{1}{2} & \frac{1}{2}\sqrt{3} \\ -\frac{1}{2}\sqrt{3} & \frac{1}{2} \end{pmatrix}$

(c) $\begin{pmatrix} \frac{1}{2}\sqrt{2} & -\frac{1}{2}\sqrt{2} \\ \frac{1}{2}\sqrt{2} & \frac{1}{2}\sqrt{2} \end{pmatrix}$ (d) $\begin{pmatrix} \frac{1}{2}\sqrt{2} & \frac{1}{2}\sqrt{2} \\ -\frac{1}{2}\sqrt{2} & \frac{1}{2}\sqrt{2} \end{pmatrix}$

(e) $\dfrac{1}{\sqrt{a^2+b^2}} \begin{pmatrix} a & -b \\ b & a \end{pmatrix}$

4 $\begin{pmatrix} \cos\theta & \sin\theta \\ -\sin\theta & \cos\theta \end{pmatrix}$

5 $\begin{pmatrix} 1 & -k \\ 0 & 1 \end{pmatrix}$; a shear in which the image of
(0, 1) is $(-k, 1)$ (or $(k, 1)$ has image $(0, 1)$), and the x-axis remains fixed.

6 $\begin{pmatrix} c^{-1} & 0 \\ 0 & 1 \end{pmatrix}$

7 $\begin{pmatrix} 2 & 3 \\ -1 & 2 \end{pmatrix}$

8 $\begin{pmatrix} 3 & -1 \\ 4 & -2 \end{pmatrix}$

9 In a matrix transformation, if $\begin{pmatrix} 1 \\ -2 \end{pmatrix} \to \begin{pmatrix} 5 \\ 4 \end{pmatrix}$,
then $3\begin{pmatrix} 1 \\ -2 \end{pmatrix} \to -3\begin{pmatrix} 5 \\ 4 \end{pmatrix} = \begin{pmatrix} -15 \\ -12 \end{pmatrix}$, not
$\begin{pmatrix} 3 \\ -2 \end{pmatrix}$. So there is no such matrix.

10 (a) $\left(\frac{25}{169}, \frac{60}{169}\right), \left(\frac{60}{169}, \frac{144}{169}\right)$

(b) $\begin{pmatrix} \frac{25}{169} & \frac{60}{169} \\ \frac{60}{169} & \frac{144}{169} \end{pmatrix}$

Exercise 5E (page 86)

1 $\begin{pmatrix} 1 & k \\ 0 & 1 \end{pmatrix}, \begin{pmatrix} 1 & 0 \\ k & 1 \end{pmatrix}$; 1, 1

2 160

3 160

4 4

5 (a) $\begin{pmatrix} 1 & 0 \\ -c/a & 1 \end{pmatrix}$ (b) $(b, d - cb/a)$

(c) The base of the parallelogram is a and its height is $d - cb/a$, so its area is
$a(d - cb/a) = ad - cb$.

(d) Start by finding the matrix of the shear parallel to the x-axis which transforms the point (b, d) to the point $(b, 0)$.

Exercise 5F (page 91)

1 $\begin{pmatrix} 5 & 5 \\ 2 & -4 \end{pmatrix}$

2 The identity matrix; the two matrices are the inverses of each other, and it makes no difference in which order you carry out the transformations.

3 $\begin{pmatrix} 1 & 3 \\ -4 & 2 \end{pmatrix}$

4 $\mathbf{A} = \begin{pmatrix} \frac{1}{2}\sqrt{3} & -\frac{1}{2} \\ \frac{1}{2} & \frac{1}{2}\sqrt{3} \end{pmatrix}$; $\mathbf{B} = \begin{pmatrix} \frac{1}{2} & -\frac{1}{2}\sqrt{3} \\ \frac{1}{2}\sqrt{3} & \frac{1}{2} \end{pmatrix}$.

$\mathbf{B} = \mathbf{A}^2$ because a rotation of $\frac{1}{6}\pi$ followed
by a rotation of $\frac{1}{6}\pi$ gives a rotation of $\frac{1}{3}\pi$;
$\mathbf{AB} = \mathbf{BA}$ because rotations about the origin
are commutative.

5 $\mathbf{QP} = \begin{pmatrix} 0 & -1 \\ -1 & 0 \end{pmatrix}$; 6 multiplications by $\mathbf{M}$ will
do because $\mathbf{M}^3 = \mathbf{P}^2$ is a half-turn about the
origin, so $\mathbf{M}^6 = (\mathbf{M}^3)^2 = \mathbf{I}$.

6 (a) $\mathbf{A}$ carries out a rotation of $\tan^{-1}\frac{4}{3}$ (53.1°)
anticlockwise about the origin; $\mathbf{B}$ is an
enlargement of factor 5; $\mathbf{AB} = \mathbf{BA}$
combines these transformations.

(b) $\mathbf{M}$ carries out an enlargement about the
origin with factor $\sqrt{a^2+b^2}$ and a rotation
about the origin of angle $\tan^{-1}\dfrac{b}{a}$
anticlockwise.

7 $\cos 15° = \frac{1}{4}\sqrt{2}(\sqrt{3}+1)$; $\sin 15° = \frac{1}{4}\sqrt{2}(\sqrt{3}-1)$

9 (a) $\sin(\theta - \phi) = \sin\theta\cos\phi - \sin\phi\cos\theta$;
$\cos(\theta - \phi) = \cos\theta\cos\phi + \sin\theta\sin\phi$

Miscellaneous exercise 5 (page 92)

1 For example, $\mathbf{M} = \begin{pmatrix} -\frac{1}{2} & -\frac{1}{2}\sqrt{3} \\ \frac{1}{2}\sqrt{3} & -\frac{1}{2} \end{pmatrix}$, since
$\mathbf{M}$ carries out an anticlockwise rotation of
$\frac{2}{3}\pi$ about the origin.

2 (a) $\mathbf{A}$ is a reflection in the line $y = x\tan\frac{1}{2}\theta$.

(b) If you carry out the same reflection twice,
the transformation is the identity
transformation.

3 $\mathbf{S}$ carries out a shear parallel to the y-axis, of
angle $\tan^{-1}2$. Its image will lie on $y = x$.
$\mathbf{R}$ carries out a half-turn about the origin.
$\mathbf{X} = \begin{pmatrix} 1 & 2 \\ 0 & 1 \end{pmatrix}$ and represents a shear parallel to
the x-axis, of angle $\tan^{-1}2$.

4 Rotation through $\frac{1}{4}\pi$ about the origin.

(a) $\begin{pmatrix} \sqrt{2} & 0 \\ 0 & 1 \end{pmatrix}$

(b) Stretch in the x-direction, factor $\sqrt{2}$.

5 $-\frac{3}{10}, -1$

6 (a) $\begin{pmatrix} \frac{1}{2} & -\frac{1}{2}\sqrt{3} \\ \frac{1}{2}\sqrt{3} & \frac{1}{2} \end{pmatrix}$ (b) $\begin{pmatrix} 2 & 0 \\ 0 & 1 \end{pmatrix}$

(c) $\begin{pmatrix} 1 & -\sqrt{3} \\ \frac{1}{2}\sqrt{3} & \frac{1}{2} \end{pmatrix}$ (d) 2

7 A reflection in the y-axis, and a stretch, with scale factor 2, parallel to the y-axis.
$$\mathbf{A} = \begin{pmatrix} -1 & 0 \\ 0 & 1 \end{pmatrix}, \mathbf{B} = \begin{pmatrix} 1 & 0 \\ 0 & 2 \end{pmatrix}$$

8 A shear, parallel to the negative x-axis, of angle $\frac{3}{4}\pi$.

(a) $\mathbf{B} = \begin{pmatrix} \frac{1}{2} & \frac{1}{2}\sqrt{3} \\ -\frac{1}{2}\sqrt{3} & \frac{1}{2} \end{pmatrix}$

(b) Rotation through $\frac{1}{3}\pi$ clockwise about the origin.

9 (a) It consists of, in either order, a shear parallel to the x-axis, in which the image of $(0, 1)$ is $(\frac{1}{2}, 1)$, and an enlargement, centre the origin and factor 2.

(b) $a = \frac{1}{4}, b = -\frac{1}{2}, c = \frac{1}{2}, d = 0$

Revision exercise 1 (page 94)

1 (a) $\begin{pmatrix} 4 & 3 \\ 3 & -4 \end{pmatrix}$

(b) $(-4, 22)$

2 (a) $\mathbf{C} = \begin{pmatrix} \frac{1}{2} & \frac{1}{2}\sqrt{3} \\ \frac{1}{2}\sqrt{3} & -\frac{1}{2} \end{pmatrix}$

(b) Reflection in the line $y = \dfrac{1}{\sqrt{3}}x$.

3 (a) $(0, 0), (3, 0), (2, 4)$
  (b) $6, 150$ (c) 6

4 (a) Convergent, $\frac{1}{3}$
  (b) Not convergent
  (c) Convergent, $\frac{3}{4}$

5 $\begin{pmatrix} 0 & k \\ 1 & 0 \end{pmatrix}$

6 (b) $1 - \dfrac{1}{(n+1)!}$

8 (a) $\begin{pmatrix} 3 & 0 \\ 0 & 1 \end{pmatrix}, \begin{pmatrix} 0 & -1 \\ 1 & 0 \end{pmatrix}$ (b) $\begin{pmatrix} 1 & 0 \\ 0 & 3 \end{pmatrix}$
  (c) A stretch with factor 3 in the y-direction

9 (b) $1 - \dfrac{1}{(n+1)^2}$ (c) 1

10 (a) Enlargement centre $(0, 0)$ and factor 2 and a rotation of $\frac{1}{3}\pi$ anticlockwise about the origin, in either order.
  (b) 32

11 (b) $56\mathbf{M} - 15\mathbf{I}$ (c) $-\mathbf{M} + 4\mathbf{I}$

12 $\frac{1}{2}n^2(n+1)$

13 $n(n-r)(1+r)$; no difference

14 (a) $(r+1)(r+2)\cdots(r+k)$
  (b) $\frac{1}{5}n(n+1)(n+2)(n+3)(n+4)$

15 (a) $(\cos\theta, \sin\theta)$ (b) $(\sin\theta, -\cos\theta)$
  (c) Reflection in the line $y = x\cot\theta$
  (d) $\begin{pmatrix} \cos^2\theta - \sin^2\theta & -2\sin\theta\cos\theta \\ -2\sin\theta\cos\theta & -\cos^2\theta + \sin^2\theta \end{pmatrix}$
  (e) $\cos 2\theta \equiv \cos^2\theta - \sin^2\theta$

6 Mathematical induction

Exercise 6 (page 104)

7 $\displaystyle\sum_{r=1}^{n}(3r(r+1)+1) = (n+1)^3 - 1$

12 $4, 9, 16; n^2$

20 $17, 391, 9503$; 17 divides every number of the given form.

21 $\displaystyle\sum_{r=1}^{n} r \times r! = (n+1)! - 1$

22 $\mathbf{A}^2 = \begin{pmatrix} 1 & 2 \\ 0 & 1 \end{pmatrix}, \mathbf{A}^3 = \begin{pmatrix} 1 & 3 \\ 0 & 1 \end{pmatrix}, \mathbf{A}^n = \begin{pmatrix} 1 & n \\ 0 & 1 \end{pmatrix}$

23 The sum of three consecutive cubes is divisible by 9.

24 $3^{2n+1} + 2^{4n+2}$ is divisible by 7.

Miscellaneous exercise 6 (page 106)

9 (a) $6, 3$ (b) $\frac{1}{3}, 2$

7 Complex numbers

Exercise 7A (page 112)

1 (a) 4 (b) $6\,\mathrm{i}$ (c) 13 (d) $24\,\mathrm{i}$
  (e) $24\,\mathrm{i}$ (f) -10 (g) 16 (h) -36

2 (a) $4 - \mathrm{i}$ (b) $2 + 3\,\mathrm{i}$ (c) $7 + 0\,\mathrm{i}$
  (d) $5 + 2\,\mathrm{i}$ (e) $5 - 5\,\mathrm{i}$ (f) $8 + 6\,\mathrm{i}$
  (g) $\frac{1}{5}(1 + 7\,\mathrm{i})$ (h) $\frac{1}{10}(1 - 7\,\mathrm{i})$ (i) $1 - 3\,\mathrm{i}$
  (j) $\frac{1}{2} + \frac{3}{10}\mathrm{i}$ (k) $\frac{1}{2}(-1 - 3\,\mathrm{i})$ (l) $\frac{1}{5}(3 + \mathrm{i})$

3 $2x - y = 1, x + 2y = 3; x = 1, y = 1; 1 + \mathrm{i}$

4 (a) 3 (b) -3 (c) 3
  (d) -6 (e) $\frac{1}{2}$ (f) -1

5 (a), (b), (d)

Exercise 7B (page 115)

1 (a) $-2 - 5\,\mathrm{i}$ (b) $\frac{1}{3}(7 - 2\,\mathrm{i})$
  (c) $\frac{1}{2}(-5 + \mathrm{i})$ (d) $\frac{1}{25}(7 + 24\,\mathrm{i})$

2 (a) $z = 2, w = \mathrm{i}$ (b) $z = 1 + \mathrm{i}, w = 2\,\mathrm{i}$

3 (a) $0 \pm 3\,\mathrm{i}$ (b) $-2 \pm \mathrm{i}$
   (c) $3 \pm 4\,\mathrm{i}$ (d) $\frac{1}{2}(-1 \pm 5\,\mathrm{i})$

4 (a) $1 - 7\,\mathrm{i}$ (i) 2   (ii) $14\,\mathrm{i}$ (iii) 50
      (iv) $\frac{1}{25}(-24 + 7\,\mathrm{i})$
   (b) $-2 - \mathrm{i}$ (i) -4 (ii) $2\,\mathrm{i}$ (iii) 5
      (iv) $\frac{1}{5}(3 - 4\,\mathrm{i})$
   (c) 5   (i) 10   (ii) 0   (iii) 25   (iv) 1
   (d) $-3\,\mathrm{i}$ (i) 0   (ii) $6\,\mathrm{i}$ (iii) 9   (iv) -1

Exercise 7C (page 121)

1 (a) s (b) $s + t^*$ (c) $s^* t$
   (d) $\dfrac{5}{s}$ (e) $s^* + i t^*$ (f) $as + bt^*$

2 (a) $\dfrac{a + z^*}{1 + bz^*}$ (b) $\dfrac{-a\mathrm{i} + z^*}{1 - b\mathrm{i}z^*}$;   (a) i (b) $-\frac{7}{5} + \frac{6}{5}\mathrm{i}$

3 (a) $-1 + 10\mathrm{i}, -1 - 10\mathrm{i}$ (b) $20 + 13\mathrm{i}, -4 - 31\mathrm{i}$

4 (a) $(z - 5\,\mathrm{i})(z + 5\,\mathrm{i})$
   (b) $(3z - 1 - 2\,\mathrm{i})(3z - 1 + 2\,\mathrm{i})$
   (c) $(2z + 3 - 2\,\mathrm{i})(2z + 3 + 2\,\mathrm{i})$
   (d) $(z - 2)(z + 2)(z - 2\,\mathrm{i})(z + 2\,\mathrm{i})$
   (e) $(z - 3)(z + 3)(z - \mathrm{i})(z + \mathrm{i})$
   (f) $(z - 2)(z + 1 - 2\,\mathrm{i})(z + 1 + 2\,\mathrm{i})$
   (g) $(z + 1)(z - 2 - \mathrm{i})(z - 2 + \mathrm{i})$
   (h) $(z - 1)^2(z + 1 - \mathrm{i})(z + 1 + \mathrm{i})$

5 $1 - \mathrm{i}, -1 + 2\,\mathrm{i}, -1 - 2\,\mathrm{i}$

6 $-2 - \mathrm{i}, 2 + \sqrt{7}\,\mathrm{i}, 2 - \sqrt{7}\,\mathrm{i}$

9 $a^5 - 10a^3b^2 + 5ab^4, 5a^4b - 10a^2b^3 + b^5$;
    $a^5 - 10a^3b^2 + 5ab^4, -5a^4b + 10a^2b^3 - b^5$

10 yes; with $n = -m$, $(z^*)^n = \dfrac{1}{(z^*)^m} = \dfrac{1}{(z^m)^*}$,
    $(z^n)^* = \left(\dfrac{1}{z^m}\right)^* = \dfrac{1}{(z^m)^*}$

Exercise 7D (page 126)

3 (a) $\pm 1, \pm \mathrm{i}$ (b) $-1, \frac{1}{2}(1 \pm \sqrt{3}\,\mathrm{i})$
   (c) $-2, 1 \pm 3\,\mathrm{i}$ (d) $-3, 1, -1 \pm \sqrt{2}\,\mathrm{i}$
   (e) $\pm 2\,\mathrm{i}, \frac{1}{2}(-1 \pm \sqrt{3}\,\mathrm{i})$

4 Line $y = 1$

Exercise 7E (page 129)

1 (a) $1 - \mathrm{i}, -1 + \mathrm{i}$ (b) $1 + 2\,\mathrm{i}, -1 - 2\,\mathrm{i}$
   (c) $3 + 2\,\mathrm{i}, -3 - 2\,\mathrm{i}$ (d) $3 - \mathrm{i}, -3 + \mathrm{i}$

2 (a) $\mathrm{i}, -1 - \mathrm{i}$ (b) $2, -3 + \mathrm{i}$
   (c) $-1 - \mathrm{i}, -3 + \mathrm{i}$ (d) $-2\,\mathrm{i}, -1 + \mathrm{i}$
   (e) $1, -2 - \mathrm{i}$
   (f) $2 - 2\,\mathrm{i}, -2 + 2\,\mathrm{i}, 2\sqrt{2} + \sqrt{2}\,\mathrm{i}$,
      $-2\sqrt{2} - \sqrt{2}\,\mathrm{i}$

3 (a) $2 + 2\,\mathrm{i}, -2 - 2\,\mathrm{i}, 2 - 2\,\mathrm{i}, -2 + 2\,\mathrm{i}$
   (b) $\frac{1}{2}\sqrt{2}(3 + \mathrm{i}), \frac{1}{2}\sqrt{2}(-3 - \mathrm{i}), \frac{1}{2}\sqrt{2}(1 - 3\,\mathrm{i})$,
      $\frac{1}{2}\sqrt{2}(-1 + 3\,\mathrm{i})$

4 $-2\,\mathrm{i}, \sqrt{3} + \mathrm{i}, -\sqrt{3} + \mathrm{i}$

5 $-1 - \mathrm{i}$; $z^2 - (1 + \mathrm{i})z + 2\,\mathrm{i} = 0$;
    $\frac{1}{2}(1 + \sqrt{3}) + \frac{1}{2}(1 - \sqrt{3})\,\mathrm{i}$,
    $\frac{1}{2}(1 - \sqrt{3}) + \frac{1}{2}(1 + \sqrt{3})\,\mathrm{i}$

Miscellaneous exercise 7 (page 130)

1 $3 - 4\,\mathrm{i}$

2 $-3\,\mathrm{i}, \frac{5}{3}$

3 $1 - 3\,\mathrm{i}$; $z^3 - 4z^2 + 14z - 20 = 0$

4 (a) 3, 3; the coefficients of the quadratic are
      not all real.
   (b) $4\,\mathrm{i}$

5 $5 - 2\,\mathrm{i}, -5 + 2\,\mathrm{i}$; they are symmetrically placed
    with respect to O.

6 $3 - \mathrm{i}, -3 + 3\,\mathrm{i}$

7 $-2\,\mathrm{i}, -2 - 2\,\mathrm{i}, -4$;
   (a) $p = -4, q = 2$ (b) $1 - \mathrm{i}, 1 + \mathrm{i}, -1, -4$

8 $z = 2 + \mathrm{i}, w = 1 - \mathrm{i}$

9 $0.28 - 0.96\mathrm{i}, 0.8 - 0.6\mathrm{i}, 1, 0.8 + 0.6\mathrm{i}$,
    $0.28 + 0.96\mathrm{i}, -0.352 + 0.936\mathrm{i}$; they are all at a
    distance 1 from O, evenly spaced round the
    circle with centre O and radius 1.

8 Roots of polynomial equations

Exercise 8A (page 133)

1 (a) $x^2 - 5x + 6 = 0$ (b) $x^2 + 2x - 3 = 0$
   (c) $x^2 - 4 = 0$ (d) $2x^2 - x - 1 = 0$

2 (a) $2, -1$ (b) $-2, -\frac{3}{2}$ (c) $\frac{1}{3}, \frac{1}{3}$

3 (a) 12   (b) 16   (c) 10
   (d) 8   (e) 2   (f) 3

4 (a) $x^2 - 3x - 2 = 0$ (b) $x^2 - 2x = 0$
   (c) $2x^2 - x + 6 = 0$ (d) $6x^2 - 2x + 3 = 0$

Exercise 8B (page 135)

1 (a) $x^2 + 6x + 45 = 0$ (b) $x^2 + 4 = 0$
   (c) $x^2 + 6x + 13 = 0$ (d) $x^2 + 6x + 25 = 0$
   (e) $5x^2 + 2x + 1 = 0$ (f) $25x^2 + 6x + 1 = 0$

2 (a) $u^2 + 12u + 63 = 0$ (b) $u^2 + 2u + 4 = 0$
   (c) $u^2 + 12u + 39 = 0$ (d) $u^2 - 2u + 49 = 0$
   (e) $7u^2 + 4u + 1 = 0$ (f) $49u^2 - 2u + 1 = 0$

Exercise 8C (page 140)

1 (a) $x^3 - 9x^2 + 26x - 24 = 0$
   (b) $x^3 - x^2 - 2x = 0$
   (c) $x^3 - 4x = 0$

2 (a) Symmetric   (b) Not symmetric
   (c) Not symmetric

3 (a) 0   (b) 12   (c) 36   (d) 3

4 (a) $u^3 + 4u^2 + 12u + 32 = 0$
  (b) $u^3 - 4u^2 + 7u - 2 = 0$
  (c) $u^3 + 2u^2 - 7u - 16 = 0$
  (d) $4u^3 + 3u^2 + 2u + 1 = 0$

5 (a) $2u^3 + u^2 - u + 4 = 0$
  (b) $2u^3 - 15u^2 + 27u + 108 = 0$

6 $2b^3 - 3bc + d = 0, \pm\sqrt{\dfrac{b^3 - d}{b}}$

7 $b^3 d = c^3, \ d^{\frac{1}{3}} r^2 + \left(d^{\frac{1}{3}} - b\right) r + d^{\frac{1}{3}} = 0$

8 $x^3 - 6x^2 + 11x - 6 = 0$
  p, q, r can be any permutation of 1, 2, 3.

9 p, q, r can be any permutation of $-1, 3, 4$.

Miscellaneous exercise 8 (page 140)

1 94, 8818

2 $-1, -1 \pm 2\,\mathrm{i}$

3 $bu^2 + 2au + 4 = 0$

4 $\alpha = 1 + \mathrm{i}, \beta = 1 - \mathrm{i}$ or $\alpha = 1 - \mathrm{i}, \beta = 1 + \mathrm{i}$

5 p, q, r can be any permutation of $-1, 1, 2$.

6 $u^3 - 2u^2 + 5u - 1, 2$

7 (a) α and β are conjugate complex numbers.
  (b) $13u^2 + 27u + 27 = 0$

8 $16, -36; x^2 - 160x + 10\,000 = 0$

9 $7, 7; u^2 - 11u + 19 = 0$

10 $u^3 + 4u^2 + 5u = 0; 3, 1 \pm \mathrm{i}$

12 $-\frac{2}{9}$

13 $\frac{2}{3}, -\frac{1}{3}, -3$

14 $b^2 (1 + u)^3 + a^3 (u + 2) = 0$

9 Modulus and argument

Exercise 9A (page 147)

2 $-1, 1, \frac{1}{2}\left(1 \pm \sqrt{3}\,\mathrm{i}\right)$

3 (a) Circle centre O radius 5, $x^2 + y^2 = 25$
  (b) Line $x = 3$ (c) Line $x = 3$
  (d) Circle centre $2 + 0\,\mathrm{i}$ radius 2,
    $x^2 + y^2 - 4x = 0$
  (e) Line $x = 2$ (f) Line $y = 2x + 3$
  (g) Circle centre $\frac{1}{2} + 0\,\mathrm{i}$ radius $1\frac{1}{2}$,
    $x^2 + y^2 - x = 2$
  (h) Parabola $y^2 = 4x$

4 (a) Exterior of circle centre O radius 2,
    $x^2 + y^2 > 4$
  (b) Interior and boundary of circle centre
    $0 + 3\,\mathrm{i}$ radius 1, $x^2 + y^2 - 6y + 8 \leqslant 0$

  (c) Half-plane including boundary, $x + y \leqslant 0$
  (d) Interior of circle centre $-1 + 0\,\mathrm{i}$ radius 2,
    $x^2 + y^2 + 2x - 3 < 0$

9 If in a triangle ABC, O is the mid-point of
  BC, then $AB^2 + AC^2 = 2OA^2 + 2OC^2$ (this is
  Apollonius's theorem).

Exercise 9B (page 152)

1 (a) 1.11   (b) −0.93   (c) 2.27   (d) −2.29
  (e) 0   (f) $\frac{1}{2}\pi$ (g) π (h) $-\frac{1}{2}\pi$
  (i) $-\frac{1}{4}\pi$ (j) $\frac{2}{3}\pi$

2 (a) Half-line from O in direction $\frac{1}{5}\pi$
    anticlockwise from real axis
  (b) Half-line from O in direction $\frac{2}{3}\pi$
    clockwise from real axis
  (c) Negative real axis
  (d) Half-line from $2 + 0\,\mathrm{i}$ in direction of
    positive imaginary axis
  (e) Half-line from $\frac{1}{2} + 0\,\mathrm{i}$ in direction of
    positive real axis
  (f) Half-line from $0 - \mathrm{i}$ in direction of
    negative real axis
  (g) Half-line from $1 + 2\mathrm{i}$ in direction $\frac{3}{4}\pi$
    anticlockwise from real axis
  (h) Half-line from $-1 + \mathrm{i}$ in direction $\frac{2}{5}\pi$
    clockwise from real axis

3 (a)   (b)
  (c)   (d) $-1 + \mathrm{i}$

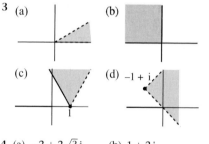

4 (a) $-2 + 2\sqrt{3}\,\mathrm{i}$ (b) $1 + 2\mathrm{i}$
  (c) $-3 - 6\mathrm{i}$ (d) $\sqrt{3} - \mathrm{i}$
  (e) $2 - 2\sqrt{3} + \mathrm{i}$ (f) $\left(1 - \sqrt{3}\right) + \left(1 + \sqrt{3}\right)\mathrm{i}$

5 (a) $\sqrt{3} + \mathrm{i}$ (b) $3 + 4\mathrm{i}$
  (c) $-3 + 4\mathrm{i}, -9 + 4\mathrm{i}$
  (d) $\mp\frac{1}{2}\sqrt{2} + \left(2 \pm \frac{1}{2}\sqrt{2}\right)\mathrm{i}$

6 $\frac{1}{5}\pi$

7 $-\frac{5}{6}\pi$

8 $\frac{1}{4}\pi$

9 $\frac{1}{3}\pi$

10 $\sqrt{5}$

11 $\frac{1}{3}\pi$

Miscellaneous exercise 9 (page 153)

1 2

2 6

3 Circle with centre $3 + 4\,\mathrm{i}$ and radius 2;

  (a) 7   (b) $2\sin^{-1}0.4 \approx 0.823$

5 Interior and boundary of the circle with centre $-2 + 2\sqrt{3}\,\mathrm{i}$ and radius 2;   (a) 2   (b) $\frac{5}{6}\pi$

6 (a) $-3 \pm 5\,\mathrm{i}$ (b) $\sqrt{34}, \pm 2.11$ (c) 10

7 (a) $-3 - 4\,\mathrm{i},\ 11 - 2\,\mathrm{i};\ -1 - 2\,\mathrm{i},\ -5$
  (b) $\sqrt{5}, \pm 2.03;\ 5,\ \pi$

10 Determinants and inverses of 3×3 matrices

Exercise 10A (page 160)

1 (a) 0   (b) -3 (c) 16

2 (a) -2 (b) 8   (c) $-2, 1$

3 (a) 13   (b) 3   (c) $-\frac{4}{3}$

4 -7;

  (a) $x = -13t,\ y = 5t,\ z = t,\ \ t \in \mathbb{R}$
  (b) $x = 0,\ y = 0,\ z = 0$

5 (a) 7
  (b) $x = \frac{32}{3} - 29t,\ y = -3t,$
    $z = -\frac{14}{3} + 14t,\ \ t \in \mathbb{R}$
  (c) No solution

Exercise 10B (page 161)

1 The pattern of signs is $\begin{pmatrix} + & - & + \\ - & + & - \\ + & - & + \end{pmatrix}$.

Exercise 10C (page 164)

1 $\begin{matrix} -34 & 37 & 11 \\ 4 & -27 & -11 \\ -28 & 24 & 22 \end{matrix}$

  (a) $3 \times (-34) + 5 \times 4 + 1 \times (-28) = -110$
  (b) $1 \times (-28) + 3 \times 24 + (-7) \times 22 = -110$

2 (a) 108   (b) -462 (c) -4

3 (a) $20 - 12k$ (b) $-22k - 28$ (c) $-1 - k^3$

4 (b) The first and second equations, when subtracted, give $0 = q - p$. If $q \ne p$ this leads to a contradiction and the equations are inconsistent. If $q = p$, then the first and second equations are identical and, from the work in Chapter 1 the equations may be consistent or inconsistent. Either way the solution is not unique.

(c) Since the equations in part (b) do not have a unique solution the determinant is 0.

(d) Consider the matrix whose rows are the columns of the given determinant. Part (a) tells you that this matrix has the same determinant as the given determinant, and part (c) tells you that this is 0.

Exercise 10D (page 170)

1 (a) $\begin{pmatrix} -3 & 2 & -1 \\ 1 & 1 & 1 \\ 2 & 0 & 1 \end{pmatrix}$ (b) $\begin{pmatrix} 1 & -1 & \frac{1}{2} \\ -1 & 1 & -1 \\ 1 & 0 & \frac{1}{2} \end{pmatrix}$

  (c) $\begin{pmatrix} -\frac{1}{2} & \frac{2}{3} & \frac{1}{6} \\ -\frac{1}{2} & \frac{1}{3} & -\frac{1}{6} \\ -\frac{1}{2} & 0 & \frac{1}{2} \end{pmatrix}$ (d) $\begin{pmatrix} -\frac{7}{6} & -\frac{1}{6} & \frac{5}{6} \\ -\frac{1}{3} & \frac{2}{3} & -\frac{1}{3} \\ -\frac{1}{2} & -\frac{1}{2} & \frac{1}{2} \end{pmatrix}$

  (e) $\begin{pmatrix} \frac{13}{2} & 4 & -\frac{9}{2} \\ \frac{9}{2} & 3 & -\frac{7}{2} \\ -\frac{7}{2} & -2 & \frac{5}{2} \end{pmatrix}$ (f) No inverse

2 (a) $x = 4,\ y = 3,\ z = 1$ (b) $x = 2,\ y = 2,\ z = 1$
  (c) $x = 1,\ y = 1,\ z = 2$

3 (a) $\begin{pmatrix} 6 & 1 & -2 \\ -4 & -1 & 1 \\ 3 & -2 & 1 \end{pmatrix}$ (b) $\begin{pmatrix} 1 & 4 & 7 \\ 2 & -1 & 3 \\ 2 & 0 & 1 \end{pmatrix}$

4 $\frac{1}{2}\begin{pmatrix} 3 & 29 & -20 \\ -2 & -14 & 10 \\ -3 & -35 & 24 \end{pmatrix}$

5 $\begin{pmatrix} 2 & 1 & 1 \\ -1 & 0 & 1 \\ 1 & 1 & 0 \end{pmatrix}$

Miscellaneous exercise 10 (page 170)

1 (a) $5, -4$

2 $k = 3;\ x = 2 - 2t,\ y = t,\ z = 1 - 5t,\ \ t \in \mathbb{R}$

3 $\mathbf{M} = \begin{pmatrix} -1 & 3 & 1 \\ 0 & 4 & 2 \\ 1 & -1 & 1 \end{pmatrix};\ \begin{pmatrix} -\frac{5}{2} \\ -\frac{1}{2} \\ 1 \end{pmatrix}$

4 (a) $28a - 84$

  (c) $\frac{1}{28a - 84}\begin{pmatrix} -34 & 6a - 35 & 4a + 5 \\ -10 & -4a + 7 & 2a - 1 \\ 28 & 14 & -14 \end{pmatrix}$,

  $\frac{1}{28a - 84}\begin{pmatrix} -8a - 44 \\ -4a - 8 \\ 56 \end{pmatrix}$

5 (a) All real numbers except 2.

  (b) $\frac{1}{10a - 20}\begin{pmatrix} 5a - 28 & 5 & 4 \\ 9a & -5 & -2a \\ -36 & 10 & 8 \end{pmatrix}$

  (c) $x = \frac{a - 7}{2a - 4},\ y = \frac{a + 3}{2a - 4},\ z = \frac{-5}{a - 2}$

6 (a) $\mathbf{I}, \mathbf{Q}^{-1}\mathbf{P}^{-1}$

(b) $\begin{pmatrix} 2a^2 & 0 & 0 \\ 0 & 2a^2 & 0 \\ 0 & 0 & 2a^2 \end{pmatrix}$, $\dfrac{1}{2a^2}\begin{pmatrix} a & a^2 & a^2 \\ -1 & a & a \\ 0 & 0 & -a \end{pmatrix}$

(c) $\frac{1}{2}\begin{pmatrix} 1 & 1 & 1 \\ -1 & 1 & 1 \\ 0 & 0 & -1 \end{pmatrix}$, $\frac{1}{8}\begin{pmatrix} 2 & -4 & 0 \\ 1 & 2 & 4 \\ 0 & 0 & -4 \end{pmatrix}$,

$\frac{1}{16}\begin{pmatrix} 6 & -2 & -2 \\ -1 & 3 & -1 \\ 0 & 0 & 4 \end{pmatrix}$

7 $\dfrac{1}{6(a-1)}\begin{pmatrix} 3a-1 & a+1 & -4 \\ 1 & 2a-1 & -2 \\ -3 & -3 & 6 \end{pmatrix}$,

$x = \dfrac{a-11}{6(a-1)}, y = \dfrac{2a-7}{6(a-1)}, z = \dfrac{5}{2(a-1)}$

8 $-2, \frac{1}{2}$

9 (a) (ii) $\frac{1}{20}\begin{pmatrix} 2 & 1 & -3 \\ 2 & 3 & 3 \\ -4 & 2 & -2 \end{pmatrix}$

(b) $x = -2, y = 6, z = -3$

10 (a) $4\mathbf{I}, \frac{1}{4}\mathbf{B}$

(b) $x = -2, y = 11, z = 18$

Revision exercise 2 (page 173)

1 $\mathbf{AB} = (a-3)\mathbf{I}, \mathbf{A}^{-1} = \dfrac{1}{a-3}\mathbf{B}$;

$x = \dfrac{-1}{a-3}, y = \dfrac{3a-4}{a-3}, z = -\dfrac{2a-4}{a-3}$;

no solution.

2 (c) $x = 28 + 13t, y = t, z = -9 - 5t, \quad t \in \mathbb{R}$

3 (a) $\dfrac{1}{1+a}\begin{pmatrix} 1 & -a & 0 \\ 1 & 1 & 0 \\ -a-5 & a^2-5 & 1+a \end{pmatrix}$

(b) $x = -1, y = 1, z = 0$

4 (a) $\begin{pmatrix} 1 & 0 & 0 \\ 1 & -1 & 0 \\ -\frac{1}{a} & 0 & \frac{1}{a} \end{pmatrix}$

(b) $\begin{pmatrix} \frac{1}{a} & 1 & -\frac{1}{a} \\ 1-\frac{1}{2a} & -1 & \frac{1}{2a} \\ -\frac{1}{2a} & 0 & \frac{1}{2a} \end{pmatrix}$

5 $c = 4$; not consistent

6 (a) 4, 16, 48, 128

(b) $S_n = n2^{n+1}$, so $f(n) = 2^{n+1}$

7 (a) $-3 \pm 4i$ (b) $1 \pm 2i, -1 \pm 2i$ (d) $2 + \sqrt{5}$

9 $-\frac{1}{2}\pi$

10 $\frac{3}{4}, \frac{2}{3}(= \frac{4}{6}), \frac{5}{8}, \frac{3}{5}(= \frac{6}{10}), \frac{7}{12}; \dfrac{n+1}{2n}$

12 (b) $1 \pm \sqrt{2}, 1 \pm \sqrt{3}$

13 (a) 10

(b) $2, \dfrac{3 \pm \sqrt{7}\,i}{2}$

14 $4 + \sqrt{3}\,i$

15 (c) $-\frac{2}{3}, \dfrac{-1 \pm \sqrt{7}}{3}$

16 (a) $p - 3$

(b) $\dfrac{1}{p-3}\begin{pmatrix} 2p-3 & -p+1 & -1 \\ -p-3 & p+1 & 2 \\ -3 & 2 & 1 \end{pmatrix}$

(c) $x = \dfrac{-5}{p-3}, y = \dfrac{p+7}{p-3}, z = \dfrac{5}{p-3}$

17 (a) $0, -7$ (b) No solution

19 (a) $A = -1, B = 1$

20 $\begin{pmatrix} 2i & 3i & -i \\ -i & 1-2i & 0 \\ -2-i & -3-2i & 1 \end{pmatrix}$

23 (a) $2 + i$ (b) $-2 \pm 3i$

(c) $i, 2 + i$ (d) $z = 2 + i, w = i$

24 Examine the argument from 2 people to 3 people.

25 (a) $0, -\frac{27}{16}, -16(\alpha + \beta + \gamma)$

(b) $\frac{3}{2}$ (repeated), $-\frac{3}{4}; -36$

(c) $27y^3 - 81y^2 + 90y - 20 = 0$

26 (a) $\frac{3}{2}, -6, 2$ (b) $\frac{57}{4}, 30$

(d) $2x^3 - 15x^2 + 24x + 7 = 0$

27 No! In part (c) it is not claimed that there are any matrices such that $[\mathbf{A}, \mathbf{B}] = \mathbf{I}$. However, if there were such matrices, $[\mathbf{A}, \mathbf{B}^m] = m\mathbf{B}^{m-1}$

Practice examinations

Practice examination 1 (page 178)

2 (i) 1

(ii) $(x + 2y, 3x + 6y), y = 3x$

3 (i) $\begin{pmatrix} 7 & 0 & 0 \\ 0 & 7 & 0 \\ 0 & 0 & 7 \end{pmatrix}$

(ii) (a) $\dfrac{1}{7}\begin{pmatrix} 1 & 0 & -2 \\ 0 & 2 & -1 \\ 2 & 1 & 0 \end{pmatrix}$

(b) $x = \frac{1}{7}a, y = \frac{2}{7}a, z = \frac{3}{7}a$

4   (ii) $\sqrt{n+1}-1$
    (iii) Not convergent, as $\sqrt{n+1} \to \infty$

5   (i) $\begin{pmatrix} 2 \\ 1 \end{pmatrix}, \begin{pmatrix} 4 \\ 3 \end{pmatrix}, \begin{pmatrix} 8 \\ 7 \end{pmatrix}, \begin{pmatrix} 16 \\ 15 \end{pmatrix}$ (ii) $\begin{pmatrix} 2^n \\ 2^n - 1 \end{pmatrix}$

6   (i) $-\frac{7}{25} - \frac{24}{25}i$ (ii) $\pm(2-i)$

7   (i) $5, 7$ (ii) $y^2 - 11y + 49 = 0$

8   (ii) 1
    (iii) $1 - 2i, -2$
    (iv), (v)

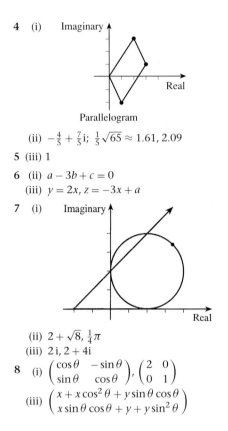

Practice examination 2 (page 180)

1   $\frac{1}{3}n(n+1)(n+2)$

2   (i) $3, 7, 15, 31$ (ii) $u_n = 2^n - 1$

3   (i) $a = \beta\gamma + \gamma\alpha + \alpha\beta, b = -\alpha\beta\gamma$
    (ii) $a = \gamma - \gamma^2, b = -\gamma^2$

4   (i)   Imaginary

Parallelogram

    (ii) $-\frac{4}{5} + \frac{7}{5}i; \ \frac{1}{5}\sqrt{65} \approx 1.61, 2.09$

5   (iii) 1

6   (ii) $a - 3b + c = 0$
    (iii) $y = 2x, z = -3x + a$

7   (i)   Imaginary

    (ii) $2 + \sqrt{8}, \frac{1}{4}\pi$
    (iii) $2i, 2 + 4i$

8   (i) $\begin{pmatrix} \cos\theta & -\sin\theta \\ \sin\theta & \cos\theta \end{pmatrix}, \begin{pmatrix} 2 & 0 \\ 0 & 1 \end{pmatrix}$
    (iii) $\begin{pmatrix} x + x\cos^2\theta + y\sin\theta\cos\theta \\ x\sin\theta\cos\theta + y + y\sin^2\theta \end{pmatrix}$

Index

The page numbers refer to the first mention of each term, or the box if there is one.